EFFECTIVE
SCHOOL
MAINTENANCE

N. L. George

PARKER PUBLISHING COMPANY, INC.
West Nyack, N.Y.

PRINTED IN THE UNITED STATES OF AMERICA
13–245449–1 B & P

TO
MY WIFE, IDA MAE

ABOUT THE AUTHOR

N. L. George received his B.S. and M.S. from the University of Oklahoma, and his D.Ed. from Teachers College, Columbia. He has been a school administrator since 1926 when he became Superintendent of Schools for Geary, Oklahoma. In 1936, he was appointed Superintendent of the Duncan, Oklahoma schools.

In 1941, the author joined the Oklahoma City Public School System where he specialized in Business Administration, becoming Assistant Superintendent responsible for the System's maintenance program. (The city has 116 operating plants valued at 135 million dollars.)

Author of two previous books and over 50 articles for professional journals, Dr. George is a nationally recognized authority in school maintenance. His services as lecturer and consultant are sought by school systems across the nation.

WHAT THIS BOOK OFFERS

The adage, "A stitch in time saves nine," is a most important concept in effective administration of school maintenance; but no stitch can save money or give the desired service until the repair or service is performed. The maintenance of school plants is more complex and difficult than the most experienced school administrator realizes.

This book will stress the practical aspects of school maintenance. It will describe, in specific detail, the principles and effective maintenance practices which will serve as guides for superintendents of schools and heads of maintenance departments. It will also be of use to administrators in maintenance personnel, to building engineers, instructors, students (studying school plant management), architects, engineers, and boards of education. Pinpointing solutions to maintenance problems requires skilled personnel who know how to perform maintenance services efficiently. The key to achieving this effectiveness can only be found in effective administrative controls.

Most school districts have programs which need updating. Larger administrative districts are a national trend. More skilled personnel and better trained central office personnel will be required to help administer the maintenance programs in the larger districts. Both situations focus attention on the need for a comprehensive treatment of maintenance problems.

Efficient maintenance of school plants is especially important because the condition of the surroundings affects education. Well-kept, attractive facilities assist in establishing the proper environment which greatly enhances any teaching effort.

Meticulous and comprehensive local planning is basic for efficient maintenance. Each school district varies in size and has localized elements. The administration of the local maintenance program combines money, men, materials, and methods into a planned program.

The book is divided into two parts. Each part treats in detail a major group of problems encountered in maintenance services. The contents are based on practical experience extending over a quarter of a century in dealing with the various phases of maintenance personnel.

Part I, The Administrative Practices, provides basic information and key factors in maintenance of the physical plant. Steps are established for organizing an efficient program, and controls are listed for these maintenance functions. The major elements in the selection, training, and retention of skilled personnel are reviewed. The management of the safety program, records, and the upgrading of personnel are described in detail. The maintenance shop with other facilities as a part of the service center plant site is examined thoroughly. Last, but not least, the key ingredients for an efficient operation are summarized for emphasis.

v

The paramount purpose of Part I is to focus attention on successful administrative practices in an efficient maintenance program. These practices have been tested and have proven efficient. Supplemental information is in the appendixes. The data included will become important as a school district evaluates its existing program. The samples of coding and machine processing techniques should become helpful as a school system installs data processing.

Part II, Daily Maintenance Problems, attempts to disclose the magnitude of the maintenance problems which may appear in a school district. A modern school plant (site and site development, building, and furniture) has about 2,000 elements to consider, which are particularized from the time the planning of a school plant starts, until it is finished and adequately equipped. About 1,200 of these factors refer to physical properties.

The major plant areas which require skilled labor or contract services are described in detail. Management of assigned maintenance tasks and maintenance of ancillary areas are important functions which are also treated. Chapter 14, Upgrading Existing School Plants, and Chapter 15, Promising Preplanned Maintenance Pointers, set the goals for effective administration of school maintenance.

Specific reading references are not given for each chapter because of the extremely close relationship existing among many of the subjects discussed. Also, the relatively few articles and books would necessitate repetition of references. The bibliography contains an annotated list of books and a selected list of pertinent articles from professional literature.

N. L. GEORGE

ACKNOWLEDGMENTS

A book of this nature is never written without advice and encouragement. Valuable assistance came from authors, educators, and publishers who graciously permitted quotations and references from their works. Many other ideas, whether directly or indirectly expressed, were garnered by participating in conferences and teaching in workshops.

I am grateful to my present co-workers who have shared with me their specialized knowledge of various phases of maintenance services. Many of their valuable suggestions are presented in this volume. They are Wallace Smith, Ruhl Potts, Roy Mullenix, and R. H. Fisher.

I would also like to thank my wife, Ida, for her help as reader; and Ruth Flaitz and Helen Ridings, typists.

N. L. GEORGE

Contents

PART I. ADMINISTRATIVE PRACTICES: KEYS TO EFFECTIVE CONTROLS

1. A PRACTICAL BASIS FOR A SUCCESSFUL PROGRAM 2

   OBJECTIVES OF MAINTENANCE   3

   FACTORS DETERMINING THE AMOUNT AND COST OF MAINTENANCE   4

   METHOD OF PERFORMING MAINTENANCE FUNCTIONS   5

   HINDRANCES TO EFFECTIVE MAINTENANCE   6

   METHODS WHICH PRODUCE MAINTENANCE ECONOMIES   7

   SUMMARY   7

2. ORGANIZING FOR EFFICIENT MAINTENANCE 8

   PRINCIPLES FOR EFFECTIVE ORGANIZATION   8
   Coordination. Functionalism. Promising Practices. Efficiency. Service.

   LOCAL DETERMINATION OF MAINTENANCE ACTIVITIES   13

   CLASSES OF MAINTENANCE SERVICES   13

   PROGRAMMING FOR MAINTENANCE   14
   Step I: Inspection by Capable Personnel. Step II: Inspection by Responsible Craftsmen. Step III: Building Principal's Annual Request. Step IV: Recommendations of Instructional Staff. Step V: Conferences. Step VI: Budget Allowance. Step VII: Establishing Priorities. Step VIII: Finalizing the Maintenance Budget. Step IX: Organizing the Maintenance Staff. Step X: Arranging for Materials. Step XI: Tooling Up for Maintenance. Step XII: Applying Constant Evaluation.

   SUMMARY   19

3. DEVELOPING EFFICIENT CONTROLS OF MAINTENANCE FUNCTIONS 20

    METHODS OF DETECTION OF REPAIRS   20
    TIME STUDY   23
    ESTABLISHING STANDARDS FOR MAINTENANCE   25
    Parts. Policies of Replacement. Frequencies of Service.

    ORDERING RIGHT MATERIALS   27
    JOB DESCRIPTIONS   27
    THE USE OF RECORDS   28
    RESPONSIBILITY FOR MAINTENANCE RECORDS   29
    BUILDING MANUALS   29
    DEVELOPING ADEQUATE COMMUNICATIONS   29
    Elements. Control. Flow of Communications. Methods. Media.

    HUMAN RELATIONS   31
    SUMMARY   32

4. ESTABLISHING SUCCESSFUL PERSONNEL POLICIES 33

    PLACE TO APPLY   33
    FREEDOMS   34
    CHARACTERISTICS OF PERSONNEL   34
    ESTABLISHING QUALIFICATIONS   35
    SPECIFIC SKILL QUALIFICATIONS   35
    Supervision. Head of Maintenance. Area Men.

    DUTIES OF AREA MECHANICS   37
    RECRUITMENT   38
    METHODS OF SELECTION, PROMOTION, AND RETENTION OF PERSONNEL   38
    WAGE AND EMPLOYEE BENEFITS   41
    Employee Benefits. Other Personal Benefits.

    SEVERANCE   42
    MISCELLANEOUS WORKING RELATIONSHIPS   43
    TRANSPORTATION   44
    GARNISHMENTS   44
    PERFORMANCE EVALUATION   45
    Employee Benefits. Administration Benefits. Scope of Qualities. Performance Evaluation Forms. Methods of Rating. Positive Steps in Rating.

    EMPLOYEE ORGANIZATION   47
    RELATIONS WITH ORGANIZED LABOR   47
    RECOGNITION   49
    SUMMARY   49

5. RESPONSIBILITY OF THE ADMINISTRATOR FOR SAFETY IN MAIN-
    TENANCE OPERATIONS 50

    SCOPE OF RESPONSIBILITY   51

    RESPONSIBILITIES OF ADMINISTRATOR   51
    *First Aid Station. First Aid—Dispatched Personnel. Fire Drills—Shop. Fire Drills—
    Schools. Disasters. Handling of Accidents. Study Causes of Accidents. Inspection.
    Mechanical Safeguard. Training in Operation Procedures. Safety Program. Teaching
    Methods and Techniques.*

    PRECAUTIONS   56
    Specific Operations. Safety Precautions for Certain Parts of the School Plant.

    STRICT ENFORCEMENT OF RULES   60
    SUMMARY   61

6. MANAGING MAINTENANCE RECORDS 62

    BASIC SCHOOL PLANT RECORDS   62
    HELPFUL RECORDS ON PARTS OF SCHOOL PLANTS   63
    RECORDS OF MAINTENANCE OPERATIONS   64
    PERSONNEL RECORDS   64
    ADEQUATE INVENTORY AND STOCK RECORDS   65
    MICROFILMING RECORDS   65
    SUMMARY   65

7. THE EFFECTIVE USE OF A CENTRAL SERVICE PLANT 66

    CENTRAL MAINTENANCE SHOPS   67
    DESIRABLE REQUIREMENTS   67
    DETERMINATION OF SUPPLY CONTROL   67
    GENERAL BUILDING REQUIREMENTS   68
    DETERMINING SIZE OF SHOP AREA   69
    SERVICE CENTERS   71
    SHOP EQUIPMENT AND TOOLS   78
    Equipment. Tools.

    HOUSEKEEPING   83
    SUMMARY   83

8. IMPERATIVES FOR EFFICIENT ADMINISTRATION 85

    SAVINGS IN THE SELECTION AND ASSIGNMENT OF MANPOWER   85
    MATERIAL SAVINGS   86

8. IMPERATIVES FOR EFFICIENT ADMINISTRATION (Continued)

SAVINGS THROUGH BETTER TOOLS AND EQUIPMENT   87
SAVINGS IN METHODS OF OPERATION   87
SAVINGS THROUGH LESS HANDLING AND MECHANIZED TRANSPORTATION   88
Within the Shop. From Shop to Locations within the District.
SAVINGS THROUGH A SAFETY PROGRAM   88
SAVINGS IN WORK TIME   89
SAVINGS IN IDLE TIME   89
SAVINGS IN CLERICAL OR ADMINISTRATIVE PAPER WORK   89
SAVINGS IN FREQUENCY OF GENERAL AND COMMITTEE MEETINGS   89
SUMMARY   90

9. UPGRADING THE PERSONNEL FOR EFFICIENT ADMINISTRATION 91

IN-SERVICE TRAINING   91
FORMAL TRAINING   92
RECOMMENDED PRACTICES   93
Visitation to Other School Districts. Testing.
USING AVAILABLE SCHOOL PLANT INFORMATION   93
SHORT TERM SCHOOLS OF INSTRUCTION   94
INSTRUCTIONAL METHODS AND SERVICES   94
Methods. Devices.
SOURCES OF HELPFUL INFORMATION   95
SUMMARY   95

PART II. DAILY MAINTENANCE PROBLEMS

10. ESTABLISHING EFFICIENT SERVICES IN SCHOOL PLANT AREAS........... 98

PAINTING SERVICES   98
Outside Painting. Interior Painting. Contract Painting. Glazing.
ROOFING SERVICES   99
Causes for Failure. Methods of Repair.
ELECTRICAL SERVICES   101
Scope. Common Problems. Lighting.
HEATING AND VENTILATION SERVICES   102
Heating. Ventilation.
MECHANICAL SERVICES   104
Sanitary Facilities. Aims of Mechanical Services. Common Problems.

10. ESTABLISHING EFFICIENT SERVICES IN SCHOOL PLANT AREAS
     (Continued)

CARPENTER SERVICES   105
Outside of the School Building. Outside Surfaces of the School Building. Inside Parts of School Building. Goals.

FURNITURE REPAIR SERVICES   106
Scope. Common Problems. Materials.

MASONRY SERVICES   107
Responsibilities. Methods of Repair. Problems.

PLASTERING SERVICES   108
Causes of Repair.

GROUNDS AND LANDSCAPING SERVICES   109
Plant Life. Site Improvements. Outside Instructional Areas. Play Equipment.

SUMMARY   110

11. MANAGING ALLIED MAINTENANCE SERVICES 111

CONCRETE SERVICES   111
SHEET METAL SERVICES   111
WELDING SERVICES   112
DRAYAGE SERVICES   112
Scope. Aims. Common Problems.

GARAGE SERVICES   113
Scope. Aims of Services. Common Problems.

THE MACHINE SHOP SERVICES   115
Scope of Services.

SNOW REMOVAL SERVICES   115
KEY SHOP SERVICES   116
VANDALISM RESTORATION SERVICES   117
FIRE PROTECTION SERVICES   117
SUMMARY   118

12. MANAGING ASSIGNED MAINTENANCE TASKS 119

INSTRUCTIONAL EQUIPMENT SERVICES   119
Drivotrainers. Electronics. Instructional Media Equipment. Sound Systems.

SCHOOL SITE MOWING SERVICES   121
RELOCATING PORTABLE CLASSROOM SERVICES   122
ELEVATOR REPAIR SERVICES   123

12. MANAGING ASSIGNED MAINTENANCE TASKS (Continued)

LAUNDRY REPAIR SERVICES   123

PEST CONTROL   123

Insects. Termites. Domestic Rodents. Birds and Flying Insects. Miscellaneous Pests.

CARPET SERVICES   125

SUMMARY   125

13. MANAGING SERVICES FOR ANCILLARY AREAS 126

DATA PROCESSING ROOM SERVICES   126

MOBILE LABORATORY SERVICES   127

SCHOOL STADIA SERVICES   127

SWIMMING POOL SERVICES   128

GREENHOUSE SERVICES   128

TELEVISION STUDIO SERVICES   129

CENTRAL ADMINISTRATION PLANT SERVICES   129

FOOD FACILITY SERVICES   130

FEDERAL PROJECTS SERVICES   130

OTHER ANCILLARY SERVICES   131

SUMMARY   131

14. UPGRADING EXISTING SCHOOL PLANTS 132

School plant's age.

EDUCATIONAL RESPONSIBILITY   133

THE USE OF SPECIALISTS   133

THE USE OF IMAGINATION   133

CRITERIA FOR JUDGING EXISTING PLANT   134

Criteria for Site. Supplemental Site Criteria. Criteria for the Building. Supplemental Educational Requirement Criteria. Criteria for Existing Construction. Supplemental Type of Construction Criteria. Criteria for Interior Building Elements. Supplemental Building Interior Criteria. Criteria for Furniture and Equipment.

MASTER PLAN   140

PLANNING THE BUDGET   140

SETTING UPGRADING PROGRAM   140

SUMMARY   140

15. PROMISING PREPLANNED MAINTENANCE POINTERS 141

TOTAL SITE LAYOUT POINTERS   142

TOTAL BUILDING POINTERS   142

15. PROMISING PREPLANNED MAINTENANCE POINTERS (Continued)

EXTERIOR FINISH POINTERS   143

POINTERS FOR BUILDING SPACES   143

POINTERS FOR INTERIOR FINISHES   143
Ceilings. Doors. Safety. Color.

POINTERS FOR CONSTRUCTION   145

POINTERS FOR ELECTRICAL SERVICES   145

POINTERS FOR MECHANICAL SERVICES   146
Water Systems. Sanitary Facilities. Heating Facilities. Ventilating Facilities.

POINTERS ON EQUIPMENT AND FURNITURE   147

SUMMARY   148

APPENDICES   149

    APPENDIX A.   149

    APPENDIX B.   169

    APPENDIX C.   203

GLOSSARY   209

BIBLIOGRAPHY   211

INDEX   216

PART
I

ADMINISTRATIVE PRACTICES:
KEYS TO EFFECTIVE CONTROLS

Chapter 1

A PRACTICAL BASIS FOR
A SUCCESSFUL PROGRAM

An intriguing phase of school administration is the development of the modern concept of the maintenance of school plants. Whether it be a one-room rural plant or a plant of many instructional areas, the ever-present problem of maintenance is a continuous challenge. The increase in the size of administration units with its many attendance units demands greater efficiency. The increasing value of the school plants in the United States requires more money for school plant maintenance. In 1966 the dollar value was in excess of $100 billion. The present rate of growth is in excess of $4 billion per year.[1] Educational administrators and school boards are faced with the problem of providing prudent policies which will protect and keep these big valuable plants functional.

Maintenance is the process of keeping the school plant and its equipment in good condition by systematized and businesslike arrangements. It is a central office staff function. The term *maintenance* implies those activities which are essential to keeping the physical plant in a good state of repair and doing the necessary functions to improve school plant facilities to enhance the educational program. The term refers to those cyclic and intermittent services intended to keep the plant near its original state of preservation, in other words, repairs and replacements.

Modern maintenance involves property protection, adaptation to the changing educational program, and continued high level efficiency for the users of the school plant. The terms most commonly used in describing these activities are *remodeling, rehabilitation, modernization,* and *repair.*

Remodeling, rehabilitation, and modernization appear confusing. The concept of alteration assists in clarifying their separate meanings.

Alterations for *remodeling* connote a change in structure or major structural or architectural improvement to the school plant for the purpose of stabilizing or protecting it. Moving or remov-

---

[1] *Schools for America* (Washington, D.C.: A.A.S.A., Commission on School Buildings, 1967), p. 131.

ing a partition and a change in the roof structure are examples. Alterations for *rehabilitation* signify a general overhauling of the complete plant or a major section thereof to adapt it for continued use. Alterations for *modernization* are designed primarily to adapt existing facilities and spaces to meet the needs of the desired educational programs.

The terms *repairs and replacements, upkeep,* and *maintenance* are synonymous. Each characterizes the continuous process of restoration of any piece of property whether grounds, buildings, or equipment. Properly conceived and executed plans for school plant restoration use new ideas and new materials to increase efficiency to meet the needs of changing educational programs. This concept of maintenance *excludes* the activities of building operations and capital outlay. Repairing sidewalks, replacing or repairing the plumbing on science tables, the rewiring of motors, and the patching of leaky roofs are good examples of maintenance. These functions exist to some extent in all districts; they only change in scope.

This book treats hundreds of items, some of which may seem elementary to the expertly qualified reader. Both practical and teaching experience reveal that many questions are forthcoming on many seemingly insignificant items. Almost all items are present in large school plant systems. Many items are present in small school systems. The ideas are presented for study and adaptation if practical in a school system of any size.

OBJECTIVES OF MAINTENANCE

The school plant, the most costly tool in the educational process, is to many people the tangible symbol of an ideal. A community, the school staff, and the students are stimulated by a well-maintained school plant, to which all point with pride. Many objectives of an effective administration of school plant maintenance activities may be listed. The objectives develop out of the educational policy of the schools. Regardless of the size of the school system, the foremost include:

Protection of Property. The protection of the public investment in the school plant is a primary objective. Definite scheduling of maintenance activities assists in the reaching of this goal.

Continued Use. This objective is the pride of most maintenance department employees. Their goal is to make certain the plant can be used each day as needed.

Attractiveness. The school plant has an added incentive when maintenance operations produce pleasant learning situations. A planned maintenance program for the site, the building, and its equipment assists in focusing pleasantness. This function makes the school plant a desirable home for the youth of the community. An attractive plant adds to staff and pupil morale. These functions also create respect and admiration on the part of the public for the school.

Healthful Conditions. The health of all people who use the building and grounds through proper heat, ventilation, humidity control, and lighting is preserved when these facilities function properly.

Safety. The maintenance of conditions conducive to safety for all people who use the school plant is an important goal. Accident prevention from any cause, the elimination of fire hazards, and the disposal of faulty equipment are important tasks.

Value as Learning Laboratory. Proper maintenance which produces conditions which foster cleanliness, well-functioning utilities, and artistic environmental conditions makes a positive impact upon the artistic and sociological pursuits of individuals who use the school.

Economies. Saving money is possible when all school plant personnel are administered according to definite programs.

Operation. Proper and timely maintenance activities affect conditions where custodial duties may be performed more easily and quickly. The conserved energy and time can then be used to perform other important duties which may prevent costly maintenance. This book of necessity mentions the custodial help in the maintenance of a school plant because of the different sized school districts throughout the nation. It is not a manual for the working custodian himself. The teamwork of school plant employees tends to reduce maintenance costs.

Maintenance. The timeliness of the correction and scheduling of frequency of the maintenance operations can produce economies. The goals of efficient school plant maintenance can be best summarized by stating that if the plant is in good repair, (1) it is easier to keep clean, (2) it is easier to heat, (3) it adds to staff and pupil morale and comfort, (4) it creates respect and admiration on the part of the public for the school, and (5) it is more economical to operate.[2] The first and final goal of maintenance, like other areas of school administration, is to improve educational opportunities for students.

FACTORS DETERMINING THE AMOUNT AND COST OF MAINTENANCE

Many factors in each district determine the amount and consequently the cost of maintenance of school plants. An able maintenance administrator examines these factors as each factor pertains to his assignment. A brief description of these isolated factors should alert administration of their importance.

Design. The maintenance of the school plant starts on the design board in the choice of materials. Materials used in the school plants should have the characteristics of (1) durability or longevity, (2) ease of cleaning and/or renovation, (3) the facility of replacement, (4) the selection of apparatus and equipment based on experience coupled with testing, and (5) an economic balance between first cost versus upkeep. The field of design for preplanned maintenance is a study in itself. An extensive list of preplanned tips for maintenance are discussed in a magazine article.[3]

Climate. Materials begin to decompose as soon as they are exposed to the atmosphere. The factors of sunshine, hail, sleet, rain, wind, smog, earth tremors, soil conditions, sedimentation, salt water, dust, and electrolysis are present to some degree causing deterioration. Each community has experiences concerning the climatic reactions which are concerns that should guide in the selection of materials in the original planning and the restoration of materials for maintenance.

Use. The kind of use and respect the public has for its property greatly determines the amount of maintenance needed in each community. Proper respect and careful use of facilities lessen the need for maintenance. Vandalism and week-end treatment of school plants have become growing concerns for responsible school administrators. Operating efficiency is an important factor. If all the equipment in the school plant is maintained and used according to instructions, maintenance functions should be lessened.

Local School Plant Situation. In a school district, the ages of the school plants may vary from those more recently constructed to those which are fifty or more years of age. The number of school plants of each age in a district determines the quantity of maintenance functions. Material obsolescence and conditions of safety as well as educational obsolescence often appear in the older plants. The types of buildings often range from all wood structures to those of all

---

[2] *School Plant Maintenance* (Washington, D.C.: American Association of Administrators, 1951), p. 24.
[3] N. L. George, "Tips for Preplanned Maintenance," *American School Board Journal,* April 1966, pp. 26–27. Copyrighted by National School Boards Association.

brick with selected impervious materials. The variables of age, number of school plants, and the type of construction materials are of primary importance in planning a maintenance program.

Updating of Building Codes. Some of the existing multi-story school buildings become hazardous where the governmental agencies adapt and/or update existing codes. "Class B" partitions and doors have to be installed in stairways to control smoke between floors. Another significant change is that fire dampers are required where ducts pierce floors.

Technological Advances. Lighting levels have changed and are changing. New instructional media are under continuous development. Different concepts of the housing of the libraries and instructional aids are evolving. These ideas are a few of the technological changes which are requiring different kinds of spaces and special provisions for storage. Additional electrical outlets and circuits are common requests.

Standards of Service. Local school districts usually establish their own standards of service. These standards are formulated and set by the responsible administrator. They may be low or high standards depending upon the conception and training of the "know-how" of the management.

Managerial Efficiency. The skill and acumen of the personnel employed to perform the maintenance functions are very important. Qualified, experienced personnel are basic to efficiency.

Wage Levels. The local wage rate is an important consideration in the cost of maintenance. If the board of education pays comparable wages to similar skill positions in the community and receives expert service for the wages, the cost may be relatively unimportant. Otherwise, if the board of education pays too low a wage to hold capable employees, the cost may become prohibitive.

Cost of Supplies, Materials, and Equipment. Efficient procurement of supplies and materials is basic to economy. Supplies and materials purchased for maintenance in the right quantity, the right quality, the right price, and at the right time enhance efficiency.

Influence of "Machine" Politics. If supplies and materials are not selected on an experience and tested basis, and if personnel are not selected on qualifications and kept on performance efficiency, operations become impaired and costly.

METHOD OF PERFORMING MAINTENANCE FUNCTIONS

The maintenance of school facilities presents a greater challenge than maintenance in most other types of operation. This function is so closely related to the educational program. Thus it behooves the administrator to use the best methods available to keep the school plants suitable for the educational processes. No one method is best for all school districts. Experience reveals that the responsible administrator may accomplish maintenance functions by using one or more of the following methods:

I. All maintenance work done by a school staff which includes custodians and a professional maintenance crew composed of one or more journeymen.

II. All maintenance work done by contract. Contracts may be on annual basis or may be for specific job.

III. Maintenance work done partly by a school staff and partly by contract.

IV. Most work done by the school staff, although occasionally journeymen are called in for specific jobs.

V. All maintenance work done by a professional maintenance crew, organized for specific planned activities.

VI. All maintenance work done by a professional maintenance crew and contracts on jobs of a certain size.[4]

Experience reveals that method VI is economical, practical, and efficient. This method allows the professional maintenance crew to work on scheduled projects at a time when the restoration is needed for economy and efficiency. Certain alterations and repairs projects which cost more than $2,000 or any selected amount can be let by contract. Replacing the entire roof on a building or converting an auditorium into a cafetorium or an instructional media center are excellent examples of contract work.

The maintenance crew operating under a flexible schedule may perform services when required and may make repeated calls to correct the same trouble.

Furthermore, full-time personnel of a maintenance crew may be employed at a slightly lower wage than the prevailing wage paid by contractors. The very nature of maintenance work defies description and often requires redirection after the work is started. The discovered change may be made without waiting for a board meeting. The school staff members have a familiarity with the plant that enables the members of the staff to proceed to assignments without loss of time. The pride of a school-employed staff working for a non-delay and smooth operation is highly commendable and favorable to this method.

HINDRANCES TO EFFECTIVE MAINTENANCE

Adept administration must deal with negative elements in the organization of maintenance activities. These negative elements may appear in the lack of planning, lack of money, or lack of staff.

Lack of Plan. School administration is deeply interested in rendering services to boys and girls in the effective maintenance of the school plant. An effective plan is required. It is not enough merely to muddle through. The plan must eliminate makeshift decisions, waste, inefficiency, shortcomings, lack of coordination, rule-of-thumb arrangements, low productivity, friction, jealousies, and high costs. Often the responsible administrative officers clash with the workers—an extremely undesirable situation. The basic need is to plan the useful work in the most systematic way that will have a practical meaning to all parties concerned with effective maintenance.

Lack of Money. The annual maintenance budget is often based on the report given by the supervisor of maintenance after a cursory inspection. No supporting data for the budget items are available. No effort has been made to estimate the maintenance budget in terms of immediate and long-term needs. These conditions, plus the stress to put all available monies into the educational programs, often hinder maintenance. Maintenance services must be planned with an estimated cost on the scheduled items. An allowance for nonscheduled items must also be made. Then an intelligent decision can be made by the responsible administration. This procedure should establish an effective plan for maintenance.

Lack of Staff. Theoretical thinking does not create an adequate staff. A study of the actual daily execution of the various activities performed creates distinct detail tasks. The required time and specific skills must be considered, prepared for, and executed specifically in every activity. The results of this method of procedure assist in planning the adequacy of the staff. A careful analysis of the maintenance needs over the long- and short-range programs should also focus on the number of staff members needed. Effective administration will decide most carefully the maintenance problems which are important enough to control. On the bases of these

---

[4] John David Engman, *School Plant Management for School Administrators* (Houston, Texas: Gulf School Research Development Association, 1962), p. 53.

data, controls will be established. Thus, no control or skimpy control will be replaced by efficient control—a guide in determining the adequacy of the staff.

METHODS WHICH PRODUCE MAINTENANCE ECONOMIES

The possible economies in the administration of maintenance services are numerous. Some methods used by the administration should include:

Standardized Component Parts. This concept is very difficult to handle in a large school district. The plants were purchased and constructed with changing school boards, changing administrations, and changing architectural conceptions within the last hundred years. Insofar as possible, maintenance items should be minimized and simplified. Such items as hardware, lighting fixtures, plumbing fixtures and fittings, motors, engines, and visual aid equipment are items which may be standardized. Standardization of locks is an asset in a maintenance program. A small but complete stock of standard repair parts, replacements, and tools accessible to staff personnel assists the proficiency of maintenance work.

Quality Checking on Materials Received. The incoming materials purchased by the school district should be thoroughly inspected by a qualified person as they are delivered to the central service warehouse or to the assigned job. This action is a protection against the substitution of inferior products. Thus the administration is assured of receiving the value for which the district pays. Good materials are an important factor in reducing future maintenance.

Purchase Locally if Practical. Secure services and equipment from dealers within the immediate community, if reasonably priced. Experience with this procedure has proven that delays in receiving parts can be eliminated.

Familiarize Responsible Personnel with School Plant Detail. The new school is ready to use. The responsible personnel should be trained so that all parts of the school plant may function as planned. Local school principals change, custodial personnel and maintenance personnel change, and the new personnel should acquaint themselves with the original plans. Operating manuals from manufacturers, plans, and specifications from the architect are all aids in alerting the users of the school plant. If all parts of the school plant are administered as planned, economies should accrue.

Time. Time is an important element in building maintenance. If a school building and equipment are kept in good repair, deterioration is greatly deferred. Often rehabilitation or even remodeling may be unnecessary until an alteration is necessary to meet a change in the educational program. Periodic treatment to certain surfaces or areas with minor and/or emergency repairs needed can forestall costly maintenance. Careful timely inspection, budgeting, and performance make possible the most effective use of local staffs and facilities.

SUMMARY

School plants require maintenance services. The kind and number of services are related to the many factors mentioned in this chapter. These services are performed by personnel employed by the school district to perform certain assigned areas of maintenance.

Schools are maintained to improve instruction—a complex process. Effective performance of maintenance services provides an attractive atmosphere for the learner as well as all school employees. In addition, the instructional areas are sanitary and safe environments.

Effective administration plans that manpower, money, machines, and methods are coordinated to bring the best environment to the youth and adults of the community.

Chapter **2**

ORGANIZING FOR

EFFICIENT MAINTENANCE

Effective maintenance is evident only when the centralized services are planned on basic operating principles. Any one of the principles is not inclusive. Each principle must be present in the effective organizational setup if the organization is to perform its function effectively. Though excellent principles are established for an ideal organization, the human factor enters into all organizational work, and the administration usually must work with the individuals available.

Determining the principles which guide the programming of maintenance in a district, regardless of its size, is basic action for effective administration. Defining maintenance activities for a school district is a second study. The classes of maintenance functions which the district purports to provide must be clearly understood regardless of the size of the district. Detailing this program is a local responsibility. The steps and essentials for programming maintenance functions in a small district of necessity may be few. Yet a definite procedure based on sound planning principles is recommended.

Figures 2–1 and 2–2 have assisted both small and large school districts in establishing effective maintenance functions. These charts can be adapted to maintenance functions according to the size of the district.

PRINCIPLES FOR EFFECTIVE ORGANIZATION

Long experience in the field of educational administration dictates that the most important principles for effective maintenance include:

Coordination.

One person who does a job has no need for coordination; the work of several people who work on the same job, however, needs coordination. In effective maintenance work, such activ-

DIVISION OF SCHOOL PLANT SERVICES

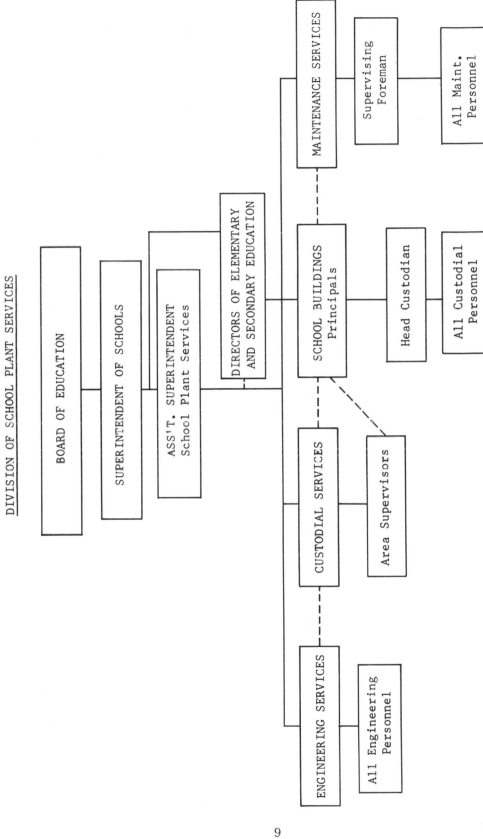

Figure 2-1. Chart of Administrative Responsibility.

9

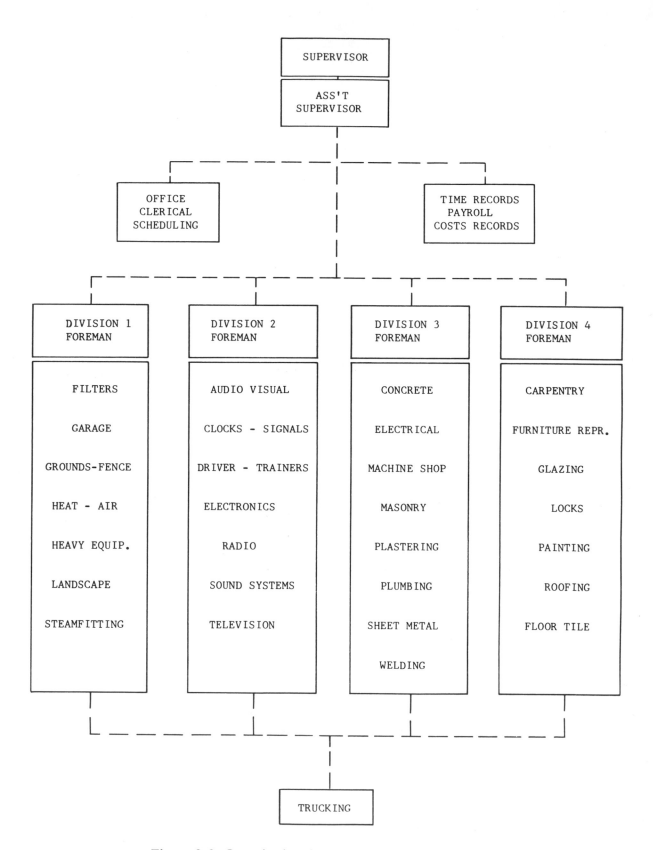

Figure 2–2. Organization Chart—Maintenance Department.

10

ities as carpentry, furniture repair, roofing, mechanical repair, trucking, and purchasing may need definite organizational steps. While the coordination of these services is mandatory, no single method of coordination exists. The plan will depend upon each local situation because of the conditions of the assigned job. Two general methods of coordination seem evident. First, the plan must subdivide responsibilities for each class of employees. Second, each worker must be able to see his task fitted into the whole plan. Neither factor is mutually inclusive, and any organization must use both methods to be successful.

Defining jobs to be done, providing the direction to see that major objectives of the maintenance organization are realized, determining how many workers are needed for specific jobs, and establishing the structure between the direction and the ultimate working conditions are all jobs of coordination. As a result, members of two or more different crafts can work efficiently together to achieve the same purpose. Thus, coordination of the different services in a school maintenance program into a combination of suitable relationships is an effective principle.

Functionalism.

The inadequacies of our language have given many meanings to *functionalism*. This book uses the term to refer to functional differentiation between types of duties. In a job of any kind, the determination that something is to be accomplished, the actual accomplishment, and the resolution of any conflicts which may occur generally appear collectively. These three factors may appear completely separated in the general structure of an effective organization.

The purpose of any organization is to achieve integrated correlation of all factors. True correlation may be realized through distinct definition of duties. The different tasks to be performed should be understood so that conflicts among the different groups can be reduced. When all members of an organization see their jobs in relation to all the jobs around them and in relation to the total purpose of the enterprise, a unity of spirit develops which is fundamental to the establishment of an effective effort.

Staff service in functionalism has three closely integrated phases: (1) the informative phase refers to that which administrative personnel should know in making its decisions; (2) the advisory phase is the actual counsel of such information; and (3) the supervision phase refers to both phases as they are applied to the details of execution. Thus, the staff is purely an auxiliary service. In effective maintenance each member of the staff must see his job both as a job itself and how his job affects the fulfillment of all the functions of the local program.

Promising Practices.

Much critical thinking has been explored regarding the placement of maintenance functions. Where should certain functions be placed? Should they be handled locally or centrally? Some functions may adjust themselves more easily to a centralized organization, while others may not. Cillie[1] found that adequate maintenance procedures prosper as well or better under centralization as they do under decentralization. The benefits of centralization[2] of services have been found to be the establishing of unified practices and standards, responding quickly to emergencies, and contributing to more efficiency and economy.

The centralized services (1) attract more competent personnel, (2) make wide sources of information available, (3) provide for greater functional specialization, (4) make possible greater opportunities for the centralization of administrative activities, (5) make possible the

[1] Reprinted with permission of the publisher from Francois Stephanus Cillie's *Centralized or Decentralized* (New York: Teacher's College Press), copyright 1940 by Francois Stephanus Cillie, p. 86.

[2] Reprinted with permission of the publisher from Paul Studenski and Paul R. Mort's *Centralized vs. Decentralized Government in Relation to Democracy* (New York: Teachers College Press), copyright 1940 and 1941, Teacher's College, Columbia University, pp. 32–51.

division of labor and the securing of better equipment, and (6) give common direction to the care of the physical properties in a system and compel the personnel to maintain maximum standards of public service. The result is the assignment of tasks to be performed in order that they can be performed more efficiently.

Efficiency.

Personal experience has revealed that the principle of efficiency in maintenance activities is very important. The expertness of eliminating waste of both human and material resources is developed by efficient administration. Facets include these provisions: (1) training for the duties and responsibilities of leadership and foremanship, (2) securing cooperation and use of talents of skilled people, (3) developing a feeling of unity in school administration, (4) providing skilled people for special jobs, and (5) upgrading people in the jobs they hold. Pooling suggestions from all workers to formulate a greater interest in the services rendered and studying methods of production are likewise positive.

The elimination of wasteful practices in the utilization of manpower and materials is enhanced by the organization of work layouts for projects and the request of correct materials for usage.

The flow of work may be enhanced by making provisions for the safety of the worker and proper maintenance of machinery and equipment necessary to perform the work stipulated in the project plans.

To achieve efficiency, goodwill is fundamental. Goodwill begins in the smallest unit of an organization. Many unexplored possibilities exist where harmony is secured by improving relations in the routine of daily work. These matters may seem small and unimportant, but if they should pile up, they will cause disruptions. The starting point of all bad labor relations is the unit of work. The sagacious leader is always focusing his attention on adjustments within his organization.

Effective organization teaches that each skill has methods and standards which each skilled person strives to maintain and improve. In pooling skills and coordinating the efforts of several skilled functions, certain phases common to all endeavors have to be routinized. The results are a facilitation and/or increase in services and an increase in production.

Service.

Past experience reveals that maintenance workers in a school system who are taught how to coordinate their work tend to develop an active cooperation between themselves and management. The pooling of ideas and efforts generally leads to better practices. Workers who develop a "trade" knowledge about the school system acquire the very spirit of improvement. They become imbued with a conscious belief that things can be improved, and thus they make possible the success of the maintenance program. This image creates for the maintenance worker a place in the school system which includes school personnel, pupils, and patrons of the community.

Another aspect of service is the opportunity that is provided for the individual worker in the maintenance organization. Steady employment, a fair wage, favorable physical surroundings, and ample fringe benefits, all serve as a motivating force. A chance to train continually to improve his skill and service and the continuous appraisal of the effectiveness of his job to the total problem are added features of motivation. These avenues of motivation of the individual worker develop a tendency to improve his contribution to the school system.

LOCAL DETERMINATION OF MAINTENANCE ACTIVITIES

Effective administration of the maintenance program depends mostly on the kinds of activities assigned to the personnel of the maintenance department. In a district with only one or two buildings, individual school building employees may be required to do minor repairs. A large school system may be able to provide full employment for a maintenance staff with a number of specific skills. Meanwhile, a small system may employ a few general maintenance personnel and contract those jobs requiring specialized labor. The size of the maintenance staff will depend largely on how the minor repairs are made. Linn[3] suggests that individual school building employees might be called upon to do minor repairs. Experience dictates that this list of thirty items is too large. The list might include:

1. Replacing broken glass in windows, doors, cases, etc.
2. Tightening screws and bolts in furniture.
3. Adjusting window shade rollers.
4. Replacing electric fuse plugs.
5. Repairing electric light switches.
6. Replacing electric light sockets.
7. Tightening loose door knobs.
8. Replacing door knobs.
9. Adjusting door checks.
10. Adjusting "adjustable" desks to pupils.
11. Cleaning and adjusting gas ranges.
12. Replacing washers in valves.
13. Regulating flow in drinking fountains.
14. Replacing or adjusting balls in toilet flush tanks.
15. Cleaning traps.
16. Cleaning a clogged toilet or drain.
17. Fastening loose trim or moldings.
18. Repairing pencil sharpeners.

The length of this list depends upon the skill of the personnel and the equipment in each school plant. The performance of these items does not require expert services in many cases. The well-qualified head building custodian or building engineer should do minor repairs as determined by the local school administration.

This book deals with major maintenance services which, when programmed, provide yearly employment. Labor is the costly item in a maintenance program, consequently a local determination of the functions which are to be included and excluded in these maintenance activities is necessary.

CLASSES OF MAINTENANCE SERVICES

This book deals with maintenance activities which fall into two broad categories, viz., scheduled and nonscheduled.

Scheduled. The scheduled program entails preventative maintenance. This kind of maintenance is a program of inspection, service, and correction which is planned for the purpose of

[3] Reprinted with the permission of the publisher from Henry H. Linn, *Practical School Economies* (New York: Teacher's College Press), copyright 1934, Teacher's College, Columbia University, pp. 288–289.

preventing expensive repairs and breakdowns before they occur. Painting exposed wood and replacing the parts of a motor at regular intervals are good examples. The crafts employed for painting, roofing, ground care (not mowing grass), some plumbing, and some ventilation projects are those which can best be used for preventative maintenance. A sound preventive program is more economical and sensible than a breakdown-replacement program. It eliminates the employment of extra personnel to handle emergency repairs. A reasonable expenditure, when needed, may insure against the school plant failure or larger expenditure later. Preventive maintenance not only decreases the cost of correction but actually helps maintain the value of the school plant. Scheduled work usually results in better job completions, and utility expenses can usually be reduced by preventive maintenance.

Nonscheduled. The nonscheduled maintenance program includes a program of repairs based on the intermittent reports of other school personnel, principals, area maintenance personnel, and head custodians. These requests for maintenance are usually emergency needs. Some of these items demand prompt attention, while others must be cared for in the immediate future. Desirable items may be postponed—if, however, they are small items which affect instruction, they should be completed as soon as practical.

PROGRAMMING FOR MAINTENANCE

Many people must be involved if the maintenance program is to be effective. The central office staff, the responsible maintenance personnel, and the school building principal have definite contributions to make. In addition each maintenance worker has a fixed responsibility and a job description to follow. The method of programming will vary from school district to school district. The following team effort has been successful for many years.

Step I: Inspection by Capable Personnel.

The first step in planning an effective maintenance program is the inspection of each existing plant. The responsible personnel who have the time and intelligence should make a study of maintenance needs in conference with the principal of the building. A thorough annual inspection of the buildings and grounds should be made. This inspection should be made in midwinter or early spring. Master check lists should guide the inspectors in making the list of needed repairs and replacements. (See Appendix A, Notes 1–11.) A school system may develop its own master check list. These check lists are useful in making inspections, because they call attention to the condition of material and equipment in each school plant. Each item needing maintenance attention should be noted. Time can be saved and copious notes eliminated by the use of line sketches of the different buildings in the school district. A 17″ × 24″ sketch of each building is made on a scale suitable to the size of the building. The rooms and areas have numbers. This sketch is put on a clipboard. The larger building sketches must be divided into quarter sheets. The inspection personnel can note on the plans the exact location of the defects which are found. (See Appendix A, Note 12.) For example, in school room 102, where the walls above the wainscot are stained by water, the 2 B 3 is noted on the exact location. This scheme assists in the review of maintenance problems of the individual school in Step V. These recorded conditions eliminate any oversight.

Step II: Inspection by Responsible Craftsmen.

The second step in planning maintenance is to have qualified craftsmen check items which use frequent periodic attentions. These reports can be made on the same master check lists.

These craftsmen should make notes of detections of the different items and report them to the head of the maintenance department. The inspection reports of the local fire departments, boiler inspectors, and insurance inspectors should be studied by responsible craftsmen and reported to the head of the department.

Step III: Building Principal's Annual Request.

The third step is to send to each building principal an annual request for maintenance. On this form should be listed modifications and repairs which are necessary for the improvement of instruction, such as the addition or removal of partitions, addition or replacement of chalkboards and tackboards, and other changes needed to improve the quality of instruction. Window shades that need repair or replacements and furniture which needs repair or refinishing should also be listed. Also community suggestions should be presented with the principal's annual request for maintenance. (See Appendix A, Note 13.)

Step IV: Recommendations of Instructional Staff.

The fourth step in planning maintenance is to ascertain the changes in the physical plant that the central office instructional staff desires in the several school plants to accommodate the instructional program for the next school year. These specific recommendations regarding the school plants are noted.

Step V: Conferences.

The fifth step in planning is to have a conference of the responsible maintenance personnel. In this conference the annual and periodic notations, the building principal's annual request for maintenance, and the requests of the recommendations of the instructional staff are reviewed item by item. The cost of repair, replacement, or alteration is estimated on each item. These estimates are based on the cost records of performance of the same or similar projects which the department has performed.

In this conference, painting schedules, replacement schedules, equipment schedules, and long-range planning for certain improvements are examined. It is important to treat all schools on an equal basis, and to be fair.

Step VI: Budget Allowance.

The sixth step in planning is to secure administrative approval of a tentative amount for maintenance. This amount is necessary in order to plan men, materials, and methods for the next year's program.

> *Budgeting for Maintenance.* The school maintenance phase of plant management is as closely related to the financial program of the school system as it is to the educational program. The long-range problems of upkeep which are related to education are of primary importance. The long-term projections for annual alterations are developed and presented to the administration in order to keep the school plants functional.
>
> This question is always present: How much of the current operating budget should be annually stipulated for upkeep of the school plant? *Schools for America* suggests that the percentage be between four and four and one-half percent.[4]

---

[4] *Schools for America* (Washington, D.C.: American Association of School Administrators, 1967), p. 135.

The size of school districts varies and each district has its own financial resources. Experience has revealed that not less than five per cent of the total amount of budget should be estimated for maintenance. This amount, if properly spent yearly, tends to keep school plants in a district on a continuous improvement level.

School districts which have good records on the cost of current replacement of the school plants may use at least one per cent of the current replacement cost as a budget item for maintenance. A few districts may use two per cent. Should the records be based on original costs, at least three per cent should be used.

These percentages are workable if a large backlog of needed repairs has not accumulated. Also, in school districts where the cost of maintenance is high, a larger percentage may be required. The suggested rates should be minimum allowances for the school budget:

Here is a sample of successful budgeting. Suppose a school system has an annual operating budget of approximately $130,000,000. Five per cent of this budget is $6,500,000.

This school system has properties which have a current replacement value of approximately $145,000,000 with about 40 per cent of the plants relatively new.

The school administration has been providing an average of $3,500,000 for maintenance and modernization for a ten year period. Through long-range planning based on annual inspections the conditions of the several properties are far above average.

Step VII: Establishing Priorities.

The seventh step in planning maintenance projects is the establishment of priorities on the requests considered in the conference where the costs of the feasible requests were estimated. Before these priorities are established, the total budget item must be reviewed by taking into account the local practices of employment for maintenance services. The number of men and materials needed for scheduled maintenance, for nonscheduled maintenance, for summer work, for extra work during the fiscal year, and the men needed for local assigned allied services must be budgeted. If annual service contracts on certain equipment are used, these items must be budgeted. An allowance should be made for the restoration of facilities if vandalism is significant in the community. These items are basic, and their priorities on new projects can be estimated. This evaluation may disclose that some very important items must be postponed. This framework allows for the long-range planning of maintenance work.

Step VIII: Finalizing the Maintenance Budget.

Once decisions have been made on the costs of the approved items in Step VII, the responsible personnel has the duty to program the work. Programming the work spells out both the man-hours (by craft) and the materials needed on each project. These calculations are very important because the costs of labor will consume a minimum of 80 per cent of the maintenance budget.[5] The division of labor according to tasks is a significant factor in determining the number of man hours for each skill.

Step IX: Organizing the Maintenance Staff.

Each school district should have an organization chart responsive to its size. The superintendent or business manager generally assumes direct supervision of school maintenance employees in small school districts. Separate maintenance staff organizations in larger schools have divergent procedures required for administration of the maintenance program. The size of the school district, the amount of needed maintenance, the money available for mainte-

---

[5] Walter C. Hawkins, *Preventive School Maintenance Program American School and University* (New York: American Publishing Co., 1949) Vol. 21, pp. 304–305.

nance, the definition of local activities for maintenance, and the availability of skilled personnel determine the district organizational plan.

Organization Charts. Good examples of organization in different sized school districts on a nationwide basis are shown by three charts, I–III, in *School Plant Management.*[6] The lines of authority for maintenance personnel must be clearly defined in order that these employees understand their relationships with other employees of the school system. The duties of the maintenance groups are different, yet they must see that each job is a part of a team effort to create an environment in which the learning process is enhanced.

An organization plan refers to the conditions that must be created and their functions as they appear in action to the people who make up the organization. The philosophy, the principles of operation, the goals, the good will, and the efficient job performance must be coordinated in the plan as these facets are developed for creating a good teaching environment.

Using the functional chart as a guide, detailed write-ups of the assignment, responsibilities, and activities of each position on the chart should be prepared for the guidance of the individuals on each assigned job.

Functional Charts. The chart in Figure 2–1 reveals the relationships in a school system large enough to have separate supervision of engineering, maintenance, and custodial (operation) functions.

A functional chart should also be made for the department itself. The chart in Figure 2–2 has been used with success for several years and has been changed several times because of changes in projects and personnel. The maintenance work of approximately 200 skeleton crew people is coordinated by this chart. No one organization will fit all school districts, however. The organization must fit the particular set of conditions which prevail for each particular school district. "The ideal organization is one in which all elements are in balance with each other and with their environment and the maximum coordination of all activities is obtained."[7]

Man-Hours by Craft. The job of estimating man-hours by craft can easily be based on the past records of man-hour requirements of like jobs in the school system.

If such records are not kept, a careful study will have to be made of the maintenance needs which can be recorded and then analyzed as to type. Another method of determining the labor amount of the budget item for maintenance, i.e., $1,250,000, is to take 80 per cent of that amount for labor which may be divided into man-hours by crafts. Some school districts attempt to employ one maintenance worker for each 200 students. This last method is very costly in systems of large enrollments.

Supervision. In school districts, small or large, supervision of maintenance activities is helpful. Proper supervision of maintenance personnel improves the quality and quantity of work, performance techniques, employee morale, and human relations. The best supervision uses common sense: teaching, helping and observing during the performance of employees' duties. In small districts the ratio of supervisors to craftsmen may be calculated as one to every two or three. In larger districts the ratio varies.

Step X: Arranging for Materials.

Top management has the responsibility to study and recommend to the administration the manner in which the best execution of the work may be accomplished. In calculating the maintenance work to be completed, the supervisor may request materials or service contracts.

---

[6] *School Plant Management—Organizing the Maintenance Program* (Washington, D.C.: U. S. Department of Health, Education, and Welfare, Office of Education, 1960), pp. 27, 29.

[7] From *Small Plant Management* by W. A. MacCrehan, Jr., copyright 1960. The American Society of Mechanical Engineers. Used by permission of McGraw-Hill Book Company, p. 187.

Materials. The procurement practices for materials for maintenance vary. In many school districts, delegated personnel in the department do the purchasing according to rules and regulations of the local administration. The better practice is for competent maintenance personnel to request materials and supplies on definite specifications for the approved projects in the maintenance budget. These requests are sent to the purchasing department which advertises, tabulates, and consults with the maintenance employees as the decision for the final purchase is made. The materials and supplies are a responsibility of the storeroom as they are received and dispersed on approved requests for materials to the maintenance employees. Experience dictates that all materials for repair be a definite responsibility of the storeroom until they are assigned to a specific job or a specific craft.

Practice reveals that an expediter may be needed to procure small parts for motors, definite parts for television sets, and other intricate elements which are not carried economically in the maintenance warehouse. The expediter can secure the necessary part and the instrument can be repaired and be ready for use.

Service Contracts. School districts, both small and large, often find that the district cannot employ the know-how to do specialized jobs at a reasonable cost. The districts find that it is both economical and expedient to contract with companies that have expert repairmen to do repairs or perform services. The upkeep of an elevator is an example for an annual service contract. These contracts will vary from one school district to another. The guide is the number of elements in all school plants, the availability of expert talent, and the cost of the service.

Step XI: Tooling Up for Maintenance.

Maintenance activities can be improved by machines, tools, equipment, and mechanization. These machines may be modified for the largest or smallest tasks. Adjustments and redesign capabilities can suit different tasks from the heaviest to the lightest kinds of work. They become ideal prospects for improvement toward effective maintenance.

Experience in a school district reveals that the top maintenance administrator who studies and knows the problems in his school district is able to request proper machines and tools. The most careful choice and selection of machines, tools, equipment, and mechanization are his prime responsibilities. He usually works with the responsible craftsmen in the separate departments in making choices and selection. Since a device must do the work at a saving, the administrator must secure all the labor-saving devices possible in order to reduce man-hours.

The concept, "any old tool will do," is false. A specific tool or machine is needed for specific performances. The specific tool enhances economies in maintenance. The alert administrator in maintenance activities will keep informed about the list of applicable machines, tools, equipment, and mechanization in nearby surplus property warehouses. He has the definite responsibility of deciding the practical use of the objects in his situation. Unless these objects do specific jobs creating economies, he should overlook the bargain potential.

Experience reveals that all portable and all fixed tools and equipment should be provided by the school district. Hand tools should also be provided by the district. These practices eliminate false economies. Definite regulations for checking in and out needed tools to workers is a most important administrative responsibility.

Step XII: Applying Constant Evaluation.

The yearly program for maintenance activities is usually established on an ideal basis. As adopted performances proceed, the progress must be checked and analyzed according to the plan of procedure. On setting the priorities for projects, those which provide better safety conditions and instructional environments are pursued first. These larger projects are usually processed during the summer. The progress on these projects should be checked at least twice a month. The progress on the scheduled maintenance by certain crafts should also be analyzed often. Too many intermittent requests deter the best of schedules. Delay in procuring materials for projects may also alter the schedules, as well as other local conditions. Therefore, the administrator of maintenance activities should avaluate the process of the planned projects as they are executed. While he is carrying out this necessary responsibility, he may delegate some personnel to check on the quality of the performance and the quality of completed work.

SUMMARY

Effective school plant maintenance is a facet of school plant management which is a segment of the school administration. The philosophy of the school administration linked with the principles of effective organization provides an understanding of the job of the maintenance of the school plant.

A methodical procedure of organizing maintenance activities in a district foretells sound administration. A thorough study of the necessary steps for organizing maintenance provides a basis for complete understanding of that task.

Chapter **3**

DEVELOPING
EFFICIENT CONTROLS
OF MAINTENANCE FUNCTIONS

In the administration of the functions of maintenance many practices may be wasteful and time-consuming. The supervisor should plan the work both to save manpower and maintain good will. Unless procedures are definitely established, much human energy and effectiveness of the program are lost. Certain facts of administration, such as methods of detection and disposition of maintenance requests; planning of efficient and effective use of the employee's time; the establishment of standards for parts, policies of replacement, and frequencies of service; ordering correct materials; job descriptions; the use and control of records and school plant documents; the provision for adequate communication, and a positive program of human relations are parts of the administrative process which require constant study. These somewhat unrelated facets are adapted and applied by each local district. The maintenance projects are classified in the planned programs, and only emergency projects are left unplanned. In Chapter 2, team planning presupposes that all maintenance projects in each plant have been planned a year in advance. Since the administration of maintenance services encompasses many details, some plan of authorization is fundamental for effective control of maintenance services. A definite procedure for handling work requests is necessary.

METHODS OF DETECTION OF REPAIRS

Authorized Personnel. During the school year all kinds of things happen which require maintenance services to the school buildings. Such work requests for maintenance emanating from the principal, the head building custodian, the area men, and the central office personnel are usually classed as emergencies. The goal of maintenance is to hold these work requests at a minimum because the costs of repair become large when a journeyman travels across the district to do a five-dollar job with a travel time of two or three hours. Definite judgments must be made in regard to pooling like requests in order to cut the costs of repair.

Work Requests. These requests are made on a form suitable to the size of the school district. The work request form in Figure 3–1 has evolved as a successful procedure in a large school district.

Maintenance Department

School_____ Code _____

Date _____

Description of Work and Exact Location (List only one item of work on each request)

_____

_____

_____

Reason for Request: emergency   vandalism   normal maintenance

Work Needed: when you have time   as soon as possible   immediately

Requested by_____ Principal_____

Do not write in this space

CRAFT_____ WORK CLASS_____

INITIATING DEPARTMENT _____

Figure 3–1. Work Request Form

Needed Information. The information on this work request should include: (1) the date, (2) the name of the school or department, (3) the location of the defect or the project in exact terms of room or area number, hall location, position on the site, etc., (4) the defect to be corrected or the desired improvement, (5) a rough diagram describing the project, (6) signature of the person requesting the work (principal, area men, custodian, and central office personnel), and (7) a separate work request number for each emergency request.

In a large school system the daily requests for emergency work accumulate. These requests are unforeseen maintenance items. (See Figure 3–2.) The supervision divides these requests into two classes. Class I comprises requests which pertain to utility items, leaky roofs, and conditions of safety. Class II items are requests for improved building conditions such as additional chalkboards, cabinets, bookshelves, and other appurtenances. Although an allowance has been made in the budget for work such as gas and water line breakage, careful consideration must be given each item because of the quantity of requests. In any district, large or small, these items need careful scrutiny in order to prevent an unbalanced budget. Definite control must be established.

Disposition. The supervisor of maintenance approves or disapproves all work requests. No maintenance work is to be performed without a work request. If the request for the project is approved by the supervisor, he writes a work order for performance. He assigns each task to the qualified person in maintenance personnel to perform the approved work.

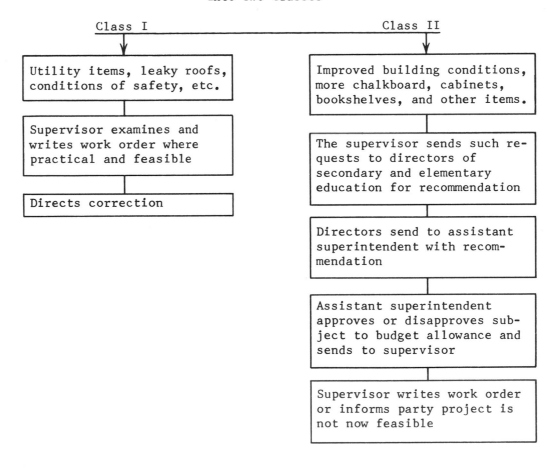

Originated by Principal,

Custodian, Area Men, Central Office Personnel,

Sent to

Supervisor of Maintenance

Who Sorts and Divides

Work Requests

Into Two Classes

Class I   Class II

Utility items, leaky roofs, conditions of safety, etc.

Improved building conditions, more chalkboard, cabinets, bookshelves, and other items.

Supervisor examines and writes work order where practical and feasible

The supervisor sends such requests to directors of secondary and elementary education for recommendation

Directs correction

Directors send to assistant superintendent with recommendation

Assistant superintendent approves or disapproves subject to budget allowance and sends to supervisor

Supervisor writes work order or informs party project is not now feasible

Figure 3–2. Flow Chart—Emergency Work Requests.

22

TIME STUDY

Manpower in maintenance services costs money. At least 80 per cent of the cost is labor. Whether the school district be small or large, 100 per cent productivity is impossible. Good supervision increases productivity. Definite planning and scheduling procedures plus work simplification and sampling methods with work measurement techniques are positive supervisory actions. The maintenance supervisor assigns the correct number of men to an assigned job. He sees that tool requirements are established and that supplies and materials are available. Then he dispatches the respective crafts to particular jobs. He also plans the jobs in proper sequence along with the knowledge of the next similar job and its location in order to avoid wasting time for further assignments.[1]

Productive time. The supervisor is interested in productive time. These components of productive time include:[2]

1. Actual time:
   a. To include only that time actually spent working directly upon the equipment being repaired or job assigned.
   b. Any work with tools necessary and incidental to the job.

2. Communications time—to include the following:
   a. Supervisor to worker instruction.
   b. Reports by workers to supervisors.
   c. Discussions between craft worker and other craft workers regarding the equipment.
   d. Discussions between craft worker and unit operators in regard to equipment.
   e. Telephone calls for equipment.
   f. Writing up time sheets.
   g. Filling out work orders.
   h. Writing requests for material.
   i. Tagging out of equipment to be worked on.
   j. Studying drawings and specifications, requisitions, bills of materials, or any written or printed information pertinent to assigned job.

3. Material procurement time—to include the following:
   a. Gathering material or tools.
   b. Hunting for material or tools.
   c. Putting away material or tools.

4. Transportation and handling time—to include the following:
   a. Walking (includes walking to get materials, tools, and instructions).
   b. Riding.
   c. Loading or unloading tools, material, or equipment.
   d. Rigging.
   e. Climbing.
   f. Use of crane to lift materials or equipment into place.
   g. Driving to and from work to haul materials or tools or equipment.

5. Cleaning time—to include the following:

---

[1] Thomas F. Sack, *A Complete Guide to Building and Plant Maintenance,* 1963. Reprinted by permission of Prentice-Hall, Inc., Englewood Cliffs, N. J., p. 492.
[2] Thomas F. Sack, *A Complete Guide,* pp. 492–497, adapted.

a. Clean-up of equipment before, during, and after repair, including cleaning and decontamination of parts.

b. Clean-up of tools after use, including decontamination.

c. Gathering and disposing of used materials and other refuse in working area.

d. Time to scrub body or hands to remove chemicals or contamination.

e. Washing hands that have become so soiled that they must be cleaned in order to go on with job. Note: Removal of machine gaskets is considered cleaning time.

Non-Productive Time. The supervisor should also be deeply concerned with the different elements which compose non-productive time. Experience has revealed that a school district which employs 200 men on the skeleton maintenance organization spends $250 per day for two fifteen-minute coffee breaks. These wages in this organization are the average paid for like crafts in the community. This example shows the importance of the management of time.

A study of the items which go into non-productive time could include:[3]

1. Delay due to others:
   a. Waiting for operator. For example: Waiting for operator to get equipment ready for repair. (Actual time to turn equipment over to craftsmen. Does not include waiting time before operator starts turnover procedure.)
   b. Waiting for transportation.
   c. Waiting for material delivery.
   d. Waiting for supervisor. For example: Waiting for supervisor to make decision as to method of repair.
   e. Waiting for other crafts. For example: (1) Waiting for other crafts to complete their portion of a job so that the observed worker can proceed. (2) Radioactive contamination and clean-up. (3) Waiting for infirmary nurse, late bus at start of shift, and materials or tool-room clerks.
   f. Waiting for work assignment. For example: Worker runs out of scheduled work and has notified supervisor but has not been given a new assignment.
   g. Waiting for co-worker. Lost time due to assignment of two people to a one-man job. (Necessary in many cases.)
   h. Protective clothing (dress and undress), personal.

2. Unavoidable delays:
   a. Attempting to use telephone but it was busy, cannot get person called.
   b. Waiting to make the several necessary packing adjustments to a pump just put back in service after a repacking job.
   c. Repair or malfunctioning equipment or tools.

3. Other delays:
   a. Lunch—includes preparation, coffee or coke break.
   b. Smoking—includes travel to and from processing area to clean area.
   c. Miscellaneous—includes the following:
      (1) Washing hands for lunch and at end of shift.
      (2) Personal needs.
      (3) Idle time when not waiting for others to perform work or for work assignments.

---

[3] Thomas F. Sack, *A Complete Guide,* pp. 496–497, adapted.

    d. Safety meetings.

    e. Union business (workman's committee, gripe sessions, phone calls, posters, talking with shop steward).

Summertime Repairs. Organization for the best use of time is probably the most important function the supervisor of maintenance, the foreman, and lead men can plan. Larger districts provide more opportunities for non-productive time because of the distance between schools. The repair work in the most distant school plants from the service center should be planned as completely as possible for summer scheduled work.

Noise. Experience also dictates that all noisy work should be planned to be executed, if possible, during vacation or summer periods. Often the machines used in repair work hinder classroom instruction.

Daily Report. Experience reveals that the daily reports showing the manner in which each employee spends his time is a basic instrument for efficient administration. Likewise, the knowledge of each worker as to the elements which are included in productive and non-productive labor becomes a basis for improvement. Furthermore, the timing of performing certain repairs in school plants is an important consideration for effective administration.

ESTABLISHING STANDARDS FOR MAINTENANCE

The standards which must be established locally depend upon the availability of parts, policies of replacement of larger components of the school plant, and the frequencies of needed services in the local district.

Parts.

Simplification and standardization of materials and equipment are an economy in a maintenance program. Responsible maintenance personnel have to accept school plants as they are. Astute administration plans for old and new school plants should have components which are similar in size and interchangeable. Technological changes and changes in school administration are both factors which hinder simplification and standardization. Among the articles which may be standarized are the following:

1. Sizes and types of glass	10. Panic bars
2. Paint supplies	11. Door closers
3. Light fixtures	12. Floor tile
4. Door locks	13. Inside doors
5. Clocks	14. Window shades and blinds
6. Pencil sharpeners	15. Door hinges and stops
7. Boilers	16. Switches
8. Burners	17. Motors
9. Plumbing fixtures and brass trim	18. Thermostats and controls

High and rising costs of maintenance have forced administrative officials to standardize the component parts wherever possible and feasible. Overstandardization can cause drabness in appearance, arrangement, and design. If carried to the extreme, standardization could hamper the educational program and destroy function.

Many manufacturers will train the responsible skilled personnel in the care of their particular equipment. Also, the lesser inventory of spare parts is an important economy.

Policies of Replacement.

The exact time at which replacement maintenance must be scheduled is unpredictable. Maintenance personnel must depend on records, regular inspections, and experience to develop the local replacement schedules. The following items may need replacing as indicated if they are kept efficient, usable, and functional.

Item	Suggested Replacement Periods
Boilers	20–25 years
Gas burners for boilers	10–15 years
Roofs	20–25 years
Plumbing	25–30 years
Resilient floor surfaces	15–20 years
Tires	20,000 to 25,000 miles
Brakes, relined	Every 50,000 miles
Motor overhaul, or exchange	Every 100,000 miles
Trucks, drayage	10 years
School buses	5–7 years
Furniture	8 years
Recoating black top play areas	4–8 years

These suggested periods of use are not exact; they merely serve as a guide in planning the maintenance budget. Replacement is not to include the substitution of complete new facilities for old facilities. These items may be kept in good condition by intermittent repairs. Many elements have much longer replacement periods.

Frequencies of Service.

The jobs and tasks in maintenance which need attention on a longer term basis than emergency items may be performed on a cycle basis. The frequency of these jobs and tasks may depend greatly on the location in the nation, the kind of fuel that is used, the cleanliness of the atmosphere, and the kind of use the building receives from its users. Some of the frequencies of services needed in a school plant are:

Item	Suggested Frequency
Outside painting	3–5 years (local conditions determine)
Outside door painting	2–3 years
Inside painting	7–10 years
Interior woodwork varnish	15–20 years
Roofs, preservative application	5 years
Window shades, blinds, curtains	4–5 years
Weatherstripping	5–10 years
Heating plants	5–10 years
Septic tanks, normal operation	2 years
Lateral disposal fields	2–3 years
Lawn rototilling	5 years

The jobs need careful analysis in each locality. The frequency will be scheduled maintenance. Once cycles are established and a careful record of the performances is made, budgeting for maintenance is facilitated. All plants are treated alike as far as repairs are concerned.

ORDERING RIGHT MATERIALS

School districts of various sizes establish individual administrative framework designating specific persons who are responsible for the procurement of supplies, materials, and equipment for maintenance functions. Probably very few schemes are exactly alike because they relate to specific personnel who hold various titles. The best schemes often fail to produce the desired results on account of the degree of training and expertness of the personnel involved.

The important idea of this phase of administration is to know the approved local procedure in purchasing and to follow it in detail. As systems increase in size, purchasing responsibilities usually fall into the hands of more people. Finally, a separate purchasing organization is established in the school district.

The purchasing department may have the responsibility of procuring supplies, materials, and equipment for the district including maintenance material. After these materials and supplies are purchased, they are delivered to a central warehouse building. Top maintenance management can then request materials and supplies for the specific jobs as they are executed. The exact practices will vary among school districts.

In the daily operation of maintenance functions the availability of materials and supplies is a consequential activity. The request for the materials and supplies must be made far enough in advance to have materials and supplies on hand when they are needed for specific projects. If they are not in stock when needed, operating losses occur.

Astute top management works closely with the purchasing office. Quantities of materials should be estimated at least three months ahead and preferably six months or a year ahead. Responsible maintenance personnel also have the responsibility of requesting materials of both the right quantity and quality to perform the various maintenance jobs in the district.

JOB DESCRIPTIONS

A job description for every maintenance employee has a definite place in the effective administration of a maintenance program. The formulation of this description saves more in waste and trouble than it costs. Each job should be planned and job routine should be organized and understood by both labor and administration. Regardless of the size of the district a job description should improve operation, eliminate friction, assist in creating a satisfactory wage structure, and tend to increase production.

Generally the description should be brief and made with the cooperation of the personnel within that division of labor. For example, a local successful description of jobs of plastering is:

A. General Foreman
  1. Supervise workmen
  2. Know how to apply scratch, or first coat, brown coat and/or finish work

B. Journeyman
  1. Do the techniques in the field of plastering
  2. Know materials

C. Apprentices
  1. Know materials
  2. Do three years apprenticeship to classify as plasterers.

D. Plasterer's Helper
  1. Know how to take instructions and mix types of mortar.
  2. Build scaffolds, service mortar boards, and temper mortar.

3. Know how to use tools

4. Know how to use level

5. Set dots and use rod

6. Some lathing where needed

3. Mix plaster

E. Laborers

1. Do assigned work

2. Know how to use tools

3. Get along with men

"A 'ready-made' job description from the *United States Director of Occupational Titles* (available from the Superintendent of Documents, Washington D. C.) may serve as a starting point or pattern to be followed."[4] The job in one school district is not the same as the job in another school district. Using both this directory and one's own knowledge as a guide, a respectable piece of work in analyzing and describing any job in maintenance may be accomplished.

THE USE OF RECORDS

Effective maintenance can be planned with accurate records which fit the local conditions. The number and kinds of helpful records for local administration vary. Chapter 6 will deal with records in detail.

School Plant Records. The list of all school property is basic for maintenance services. Bulletin 22 of the U. S. Department of Health, Education and Welfare, Office of Education, entitled *Property Accounting for Local and State School Systems*[5] is an excellent guide for property accounting in local school districts. The architectural drawings and specifications on school projects should be preserved in good condition in order that maintenance personnel may review these documents as problems arise. "As-built" plans for each project are excellent records. This record shows the depths of utility lines in the ground and their locations.

Inventory Records. All equipment, furniture, maintenance materials and supplies, and maintenance tools and equipment are listed to give an accurate accounting of these items with respect to type, quantity, location, condition, and value.

Cost Records. Local officials should keep itemized records of job costs to show the amounts for labor and materials. The many details on these cost reports will be locally determined. A good guide for the data needed for these records is found in *School Plant Management.*[6] These records contain basic information which may be used to estimate the costs of scheduled maintenance. They also may be used to compare the economy of work performed by the school maintenance personnel and the work let out on contract. The efficiency of the work of employees should improve because they know that a check is being made on their work. Finally, these records will show evidence that the available funds were spent on needed projects.

Control Records. Each particular school district has its own pattern of maintenance procedures. These records need to be kept current so that the maintenance program can be kept under control. The school plants in their several locations have a chance of receiving fair treatment. Separate sections of the control records should be divided among site, buildings, and equipment. The information will be discussed more fully in Chapter 6.

---

4 From *Small Plant Management,* 2nd ed. by W. A. MacCrehan, Jr., August 1960, The American Society of Mechanical Engineers. Used by permission of McGraw-Hill Book Company, p. 282.

5 Paul L. Reason and George G. Tankard, Jr., *Property Accounting for Local and State School Systems* (Washington, D. C.: U.S. Government Printing Office, Bulletin No. 22, 1959).

6 R. N. Finchum, *School Plant Management: Organizing the Maintenance Program,* U. S. Department of Health, Education, and Welfare, Office of Education (Washington: U. S. Government Printing Office, Bulletin No. 15, 1960), p. 68.

Contractual Records. The contracts on large projects for maintenance work are usually kept by the business department. They have to meet all legal requirements of the state in which they are executed. A copy of these contract documents with warranties attached should become a part of the school district's maintenance record.

RESPONSIBILITY FOR MAINTENANCE RECORDS

Each school district, depending on its size and the number of employees, has to determine what records are needed and who is to make these records. Experience reveals that often too many records are kept. They are made but never used to guide future action. In most emergency work some records cost more than the information is worth. Essential records may be kept by several people. Determining the number of copies of each record depends upon who uses the records that accumulate. The designated people who may be responsible are principals, foremen, maintenance supervisors, transportation supervisors, assistant superintendents, and others. The size of the school district, the adjacency of offices, and the kinds of records needed are important considerations in determining who shall record the different data.

BUILDING MANUALS

Experience has revealed that the compilation of school building manuals detailing the kinds and brands of mechanical and electrical materials which are approved is economical. Somewhere in the housing of the administrative personnel a definite place should be designated to keep a record of the final approvals on each construction project. In the mechanical part of the manual, an example of the item of "Double Duct Mixing Unit Boxes" shows who manufactured these items, who installed these items, sizes, location, pictures of these items, and how they are installed. For example, an electrical item in the manual such as a grounding type device has the catalogue number of the item installed, its size, and installation in a picture. Should a failure in this type of equipment occur, the manual is a ready guide to find specifications for repair or replacement. Incalculable savings in time alone can be realized during the lifetime of the building.

DEVELOPING ADEQUATE COMMUNICATIONS

Maintenance at its best is teamwork. Responsible central office employees, principals, maintenance area men, and other building service employees have by necessity a common undertaking to perform. Whether the territory of the school district be large or small, the importance of keeping communication channels open cannot be overstressed. The needed cooperation is to provide the best possible environment for the pupils of the school district. Also, experience has revealed that the employees within the maintenance organization must have definite communication channels to operate efficiently. Poor communications hinder efficiency; improved communications tend to eliminate frictions.

Elements.

The day-by-day handling of communications and relations within a maintenance organization must be definitely planned to be effective. Regardless of size of the district, a complete plan should include the purposes, methods of procedure, duties assigned, authority granted, and the subjects approved for the inter-communication program.

Control.

Proper communications within the organization must be controlled to keep all members of the team informed. Otherwise, certain ambitious personnel may use too much time of other maintenance employees obtaining information which is similar or at cross purposes.

Flow of Communications.

A most significant practice in establishing the flow of information in a maintenance department is to be certain that information can flow upward, be exchanged, and flow downward.

Upward. Definite steps should be planned so that the employee who hauls trash for a school district can relay information to top management. It is very important that both good and bad news should be channeled in order that top management may know what is happening in the organization. Often the maintenance worker does not have the ability nor the inclination to write communications to top management. Top management personnel should, therefore, try to make personal contacts with all the workers as often as possible. Experience reveals that provision should be made for encouraging written suggestions from any employee who has something to communicate to top management. This may be handled through the means of a suggestion box. Top management should also circulate among employees and hear and see their good and bad conditions. Meetings within crafts and with people of like responsibilities give an opportunity to hear the comments of these workmen.

Exchange. An important consideration often overlooked is the provision for an adequate exchange of information between personnel at the same level. In many cases, basic exchange of information is needed between plumbers, carpenters, plasterers, and electricians. The form of lateral communication places an emphasis on consultation rather than on direction.

Downward. Top management in maintenance usually communicates with employees by means of general meetings, by crafts, or by divisions. A common medium is written statements and bulletins. Astute handling of personnel is the most important single factor in the effective administration of maintenance activities, and personal contact by management is of prime importance. A strengthening practice is to contact the family as well as the employee. In practice, the contact by top management personnel made in the home of employees clarifies many questions and creates good rapport. Workers are human beings with divergent interests, as well as varied religious, social, and racial backgrounds. Top management must be aware of the varied backgrounds of the individuals to understand their personal problems.

Methods.

Maintenance employees like to know about changing conditions in the school organization which may affect them. Management is responsible for releasing this information as it develops. Also, management has the responsibility to anticipate and answer questions which pertain to the problems of the maintenance employees. The establishment of a system of communications gradually and naturally is very effective.

Media.

Top management has a definite responsibility to communicate with responsible employees when these employees are deployed over wide areas of the district. "Two-way communication facilities between field crews and the central office will be helpful in reducing man-hours and transportation costs for the maintenance personnel. For example, requests for emergency service are often received at the central office after work crews have departed for the day's work. Such requests can be relayed to these crews while they are in the field, thus permitting them to proceed from job to job without loss of time and excessive travel. Furthermore, if materials or supplies are needed for the jobs encountered, the foreman of the field crew can request the maintenance office to send them out to avoid wasted time in waiting for supplies."[7]

Telephone. Different plans have been developed to assist in two-way communication. The most common plan is to have telephone communication installed on every school site. This practice is very effective inasmuch as most necessary contacts can be obtained within thirty minutes.

Radio. Baker and Peters[8] relate that the two-way radio installed in cars in school districts which are large and have scattered school plants is both effective and economical. This device saves miles of extra transportation and hours of waiting caused by coming to the shops for orders and often passing jobs on the way in and out. Other school systems have installed the radio in specific cars. Experience reveals that each school district should study how the communications in its system can be improved and use whatever devices will perfect or improve performance and economies.

HUMAN RELATIONS

The establishment of a program of human relations is essential for effective administration of the maintenance administration in schools. Employees of various sized schools have different problems. The maintenance program develops more smoothly, efficiently, and economically when management recognizes important facets of human relations.

Public Authorities. In the development of efficient controls of maintenance functions, certain phases of maintenance are regulated by ordinances of town, city, county, and state authorities. Some school districts have as high as seven municipalities within the territory of their school district. These authorities have to be seen, consulted, and petitioned to grant certain rights, permits, and privileges. In many cases certain concessions have to be made. A frank, straightforward approach is the recommended procedure. This kind of approach in all contacts with the pertinent authorities and compliance with regulations usually proves beneficial.

Top management can also strengthen human relations by participation in civic affairs. Willingness to participate in activities which are considered best for the community is a manifestation of desire to be a part of the total community.

Salesmen. In this technological age new materials and supplies are constantly put on the market. Top management has the responsibility of keeping up to date with materials and supplies. When salesmen appear, management should welcome a brief presentation of their products. This action creates good relations even though the product may not be recommended for purchase. The salesmen are interested in sales, but it is still the responsibility of top management to make the recommendation for purchase.

School Personnel and General Public. The maintenance personnel in school districts have a definite responsibility to perform their work in a quiet dignified manner. The men should be

---

7 "Organizing the Maintenance Program," *School Plant Management* (Washington: U. S. Department of Health, Education and Welfare, Office of Education, 1960), p. 81.

8 Joseph J. Baker and Jon S. Peters, *School Maintenance and Operation* (Danville, Illinois: The Interstate Printers and Publishers, Inc., 1963), pp. 60–64.

gentlemen at all times when they do their assigned tasks. They are a part of the total school organization, and their images are created by efficient and skillful completion of their tasks. Word about their work performance travels swiftly to all parts of the school organization, and the general public exercises vigilance in observing the decorum of maintenance personnel. Thus, each employee should be courteous in all situations. This action may be difficult when conditions are severe as they sometimes occur in school systems. Good human relations are extended when the employee knows his responsibilties and executes them according to his assignment.

SUMMARY

Scheduled maintenance is planned by top management. Adequate emergency maintenance is maintained when authorized personnel make work requests. These requests are forwarded to the supervisor of maintenance. Each school district will make a definite plan for handling work requests.

Top management has the responsibility of scheduling and making arrangements so that the men put in as much productive time as possible. Continuous vigilance is necessary for effective administration. Maintenance projects should be timed in order to avoid interference with school activities as much as possible.

The establishment of standards, job descriptions and records, and the use of present records are aids to the smooth and economical administration of maintenance functions.

Adequate communication must be planned within the department and human relations must be stressed. The image of the maintenance personnel is enhanced by definite plans.

Top management can operate efficiently and economically when men, materials, and methods are synchronized. The right kinds of materials put in the hands of appropriately skilled workers at the right time make possible effective administration of maintenance.

Chapter 4

ESTABLISHING SUCCESSFUL
PERSONNEL POLICIES

Effective administration of school maintenance is measured largely on the basis of selecting and motivating qualified personnel. The high level of competency is required because of the complicated and demanding jobs the employees perform. The school administrator deals with these employees in straightforward ways. Oral and written communications are basic instruments. Written policies for these employees become necessities. Maintenance of school plants is a segment of general school administration. To keep the personnel motivated and happy, the contents of the policies for maintenance personnel should be comparable to the policies which pertain to other personnel of like segments. Good rapport is established when personnel are selected on the basis of merit, treated fairly, and recognized. Each school district will have different policies because of the differing conditions of employment under local administration.

The author chooses to discuss the various aspects of personnel policies in a random fashion. He feels that each is important when it is considered for various school districts of many sizes; and he recognizes that many of the aspects are optional. Each phase should be mentioned because administration should know about personnel practices elsewhere. Special notation is given to the practices which seem to increase employee morale. This chapter lists many of the ingredients of successful policies.

PLACE TO APPLY

The different states have varied laws governing the administration of schools. Also, different districts within these states have different policies. Generally speaking, these types exist:

Independent Unit Organization. In this type of organization the personnel office usually receives the applications of candidates for the maintenance department. In small administrative units, the office of the superintendent or some designated division of administration receives the application.

Dependent Organization. Practices vary as to the department which receives the application. In some states the Civil Service Commission receives the applications and maintenance personnel are chosen from eligible lists.

Practical experience dictates definite procedure and that a definite place to appear be chosen in order to assist the selection on the basis of qualifications. This practice helps keep performance efficiency on a high standard.

FREEDOMS

A maintenance employee can best grow and improve his status when he knows that he has stipulated freedoms which are regulated by policy. The freedom of employment and the freedom from pressures are two basic conditions.

Employment. The freedom of employment is a factor which aids efficiency in maintenance operations. The employee has the privilege to leave the employment of the school system whenever he sees fit. Under this arrangement the employer also has the privilege to discharge any workman when circumstances arise which hinder efficiency or when insubordination exists. The discharged employee retains the right to appeal the decision for dismissal to the top school administration and board of education.

Pressures. A policy which eliminates the factors of race, creed, and national ancestry is recommended. These factors are avoided in the appointment, assignment, promotion, salary determination, and other terms of employment. The process of selection must be free from all pressures considered detrimental to the best interest of public schools. The ability to fulfill the responsibilities of the position effectively as judged by all pertinent standards is the sole basis for selection. The use of political, social, and other pressures automatically disqualifies the applicant from further consideration.

CHARACTERISTICS OF PERSONNEL

Each person of an efficient maintenance department must possess certain characteristics. In the first place he must be unquestionably honest. The responsibilities in the care and accounting for tools, the disposal of salvage, the reporting of deficient materials, the waste of materials, and the returning of unused materials and supplies give ample opportunity for filching. He must be honest about his time. In a scattered organization opportunities exist in which time may be wasted. Top management must be honest. All personal favoritism or use of time or material must be eliminated.

In the second place, the employees must be proficient in their respective lines of labor. Another salient characteristic is that the workmen must be willing to assist other workmen in other lines when circumstances are such that cooperation is needed to execute a task economically. These workmen are subject to call twenty-four hours a day to care for emergencies, such as fire and water damage and heating failures. Many repair jobs are disagreeable and/or unpleasant; yet these jobs must be completed by willing workmen.

These men often meet pupils, school personnel, and the public. Good moral character is thus a basic characteristic for each employee. Neatness and good manners are of prime importance.

Effective administration is forthcoming when these men are industrious and intelligent so that a minimum of close supervision is required.

ESTABLISHING QUALIFICATIONS

In the effective administration of this segment of general school administration, certain guidelines for qualifications should be established. Local practice and economic conditions largely determine the available qualified personnel who are skilled for maintenance responsibilities. A successful list includes the following:

Residence. The prospective employee should live within the district in which he works. To be most effective he should be a part of the school district which pays him.

Age. The employee should be at least twenty years of age and should have at least ten years, preferably longer, before retirement.

Physical Ability. The stamina, height, weight, and other health conditions should be at such a standard that the prospective employee is able to perform his assigned work. A health certificate should help establish his physical condition.

Level of Education. The nature of the work to be performed is a determining factor. For laborers, at least a grammar school level is desired; for journeymen and above classifications, at least a high school education or better is a good standard.

Intelligence. The demands of the job for which he is employed largely determine this standard. The minimum requirement should be that the candidate have average intelligence.

Experience. Previous experience in a similar job is helpful; good work at any previous job is desired; previous training for the desired job is an asset; desired high classifications necessitate more experience and more training; license required when and where local conditions demand.

Attitude. Desire to succeed is foremost; willingness to take training and instructions, both written and oral, and special training are very important.

Working with Others. Ability and willingness to perform on a team are basic considerations.

Relatives. Blood or marital relationships to present personnel are factors which astute administration must consider.

The above practical list of qualifications should be supplemented by determining the day-to-day conduct of the prospective employee. Practice reveals that these items are most important:

Personal Appearance. Maintenance workers must be as neat and clean as possible when they work around students and other school personnel. They should keep their clothing as clean as possible as they do their required tasks.

Smoking. Workers should refrain from smoking around boys and girls and other school personnel. Smoking may be allowed in specific areas. Safety rules should be strictly observed at all times.

Drinking. Workers should be in first class condition when they present themselves ready to render services. Drinking is not to be tolerated on the job. Evidence of liquor on person or breath renders the offender liable to immediate dismissal.

Dependability. Workers must be prompt in effective administration. They must report to work at a stated time, give notice of emergency absence, and seek permission for leaves of absence.

SPECIFIC SKILL QUALIFICATIONS

A significant practice in effective administration of school maintenance functions is to define clearly the duties and necessary attributes which pertain to the different classes of employees in the department. In the presentation of this concept a brief discussion of some fundamental principles of supervision is practical.

Supervision.

The real job of a supervisor should be that of assisting workers to see the underlying principles of actions and convincing them of their soundness. The worker must be helped in a sufficient number of applications to duty until he forms the habit of self-help by reference to fundamental principles.

A good summary of these principles is presented by Brainard. The individual who performs these services should consider these carefully. Persons selected should have the potential to become proficient in a short time and require only occasional supervision.

Authorities in the field of supervision have pointed out the following principles:

> Supervision should not be based on the power of position or personality.
> Supervision should never be divorced from a constant recognition of goals of the job to be performed.
> Supervision should not, as a rule, be largely concerned with the details of a particular assignment.
> Supervision should never be nagging.
> Supervision should not be impatient of results.
> Supervision should be characterized by simplicity and informality.
> Supervision should use only the simplest machinery.
> Supervision should begin with conditions and practices as they are.
> Supervision should be adapted to the capacities, attitudes, and even prejudices of the employee.
> Supervision should be gradual, progressive, and persistent.
> Supervision should be cumulative in its result.
> Supervision can well follow the original plan existing in a school district.[1]

The principles are basic ones to follow. Especially noted is the emphasis on the attainment of the maintenance functions.

Head of Maintenance.

This position is held by responsible persons who have many titles. The superintendent of schools, the assistant superintendent, the director, the supervisor, or the head of the maintenance department are titles used. Regardless of title, the attitude of this man automatically sets the attitude of the maintenance personnel. His duties vary among school districts. His approach must be logical, honest, and reveal astuteness. He must:

1. Select and manage the personnel of his department.
2. Organize the department for effective work.
3. Clarify responsibilities and assignments.
4. Inspect the physical conditions of school plants for maintenance purposes.
5. Organize the findings of inspection into a periodic workable program.
6. Participate in setting the budget for maintenance.
7. Dispatch the work to the respective staff and workers.
8. Recommend adequate supplies and materials to purchase.

---

[1] A. D. Brainard, Proceedings, Association of School Business Officials of the United States and Canada (Forty-first Convention, 1955), p. 286.

    9. Organize system of adequate records.
  10. Develop the techniques of communication within the organization he supervises.
  11. Inspect the quality and quantity of maintenance work as time permits.
  12. Organize programs for in-service training.
  13. See that the personnel know and are trained in safety practices.
  14. Have the interest and welfare of his personnel and school system foremost.

The head of maintenance is faced daily with decision making. He knows how to work with school administrators who make policy decisions in setting forth goals and general courses of action. He also cooperates in making administrative decisions in determining the means to be used in trying to achieve the goals. He alone makes multitudinous executive decisions which occur on a day-to-day basis as the particular cases occur.

Area Men.

In practice, an effective part of the administration of maintenance is to divide the total school district into areas and assign a man whose general responsibility is to have a more intimate knowledge of the school plants to which he is assigned. He can be the contact person for the principal of each school. He may have the title of area carpenter, area mechanic, or other title that fits his responsibilities. Many small maintenance problems may be corrected by this employee and long-term economies result.

DUTIES OF AREA MECHANICS

In addition to his broad duties as an area representative of the maintenance department, he may also be required to:

1. Inspect thoroughly each school at periodic intervals, noting conditions of the site, building, and equipment which need immediate attention of certain crafts.
2. Make minor repairs to the plumbing and electrical fixtures, adjust door closers, tighten loose screws, and many other similar items.
3. Consult with the principal of the building as to the feasibility of certain maintenance jobs, if requested.
4. Report to the supervisor of maintenance such mechanical or structural failures which could lead to potential damage to the building or danger to the occupants.
5. Fill out and send to the supervisor of maintenance the "Self-Inspection" insurance forms each May 1 and November 1.
6. Participate in the annual review of maintenance needs for the school plants to which he is assigned.
7. Check the drainage conditions around the first twenty feet adjacent to the school building or buildings.

Foremen. In practice the foremen are key people in the maintenance organization. They must be knowledgeable of the responsibilities of several crafts which are assigned to them. The number of general foremen has to be scrutinized in school districts which are large and continue to grow. In practice the foreman assigns the work on the basis of priorities to the head men of the several crafts, requests materials and supplies, and sees that the head men have enough personnel to perform their jobs both expeditiously and economically. Should more than one approved craft work order be at the same location, the foreman assigns all the work to be performed by one craft at one location. In addition, he must be able to read plans and specifications and should inspect all completed work. Duties of the foreman will vary from one district to another.

Journeymen. These men do the actual work on their respective jobs. Each craft has special techniques of performance for their crafts. These techniques are spelled out in their job classifications.

Other Labor. As maintenance projects vary, the tasks within the projects vary. In some repair projects economy results when common labor can do a part of the work which comprises the project.

RECRUITMENT

Significant practices in the procurement of qualified personnel include such sources as:

1. *Industry.* Skilled people work in industry on a full- or part-time basis. Business becomes slack and industry reduces its operations. The skilled persons prefer a steady job with good wages and fringe benefits and may be applicants for work in a school district.
2. *Apprenticeship.* Applicants shall be willing to serve apprentice time in a school organization and progress to the status of journeyman.
3. *Trained.* Educational institutions in the community may have adult programs which train people for particular jobs which are similar to maintenance jobs in schools.
4. *Within the School District.* Often a qualified person for the maintenance program is found in the custodial (operating) department of the school district. This person may have the ability, the know-how, and the inclination to be an effective craftsman. Sometimes a teacher for various reasons chooses to change his work. These people, if qualified, make excellent employees in most cases because they already have partial acquaintance with the operation of the school district.
5. *Specials.* Sources to secure supervision and top management people are varied. Probably the best source is industry, where good leaders may have similar experience to maintenance functions of school districts. Applicants for these places are difficult to find.
6. *Civil Service Commissions.* In states and municipalities where this source is mandated by statute, lists of eligible personnel for appointment are furnished school officials. School districts may select candidates for positions from the certified list.
7. *Union Referrals.* The offices of organized labor usually have a pool of unemployed approved personnel. The responsible school maintenance administrator may contact the separate offices for employees as he needs them.
8. *Miscellaneous.* The administration may advertise for applicants, use employment agencies, or contact fraternal organizations, lodges, and churches. These sources may be fruitful in suggesting candidates.

METHODS OF SELECTION, PROMOTION,
AND RETENTION OF PERSONNEL

Firm rules and policies are necessary for the procurement and retention of qualified personnel. This procedure will vary according to size of district. In most school districts the person desiring employment makes an application on a form. (See Figure 4-1.) This application is filed at the designated office in the school district.

```
┌─────────────────────────────────┐
│   APPLICATION FOR EMPLOYMENT    │
│   THE BOARD OF EDUCATION        │
│   MAINTENANCE DEPARTMENT        │
└─────────────────────────────────┘
```

Name:_____ Address_____

Telephone: _____ Job Applied For _____

Check All That Apply:
☐ Male   ☐ Female   ☐ Single   ☐ Married   ☐ Divorced   ☐ Separated   ☐ Widowed

Height_____ Weight _____ Color of Hair_____ Color of Eyes_____

Date of Birth:_____ Age:_____ Social Security No:_____

Do You Have Any Relatives Now Employed By The Board Of Education, ☐ Yes   ☐ No

If So Where_____ Name_____

Job Desired: _____

Other Work For Which You Are Qualified: _____

Salary Expected: _____

Have You Any Physical Defects? ☐ Yes ☐ No	If Yes Explain
Have You Ever Been Arrested? ☐ Yes ☐ No	If Yes Explain

	Name	Year Graduated
Grade School	_____	_____
High School	_____	_____
College	_____	_____
Other Training Or Skills	_____	_____

	Name	Address
List The Last Three Places Where You Have Worked	_____	_____

Certificate of Applicant

I hereby certify that all statements made herein are true and correct, and I agree and understand that any misstatement will be grounds for forfeiture on my part to any employment by the Board of Education.

DATE: _____   _____
                                              Signature

Figure 4–1. Application for Employment.

39

Review of Applications. When a vacancy exists, top management secures the applications and reviews them. Should a likely, capable application be on file, he will call the person in for an interview.

Interview. The purpose of the interview is to secure information, give information, and establish a friendly relationship. The interview is a means of obtaining from the applicant the facts about his experience and qualifications on which selection and placement are based. The interviewer should picture the unfilled position in the school district organization and the disadvantages and opportunities connected thereto. The interview should not be a rush affair because both should be friends when the interview terminates.

Tests. Some school districts desire further information by means of written and performance tests. In practice, flourishing economic conditions diminish the supply of applicants for maintenance positions and this requirement is frequently waived.

Selection. The administrator selects the applicant who has the ability and experience which seem best to fit into the district maintenance organization. Thus, the best qualified available person is recommended to fill the vacancy. The legal procedure of actual employment varies from state to state and in the several school districts.

Induction. An employee who is hired to fill a position in a school system has many things to learn. Administration should provide information which will assist him in orienting his activities. Among the things that could be provided include:

1. A map of the school district showing the location of the school plants.
2. All the written instructions and policies which pertain to his duties and responsibilities. Safety practices should be included.
3. Information on the fringe benefits operating in the school system.
4. Explanation of the organization procedures and to whom he is definitely responsible.
5. A buddy, preferably some person of equal rank in the organization, whom he may counsel in learning the methods and procedures which govern the maintenance department.

Retention. Capable employees who apply themselves to their assigned tasks are the "warp and woof" of a maintenance program. The employees should know as long as their services are satisfactory that they will be welcome in the organization. This continuity of service breeds economy, efficiency, and good will. State laws and local ordinances determine the manner in which employees are notified of retention.

Promotions and Transfers. Employees should know that promotions will come to those who are capable and apply themselves. Faithful and economical performance is the basis for promotions. The policy on transfer concerns moving employees from one position to another without effecting any significant increase in duties, responsibilities, skill required, or compensation. Local policies have to be definite in these respects.

Terms of Employment. A new employee usually is employed on a four to six month probation. If his services are satisfactory during this period, his classification changes to a regular employee status.

Length of Day. The eight hour day and five day week is recommended and is an accepted practice. The regular schedule is 8:00 A.M. to noon and 1:00 to 5:00 P.M. with an hour for lunch. If a half hour is taken for lunch, the quitting time may be 4:30 P.M. Often staggered schedules are necessary to avoid interruptions. Hours before school, after school, during lunch hour, and during the evening must be planned. Emergency schedules are frequently necessary to care for special items.

Summer Hours. The periods of work each day may be adjusted by the supervisor of maintenance during the summer months.

Overtime. The supervisor of maintenance may authorize overtime when the central office approves. The overtime rate shall be paid at the rate of one and one-half regular time during the week days and double the regular rate if work has to be performed on Sundays.

WAGE AND EMPLOYEE BENEFITS

School districts adopt a policy that employees in the maintenance services be paid at the prevailing rate of wages for comparable work in the community. This wage information is available from state employment security commissions which make annual occupational wage surveys. This policy is fair to both public and employees. Paying less than prevailing wages over a long period tends to recruit substandard personnel. Substandard pay can increase the costs of maintenance and education through inefficient, incompetent employees of low morale.[2] Law determines some features of wage policy, such as minimum wages and the time and manner of payment.

Employee Benefits.

The personnel policies of each school district should govern the benefits which a non-certified or non-instructional employee earns and enjoys. The items therein should cover holidays, payroll deductions, leaves of absence with and without pay, vacation time, jury duty, and subpoenas. Other items of policy may include accident or injury on duty, blood donations, conventions, examinations, and graduations. These policies will vary. In practice, these employees desire to know these policies in detail.

Experience proves that maintenance employees desire policies of treatment in these aspects common to the certified employees based on job similarities, training, and experience.

In the administration of employee benefits a special provision for emergency absence or leave, not to exceed two (2) days per calendar year, granted to an employee where circumstances make it impossible for him to be on the job, has improved employee morale. A fire in the home, broken resident water lines, and stopped-up sewer lines are good examples of emergency leaves.

Another much appreciated policy is the increase in vacation time as seniority increases. This provision permits the employee to make more extended trips or have longer free time for diversion or work as he chooses. Experienced employees really appreciate this provision.

In concluding this discussion of employee benefits, experience evinces that local policies should be as liberal as possible. They should be kept in line with policies of industry and other nearby educational institutions. These benefits assist greatly in making the employee proud of both his job and the school system.

Other Personal Benefits.

Each state and each local school district has laws and policies which pertain to the welfare and security of the employee. The state retirement system, social security, optional deductions

2 Robert Fisher, Annual Volume of Proceedings, Association of School Business Officials of the United States and Canada (Forty-ninth Annual Meeting, Chicago, Illinois), p. 214.

for Blue Cross and Blue Shield insurance, U. S. Savings Bonds, tax sheltered annuities, and credit union saving and loan accounts are among the major items. Some states require compensation insurance. The written details of these different plans become cumbersome. Each school district should furnish and explain these personal benefits to the employees by oral and written communications.

Maintenance employees appreciate the provision for district-carried insurance which covers them for a twenty-four hour day. By necessity they must travel between jobs and execute many projects which may entail many elements which are and may become hazardous.

SEVERANCE

Significant practice spells out in detail the policies which govern employee severance in the cases of resignation, death, discharge, and suspension.

Employee Resignation. The employee who voluntarily leaves his job completely divorces himself from all benefits, such as vacation pay, sick leaves retirement benefits, etc. Some insurance policies may make an allowance that he may continue at his own expense. Absolute severance precludes any further claim on the employer for seniority or other accrued rights.

Death. All seniority and other accrued rights cease when an employee dies. Also, his pay ceases on the day of his death.

Discharge. This most drastic disciplinary measure means that the school loses the services of an experienced employee whose training and experience have largely been gained at the expense of the school district. Ill will is bound to occur. The worker himself, the administration, his immediate friends, and in many cases other employees will take exception to this action.

This action demands predetermined policies which should be described completely in the employer's handbook or other school regulations.

The reason for dismissal is a prime necessity. A helpful guide in listing reasons for dismissal is in this summary:

> The increasing judicial nature of dismissal procedures has required boards of education and school administrators to seek causes for dismissal that are as concrete as possible. In other words, there is an increasing trend to require legal proof that specific wrongful acts were committed or that there were actual instances of misfeasance, malfeasance, or non-feasance of duty. The results have been that the rules of Civil Service jurisdictions have tended to list specific charges for dismissal. The following is a composite list prepared by selecting those that occurred most frequently in a number of documents.
>
> 1. Incompetency and inefficiency in performance of duty.
> 2. Wanton carelessness or negligence.
> 3. Damaging public property or wasting public supplies.
> 4. Bribery.
> 5. Dishonesty.
> 6. Brutality and offensiveness toward fellow employees and the public.
> 7. Permanent or chronic physical or mental ailments or defects impairing proper performance of duty.
> 8. Violation of any lawful or official regulation or order.
> 9. Insubordination.
> 10. Refusal to testify before a commission.

11. Being convicted of a criminal offense or of a misdemeanor involving moral turpitude.
12. Conspiring to commit an unlawful act.
13. Employment elsewhere during working hours.
14. Failure to report to work without reason.
15. Failure to report back to work without reason.
16. Failure to pay just debts without reason.
17. Engaging in political activities during working hours.
18. Using or attempting to use political influence to secure promotion.
19. Conduct unbecoming an employee.
20. Immoral conduct.
21. Drunkenness on duty or habitual intemperance.
22. Causing a low morale in the organization.[3]

The administration must be fair in a dismissal case. A diary of written proof starting the exact time the event occurred is effective. The basis of proof should be a record. Should a dismissal hearing become necessary, written statements are important. Dismissal cases become matters of public record and care should be taken with the word content of the dismissal statement. The dismissed employee may hire an attorney for the case which forces the board of education to prepare adequately in presenting the reason for dismissal. A wise action is to treat dismissal problems as early as possible. Consistent and honest evaluations of the manner in which the services in question affect the school is the forthright action. Effective administration must face these problems even though much unpleasantness may result.

Suspension. An action which is sometimes used to discipline a maintenance worker is to suspend the employee for a short period without pay for a minor violation of rules and regulations. This practice is effective; however, the needed caution is to use suspension as little as possible. Often a suspension has a good effect on other employees.

MISCELLANEOUS WORKING RELATIONSHIPS

In the effective administration of school maintenance many small but significant policies assist in the good will of employees. These policies assist each worker in understanding how the department operates. Each district should create policies which induce efficient operation within the district.

Personal Mail. Insofar as possible all personal mail should be sent to the home address of the employee. Some personal mail will come to the school offices. Top management should assume the responsibility of seeing that an employee's personal mail reaches him. If the employee has personal mail, it is his responsibility to post it.

Change of Address. The employee who changes his residence should immediately notify top management in writing. His new address and telephone are basic items of personnel administration.

Telephone Calls. Insofar as possible personal telephone calls should be made at the residence of the employee. Should a personal long distance telephone call become necessary, the charges should be made to the home phone of the employee.

---

[3] Louis Cohen and Ridgley M. Bogg, *The Administration of Non-Instructional Personnel in Public Schools* (Chicago: Research Corporation of the Association of School Business Officials, 1964), p. 60.

Emergency Telephone Numbers. Each school district should designate certain telephone numbers to be used only in the case of emergencies. These numbers should be concealed and not used by anyone for personal business. The families of the workmen may have the numbers as a means of contact in an emergency. Workmen may use these numbers to request materials, to advise the maintenance office of their whereabouts, and to contact their foremen for instructions.

Talkfests. Employees should avoid grouping and talking while they are on duty.

Keeping Informed. All important announcements should be placed on designated bulletin boards which each employee should read. Written communications are very important. A monthly house organ covering the news of this department is recommended.

Personal Visitors. Only in cases of emergency should personal visitors come to the work station of an employee. Then, the visitor should seek permission from the foreman in charge before entering.

Subscriptions. Agents who take subscriptions to periodicals should canvass the personnel at their homes.

Solicitations. The general school administration should approve solicitations for money or materials before these requests are presented to the employees of the maintenance department. A good policy is to limit the requests to one or two a year.

Use of Shops. Regardless of the personal inconvenience of the worker, the use of the shops should be only for the use of work of the school district. This policy forbids the use of the shops and equipment for personal use before, during, and after working hours.

TRANSPORTATION

Maintenance workers in the school district by necessity must travel to the different school plants in order to perform their duties. In addition, the workmen must carry with them their basic tools and equipment, and, in some cases, supplies and materials for the repair work. Provision must be made to enable these men to travel expeditiously without undue waste of time. Top management has the responsibility of assigning available trucks and setting travel allowances. The deploying of all workers in the most expeditious manner is the one responsibility of management which must be carefully planned in the day-by-day operation of maintenance activities.

GARNISHMENTS

An employee may have delinquent personal bills for goods and services for which he is unable to pay, in which case the supplier of these services may garnishee the wages of the employee. This legal action is served on the school district warning the district not to pay or deliver money or effects to the employee, pending a judgment of a court. Both the employee and the payroll department spend needless time in caring for this situation. The employee has the responsibility to arrange for the payment of his personal debts. Continuous garnishments are good bases for severance.

The discussion of these various items in working relationships may seem small and unimportant. Experience has revealed that detailed policies relating to these minutiae eliminate much misunderstanding.

PERFORMANCE EVALUATION

The administration of a performance evaluation program on the work of the employee furnishes a good basis or starting point for top management and maintenance personnel. The purposes must be carefully defined.

Employee Benefits.

The employee is entitled to know how well he is measuring up to expected standards of job performance. The employee should know in what areas he is weak in order that he can strengthen these aspects.

Administration Benefits.

Top administration can use employee performance evaluations to form the fairest and best basis for decisions in considering salary promotions. The supervisor can use performance evaluations in individual interviews and make suggestions for the improvement of the work of this individual. The supervisor can also learn the characteristics of the individual on the basis of judgments through comparison and opinion. These judgments of an employee's individual effectiveness form a basis for use in training and supervision.

Scope of Qualities.

A performance evaluation should contain only those traits which are pertinent to the job. Five major qualities pertaining to employees that should be evaluated by top management are: (1) performance abilities, (2) mental abilities, (3) supervisory abilities, (4) personal abilities, and (5) capacity for further development.[4] An administration may add other qualities. A definite decision on the qualities desired for each job classification is a direct responsibility of the administration.

Performance Evaluation Forms.

Three general types of forms must be used.[5] Each form has its advantages and disadvantages. The personal quality type of form provides an excellent basis for broad training programs dealing with the fundamental qualities necessary for success. The job performance type of rating is concrete, easy to understand, and easy to use in interviews with employees. The third common type is an overall evaluation form which rates the entire job performance and is easily understood. Local administration may formulate a form. (See Figure 4-2.) In the administration of this form, called "Progress Record," the raters have designated the following points to prevent over-rating (creating a halo): Far Exceeds—5 points, Exceeds—10 points, Meets Requirements—15 points, Partially Meets Requirements—10 points, and Does Not Meet Requirements—5 points. This guide is a measure used for promotion.

Methods of Rating.

The most common performance rating methods include:

Ranking Method. The comparison is made by selecting the best employee, then

---

[4] Cohen and Bogg, *The Administration of Non-Instructional Personnel in Public Schools,* p. 43.

[5] Cohen and Bogg, *The Administration of Non-Instructional Personnel in Public Schools.*

Name _____ Date _____

Employee's Position _____ Job Grade _____ Job Class _____

Note: This rating will represent in a systematic way your appraisal of the employee in terms of his ACTUAL PERFORMANCE ON HIS JOB. In the interests of furthering careful analysis, the following suggestions are offered regarding the use of this form.

1. Consider only one factor at a time.
2. Study each factor and the specifications for each grade.
3. Review upon completion to see that the rating of each factor applies exclusively to the individual's ACTUAL PERFORMANCE ON HIS JOB.
4. Comment fully at bottom of the page and on reverse side upon any matter which in your opinion needs explanation.

PERFORMANCE

PERFORMANCE FACTORS	FAR EXCEEDS Requirements of this job	EXCEEDS Requirements of this job	MEETS Requirements of this job	PARTIALLY MEETS Requirements of this job	DOES NOT MEET Requirements of this job
QUALITY OF WORK Accuracy Economy of Materials Economy of Time (His own & others) Neatness Thoroughness	Consistently Superior ☐	Sometimes Superior ☐	Consistently Satisfactory ☐	Usually Acceptable ☐	Consistently Unsatisfactory ☐
DEPENDABILITY Follow instructions Judgment Punctuality & Attendance Safety Habits	Consistently Dependable ☐	Dependable in most respects ☐	Ordinarily Dependable ☐	Frequently Undependable ☐	Consistently Undependable ☐
COMPATIBILITY Attitude toward the Board Attitude toward Supervision Cooperation with Fellow Employees	Inspires others to work with & assist co-workers ☐	Quick to Volunteer to work with & assist others ☐	Generally works well with & assists others ☐	Seldom works well with or assists others ☐	Does not work well with or assist others ☐

RECOMMENDED CLASSIFICATION BE: JOB GRADE _____ JOB CLASS _____

SIGNED _____ (USE BACK OF THIS SHEET FOR ANY COMMENTS)

Figure 4-2. Progress Record.

the next best employee, the poorest, then the next poorest, and find the rank with others.

Forced Choice. Great skill and technical knowledge are required by the rater when he has to make two choices from a group of descriptive statements. Each job has to have a rating form and a scoring key.

Self Rating. This method is an excellent means of causing employees to think in an organized way about their job performances. The actual merit rating of the employee is not valid but this device can be of great value if it is properly used in connection with other rating forms.

Positive Steps in Rating.

The administration should plan carefully the performance valuation techniques. The effectiveness of the program depends on how thorough the plan is made. Included in the steps should be:

1. The selection of appropriate methods of rating to insure fairness and objectivity is a first essential.
2. The selection and the training of raters are basic for proper execution.
3. The standards for rating should be thoroughly discussed by those affected.
4. The administration must recognize that the rating techniques have value, and he must be aware of the limitations therein.

Significant practice in performance evaluation demands that ratings be made carefully and objectively on decisions which are fair to the employee. If successful, the decisions boost the morale of the organization both individually and collectively.

EMPLOYEE ORGANIZATION

Maintenance employees perform significant services in the job of educating children. Other segments of the school employees organize for self-betterment. The board of education should adopt rules which guarantee the right of each maintenance employee to belong or refrain from belonging to his employee organization. This policy should provide that the organization should file a statement of purposes, rules and by-laws, and the names of their responsible officials. The policy should include provision for appearing before the administration and the board itself. The responsible officers may present the interests and aspirations of the membership. Definite subjects such as compensation, fringe benefits, working conditions, grievances, and disciplinary matters should be included in the policies.

Long experience with an organization of this type has eliminated endless days of quibbling, has removed the need for employee political activity, and has permitted both employees and management to proceed with their respective jobs. The grievances of employees have been at a minimum.

RELATIONS WITH ORGANIZED LABOR

The administrator of maintenance functions in some school districts works with organized labor. The present militant attitudes of all public school employees are being expressed in articulate fashion. Increasingly these attitudes are expressed to both leadership and management by means of organized effort of local, national, or international unions. The present trend points toward more relationship with labor through the process of collective bargaining.

Organized labor has many union organizations. Those unions most likely to perform for schools are the individual craft union, building trades union, blanket union (teamsters), and the industrial or maintenance workers union.

The employees group organizes and joins an established union to achieve security—economic, social, and emotional. The worker expects good treatment in his job situations. The improvement in social and economic security is the primary goal of organized labor. The achievement of this goal is provided by adequate wage rates, pertinent fringe benefits, and requests for changes in working conditions.

Astute leadership in organized labor realizes that most schools are financed on a tax limited fiscal year basis. Therefore, the union has to put its thrust on fringe benefits and improved working conditions. A push for higher wages receives constant union attention by concentrated effort in both personal voting and supporting positive legislation.

Some states have labor-management framework mandated by laws. Others have optional plans or no directions. Local union leadership is generally well versed in all the pertinent state and national laws. No general formula exists at present as how best to work with organized labor. In most states no particular rules are established by law for public schools.

The maintenance administration usually works as a representative of the chief school officer of the district. State school laws define the responsible school district officer. The responsible administrator becomes deeply involved in the renewal of working contracts, administering the contracts, handling of grievances, and handling irresponsible labor personnel.

The able maintenance administrator is compelled to become knowledgeably informed about sources of labor law and court decisions. Furthermore, statutes, regulations, administrative decisions, and rulings or labor laws add to the effect of the labor law. In addition, he should thoroughly know the union policies of the organization which has a contract with the district. The employment of a qualified legal counsel is a high priority.

School administrators who are confronted with an initial organization could profit by following definite policies. The first and foremost responsibility is to keep a written dated record of all communications pertaining to labor relations. The second is to conduct all negotiations in a businesslike, calm, and rational manner.

Some suggestions for procedure which may have positive value are briefly stated:

1. Receive and date letter of organized labor request to meet with school official.
2. Set convenient date and write a prompt courteous reply.
3. Plan the meeting with time for adequate communication and exchange of ideas and information. Notes should be taken on items discussed. The school official should request a list of officers of the local union, a constitution of its bylaws, and a report of its activities.
4. Ascertain the goals of the proposed contract with the school system.
5. Immediately communicate the above information to the chief school official and board of education.
6. When authority is given to proceed with the preparation of a written proposal for a working relationship, some important elements, briefly stated, should include:
   a. Where are meetings to be held?
   b. What is the schedule of meeting dates?
   c. Time of day meeting is to be held.
   d. Who will speak for union? Maintenance employees?

    e. What should be the contents placed in the document?
        (1) Detail requests for wage increases?
        (2) Detail requests for specific fringe benefits?
        (3) Detail requests for improved working conditions?
        (4) Should a statement of "no strike clause" be inserted?
    f. When should cases be arbitrated?
    g. How should grievances be handled?
    h. Who is to prepare and read document?
    i. Who ratifies document?

These briefly stated suggestions may be extended by legal counsel. This relatively new phase in the personnel administration of school maintenance challenges the ingenuity and acumen of all officials. Precise roles of administrators and superiors are difficult to outline in labor relations. Such experiences should be interesting, positive, and useful—destined to strengthen effective administration.

RECOGNITION

Maintenance employees of a school system are far removed from the central administration of the school. Better conditions prevail when a custodian keeps a clean building because people see and appreciate his performance. The employee of the maintenance department who patches the roof has very little chance of public notice because of the job (good or bad) which he has performed. His services are taken for granted. Astute administration plans to recognize good work as it progresses and is completed. Various devices, such as certificates of administrative commendation, are a small means of producing good morale.

SUMMARY

The daily practice of personnel administration in the maintenance department must be guided by frank and fair policies. These employees should be recognized in an organized manner. The policies on compensation and fringe benefits must be fair and induce competency. Selection and promotions must be made on the basis of the best man for the place. Definite policies on grievances and discipline are a basis for effective administration of maintenance. The manpower in maintenance is the most costly expenditure. Liberal personnel policies act as a "crutch" in the retention of qualified personnel in the maintenance department.

Chapter 5

RESPONSIBILITY OF THE
ADMINISTRATOR FOR SAFETY
IN MAINTENANCE OPERATIONS

The safety program is the definite responsibility of the school administrator. This job entails the direction of the activities within this division which will arouse an interest in methods of accident prevention. Injuries and deaths become a cost to the employee, employer, dependents, and consumer. The responsibility of the administrator is at least threefold. He is interested in the safety of the *maintenance personnel*, the *school plants* for which he is responsible, and the safety of the *occupants* of these school plants. This chapter outlines his responsibilities to the first and second items.

In order to establish a program for prevention and correction, the school administrator must understand why people act as they do. Experience reveals the personnel causes of accidents in school maintenance operation as:

1. Failing to follow instruction.
2. Lacking the know-how before performance.
3. Tinkering with safety devices.
4. Failing to use safety precautions.
5. Taking unsafe positions or posture.
6. Working on moving equipment.
7. Moving or working at unsafe speeds.
8. Using unsafe equipment or substitutes or hands instead of equipment.
9. Pranking, bothering, and scaring fellow workmen.

Certain bodily and mental circumstances of individual employees add to the causes of unsafe acts. A careful analysis of the bodily reactions of a person may include one or more of these defects: crippled, heart or other organic weakness, hernia, muscular weakness, poor eyesight, defective hearing, and intoxication.

A worker may possess or create an improper attitude which may occasion an unsafe act. An analysis may reveal that the worker may be excitable, nervous, absentminded, and restless. He may also have a violent temper and possess a wilful intent to injure. In addition he may also deliberately disregard instructions.

The conditions of the working environment of a person may contribute to unsafe acts. Areas in which work is performed may have improper illumination and/or improper ventilation. Machines, tools, and equipment may be improperly guarded and/or have defective parts. The worker may be improperly dressed. Out of the way and high work hinder ease of performance. The standard of housekeeping in all areas where a worker performs his task is a very important consideration.

The administrator is under a continuous obligation to arouse the interest and cooperation of all maintenance personnel to an active part in every plan of removing hazards and reducing the frequency and severity of accidents.

SCOPE OF RESPONSIBILITY

School maintenance activities are scattered. The activities in the maintenance shop area, in the several school plants, and in transportation to and from these areas are many and varied. These activities allow for many events in which injuries may occur. This complex wide-spread geographical area demands effective administration of a safety program. The program includes instructions, actions to follow to prevent accidents, and plans to follow in case of accidents.

RESPONSIBILITIES OF ADMINISTRATOR

The essentials of a safety program for maintenance operations will be administered differently in the various school districts. Regardless of who administers the essentials or how the essentials are planned and administered, they are present in effective administration.

First Aid Station.

A definite space in the shop area properly equipped with furniture and first aid medical supplies is a basic consideration. Personnel in shops may have accidents or become ill. Some specific person should be trained and responsible for the administration of this facility.

First Aid—Dispatched Personnel.

Both instructions of the proper course of action to take and some minimum supplies for first aid should be provided for workers. Often gangs of workmen are present on maintenance jobs throughout the school district. The foreman or leadman has definite responsibilities regarding safety practices in this situation.

Fire Drills—Shop.

The men should be drilled for speedy evacuation in the event of a fire in the shop. Some shop activities have critical operations which may produce a fire. Management must see that "there is a place for everything and that everything is in its place." In essence, they must insist on good housekeeping. If a fire occurs in the maintenance shops, a call should immediately be made to the fire department, and then the existing fire extinguisher equipment should be used.

Fire Drills—Schools.

All maintenance personnel who work within the individual schools should become familiar with the fire exit drill regulations which pertain to that building.

Disasters.

The entire maintenance staff should become familiar with the activities which take place around school plants during and after any disaster. Cyclones, tornadoes, earthquakes, explosions, and air raids may occur. Many administrators have preplanned written regulations for these disasters.

Handling of Accidents.

Management has a definite responsibility of providing first aid instructions. This list should be posted in various critical areas of the maintenance shop. A good source for this kind of information is the Red Cross. Astute administration will designate some person or persons among the maintenance shop employees to take the first aid course taught by the Red Cross and assign him or them to assist injured employees. The following check list of first aid instructions, which has been a successful guide, was taken from some unknown source.

Checklist of First Aid Instructions. If the injury is a cut, burn or other injury small enough that the patient may safely work and later be taken to a doctor of his own choice, take him to a doctor or to the closest receiving hospital listed on a large card kept near the telephone in the main office. (Notify his family.)

If the injury is very serious or there may be broken bones, do not move the patient. Call or send someone else to call the nearest emergency hospital listed on a card by the telephone to request that an ambulance come to the school or shop for the injured person. Recommended local procedure may be to call the Police Department for an ambulance. (Notify the injured person's family.)

Reporting. A significant responsibility in the management of safety is to have an adequate procedure for reporting accidents. Generally speaking, accidents don't just happen. Psychological, emotional, and physical conditions cause accidents. Effective administration has a definite plan of reporting accidents. See Figure 5-1. Most states have a regulation form which must be used for filing accident reports for workmen's compensation.

Study Causes of Accidents.

The reports of accidents do not mean anything unless capable people study them and make a thorough inquiry when they occur. The study will be time-consuming, but the facts obtained should enable management to know the individual characteristics of the persons involved.

Maintenance Areas. Accidents occur in the areas of the maintenance plant. Whether the accident be minor or critical, management should know as far as possible the causes of the accident.

School Plants. The study of the causes of accidents which occur in school plants is likewise important. Most careful performance in the execution of future projects may result.

<table>
<tr><td rowspan="2">

Standard Form For

**EMPLOYER'S FIRST REPORT
OF INJURY**

</td><td>

State's
Number
For:

</td><td>

File:_____
Carrier:_____
Employer:_____

</td></tr>
<tr><td colspan="2">

Carrier's File No._____
(The spaces above not to be filled in
by employer)

</td></tr>
</table>

Employer	1. Name of Employer _____ 2. Office Address: No. and St._____City or Town_____State_____ 3. Insured by_____Address_____ 4. Give Nature of Business (or Article Manufactured)_____
Time And Place	5. (A) Location of Plant or Place Where Accident Occurred_____ _____Department_____State if Employer's Premises_____ (B) If Injured in a Mine. Did Accident Occur on Surface, Underground, Shaft, Drill or Mill_____ 6. Date of Injury_____19___Day of Week_____Hour of Day_____A.M._____P.M. 7. Date Disability Began_____19____A.M.____P.M.. 8. Was Injured Paid in Full for this Day_____ 9. When Did You or Foreman First Know of Injury_____ 10. Name of Foreman_____

Injured Person	11. (A) Name of Injured_____(B) Is Injured Related to Employer_____
	       (first name) (middle initial) (last name)
	                     (C) Social Security No._____
	12. Address: No. and St._____City or Town_____State_____
	13. Check (√) Married___. Single___. Widowed___. Widower___. Divorced____. Male_____. Female_____.
	14. Speak English?_____If Not. What Language?_____
	15. Age_____Did You Have on File Employment Certificate or Permit_____
	16. (A) Occupation When Injured_____(B) Was This His or Her Regular Occupation_____
	   (If Not, State in What Department or Branch of Work Regularly Employed)_____
	17. (A) How Long Employed by You_____(B) Piece or Time Worker_____(C) Wages Per Hour $___
	18. (A) No. Hours Worked per Day_____(B) Wages per Day $_____
	   (C) No. Days Worked per Week_____(D) Average Weekly Earnings $_____
	   (E) If Board, Lodging, Fuel or Other Advantages were Furnished in Addition to Wages, Give Estimated Value
	per Day, Week or Month_____(F) How Many Children Under 18 Years of Age_____
	                Minnesota Only: How Many Children Under 16 Years of Age_____

Cause Of Injury	19. Machine, Tool or Thing Causing Injury_____20. Kind of Power (Hand, Foot, Electrical Steam, Etc.)_____21. Part of Machine on Which Accident Occurred_____ 22. (A) Was Safety Appliance or Regulation Provided_____(B) Was It in Use at Time_____ 23. Was Accident Caused by Injured's Failure to Use or Observe Safety Appliance or Regulation_____ 24. Describe Fully How Accident Occurred, and State What Employee Was Doing When Injured_____ _____ 25. Names and Addresses of Witnesses_____

Nature Of Injury	26. Nature and Location of Injury (Describe Fully Exact Location of Amputations or Fractures, Right or Left)___
	_____
	27. Probable Length of Disability_____28. Has Injured Returned to Work_____
	   If so, Date and Hour_____At What Wage $_____
	29. At What Occupation_____
	30. (A) Name and Address of Physician_____
	   (B) Name and Address of Hospital_____

Fatal Cases	31. Has Injured Died_____If So, Give Date of Death_____

<table>
<tr><td>

Date of This Report

</td><td colspan="2">

Firm Name

</td></tr>
<tr><td></td><td>

Signed By

</td><td>

Official Title

</td></tr>
</table>

Figure 5–1. Employer's First Report of Injury.

53

Inspection.

Safety inspection of all the school plants in a school system may become perfunctory. The responsible people in the school plants, such as the principal and the head custodian, have definite obligations for safety inspection and reporting. When maintenance management gives a thorough yearly inspection to each plant, safety feature inspection should be noted. Responsible maintenance personnel should check the areas of their responsibility for safety. The fire department in many school districts checks the building for safety. The American Insurance Association requires periodic checks for safety and deficiencies or malpractices. The report of these inspections tends to alert all school personnel about the safety conditions of the respective plants. The reports of the separate inspections serve as good material for plant correction to provide accident prevention.

Florio and Stafford[1] designate twelve key hazards:

    a. Chemical hazards—unlabeled acids, improper handling of caustics, etc.
    b. Electrical hazards—open switches, defective portable lights, etc.
    c. Fire hazards—improperly stored oily rags, flammable liquids used near a flame, etc.
    d. Faulty fire protection equipment—unsafe fire escapes, defective fire extinguishers, etc.
    e. Machine operation hazards—defective equipment, failure to use guards on saws, power presses, grinding wheels, and other dangerous machines, etc.
    f. Material hazards—defective trucks, conveyors, etc.
    g. Power-transmission hazards—unguarded belts, defective pulley, etc.
    h. Poor lighting.
    i. Poor housekeeping—unproperly stored tools, scraps left on work bench, etc.
    j. Poor ventilation.
    k. Yard hazards—unguarded railroad crossing, etc.
    l. Seasonal hazards—icicles, slippery walks, etc.

This non-inclusive list of 12 items serves as a stimulus for noticing unsafe conditions which may occur around all school plants.

Mechanical Safeguard.

Every worker who has a machine which requires a safety guard for safe operations should use the guard at all times. A good practice is to paint the guard a bright color. The user is thus made conscious of its presence. Other protective apparel as aprons, goggles, safety shoes, and work gloves should be provided as normal requirements in protecting the employee from the hazards involved in using various machines and tools.

Training in Operation Procedures.

Each machine requires procedures which permit the employee to perform the most satisfactory work with least expenditure of energy and with a minimum of risk. These procedures have been scientifically determined by safety engineers and efficiency experts. Each new employee who is to work on new machinery should be trained to run the machine. The training is usually divided into three phases. First, the worker reads the Manual of Operations prepared

---

[1] From *Safety Education* by A. E. Florio and G. T. Stafford, copyright 1962. (McGraw-Hill Book Co., Inc., New York.) Used by permission of McGraw-Hill Book Company, p. 225.

by the manufacturer. Second, the supervisor or foreman demonstrates these procedures step by step. Third, the worker practices manipulation of the machinery under supervision until he is thoroughly acquainted with the requisite techniques. All manuals of operations should be kept in the office of the head of maintenance operations when the instructions on the individual machines have terminated. This practice assists in the instruction of future employees. Safety rules which govern the machines should be conspicuously posted. Only properly trained people should operate machinery.

Safety Program.

The operations of maintenance activities are performed by adult male employees. The safety program consists largely in the development of safety habits, attitudes, skills, insights and appreciations of these employees.[2] The objectives are to avoid accidents which will injure their bodies or other people, avoid the loss of time on the job, and be efficient in their work. The maintenance personnel should be alerted to take proper precautions in performing hazardous work. Two men should be together when the project is located in out-of-the-way places, high work, and work on electrical currents. The foremost safety task of the administrator of maintenance is to involve the personnel in such organizational groupings that the time and efforts are effective. The foremen and leadmen are key personnel in working with journeymen and other labor personnel. The group must be small enough that each individual can study and receive help on the weakest aspects of his performances. Also safety appeals must be addressed to the individual. "The supervisor also has the opportunity to observe unsafe acts, faulty attitude, and faulty performance."[3] The total emphasis of a safety program should be to make each individual safety conscious.

Teaching Methods and Techniques.

The methods which are chosen to instruct the maintenance personnel are the responsibility of the management. The implementation of the methods depends upon the number and kinds of educational institutions in the community. Opportunities exist for adult classes on safety under the auspices of colleges and universites, vocational courses in safety, safety institutes, lectures, talks, and conferences on technical aspects of safety education.

A significant practice is to organize the maintenance personnel into safety committees, especially the foremen and leadmen. These leaders may use forms or discussion conferences on safety, motion pictures, safety signs, symbols, posters, slogans, and billboards to impress the importance of safety. Other techniques include demonstrations, charts and graphs, and intensive use of campaign media. In these meetings on safety the importance of safety in transportation, safe handling of materials, and safe performance of assigned jobs must be correlated.

In establishing an effective program of safety in this department, three essentials must be carefully planned. First, the administrator must understand that the safety rules must pertain to the activities of this department. The safety rules which pertain to the general operation of the school system will have to be studied for conformance. Second, he must schedule the time, place, and frequency of meetings, and third, he plans the program and requires attendance at these meetings.

[2] *Safety Education:* Eighteenth Year Book (Washington, D. C.: American Association of School Administrators, 1940), p. 190.
[3] Herbert J. Stack, Elmer B. Siebrecht and J. Duke Elkon, *Education for Safe Living,* Fourth Edition, copyright 1966. Reprinted by permission of Prentice-Hall, Inc., Englewood Cliffs, N. J. p. 184.

A particular phase of safety which should be carefully considered is driving. All the personnel should be alerted to safety in driving to and from work in private cars. The specific personnel who drive trucks or vans to school plants should have specific instructions even though they have a chauffeur's license. Another group of employees may drive buses, mowers, and all kinds of transit equipment to jobs. The last two classes of drivers have extra responsibilities for safety which should be understood by each.

PRECAUTIONS

The leadership in maintenance activities should develop safety rules and regulations for each operation in the maintenance program.

Specific Operations.

Precautions can be emphasized by using past experiences of specific trades, learning precautions from industrial divisions of insurance companies, and local experiences.

Plumbing. A good example for the operation of the plumbing department is listed in *Safety Education*.[4] Accident prevention in plumbing includes:

1. Safety guarding against cave-ins.
2. Guarding against damages from sewer gas.
3. Wet load.
4. Iron and concrete chips.
5. Gasoline dangers.
6. First aid in burns and accidents.
7. Cuts from mushroomed heads of caulking and chests.
8. Care in using scaffolds and ladders.
9. Care in building ladders and scaffolds.
10. Too rapid filling of waterline.
11. Explosive dangers of marsh gas.
12. Danger of open flame when examining septic tanks or opening sewer line.
13. Artificial and natural gas dangers and carbon monoxide dangers.
14. Handling equipment and fixtures.
15. Wet solder.
16. Care of eyes in using welding equipment.
17. Care of handling gas and acids.
18. Care in use of solvents and lyes.
19. Necessity for immediate care of cuts and abrasions.
20. Wash hands before eating.
21. Cleanliness in relationship to repair work.
22. Scalding water or steam burns.

Power Saws. Another example of safety precautions in a specific maintenance operation is the recognition of the potential dangers involved in operating power saws. The rules are typical of safety codes used to guard employees who are assigned to work on these machines.[5]

1. See that the saw is firmly tight on the arbor.

---

[4] *Safety Education* (American Association of School Administrators, Washington, D. C., 1940), p. 208.
[5] General Safety Handbook, Western Electric, Chicago. pp. 97–98.

2. Do not use a cracked saw, it may break, and flying pieces may cause injuries.
3. Before placing the saw in the machine, test it for cracks. If you have any suspicion that the saw is cracked, see your supervisor.
4. In sawing material in small pieces, or narrow cuts, the stock should not be fed with the fingers. A stick of hard wood made for the purpose should be used.
5. Keep your hands away from the blade.
6. Be sure that the guard is correctly adjusted and placed as close to the cutter as possible.
7. When a saw binds in a cut, shut off your machine before trying to release the lumber.
8. Pile your work so that it will not fall.
9. While being sawed, material should be held firmly against the gauge with the hands at a safe distance from the saw.
10. In no case should the hands be placed back of the saw or hook be pulled from the back, as this is apt to bring your hands too close to the saw to be safe.
11. Learn to work at one side of the saw as much as possible. Occasionally pieces of wood are shot back from the saw. They can cause serious injuries.
12. Do not remove pieces with your hand. Use a stick. Keep the small pieces away from the back of the saw.
13. Do not stop the saw too quickly in forcing a piece of wood against the cutting edge when the power is off.
14. Many injuries have resulted when attempting to use a rip saw for cross cutting work and vice versa.
15. Do not reach over a saw to get finished material from the other side, as there is danger of contacting the saw.
16. When using a rip saw see that the guard and fence are in position and in working order.
17. Be sure the splitter guard is in place when using the rip saw.
18. Care should be taken when cutting on knotty wood so the loose knots do not come in contact with the back of the saw.
19. Keep the floor around the machine clean.
20. Be careful not to bump any operators working at their machines.
21. If you see an operation being performed in a dangerous manner, report it to your supervisor.

Safety Precautions for Certain Parts of the School Plant.

Experience discloses many hazards occur during the operation of maintenance functions of the school plant. The original choice of improper materials and appurtenances is a source of hazards. Also unsafe practices around certain parts of the school plant create many hazards.

Grounds. The conditions which help to eliminate accidents on school sites are:

1. Barricading of excavations as they are made.
2. Flaring the excavations during off working hours.
3. Signaling old wells or caves on the school site.
4. Periodically checking the condition of fences around cesspools.
5. Mowing grass while children are kept away from the mower.
6. Keeping sidewalks level to eliminate tripping.
7. Cautioning teachers when backing on school grounds.

8. Eliminating protrusions of any materials on playgrounds.

Electrical Components. Electrical hazards occur in school plants and are often left unattended. Close attention must be given to those hazards or someone may be injured or killed. Some of the most important precautions are:

1. If schools have overhead leads to buildings, notify proper authorities at once if any defect is detected.
2. Always kill a circuit before an attempt is made to repair.
3. All electrical panels should have a three-foot clearance around them.
4. When an electrical switch is pulled, lock it open. The worker should put the key in his pocket.
5. Ground all electrical power tools and machines.
6. Watch for beryllium when destroying fluorescent lamps. Federal law prohibits the use of beryllium.
7. Use safety tools and all necessary protection when working on electrical wiring.
8. Cover plates over outlets should be kept firmly in place at all times.
9. Qualified personnel is a must for electrical repairs.
10. Lightning arrestors are grounded.

Mechanical Elements. Important safety precautions relating to various parts of the mechanical system and mechanical devices include:

1. Replace porcelain handles with metal handles on faucets.
2. Replace all glass soap dispensers with metal dispensers.
3. Check for gas or bad air before cleaning or repairing a tank or entering a tunnel.
4. Hot pipes should be insulated or out of reach.
5. At least two inches should be maintained between furniture and a heating unit.
6. The area around a gas water heater must be free from all combustible materials.
7. Never throw a moving belt by hand.
8. Drain and adjust valves on air lines to avoid build-up pressure. (Same applies to steam lines.)
9. The master gas valve should be installed outside of the building for use of the fire department.
10. Remove gas piping under school building.

Door hazards. Next to the floor, doors are the most often used part of a school building. To prevent accidents caused by doors, the precautions are:

1. Check the condition of all outside door checks periodically.
2. Frequently check the conditions of locks and door checks.
3. Clear glass below the panic bars in doors should be replaced with wire glass or aluminum, or tempered glass or steel panel.
4. Check frequently the mechanism on overhead door.
5. Openings in classroom doors should have wire glass.
6. If door checks are used on interior doors, the door should be completely open with 180° swing or closed.

Boiler Room Hazards. The boiler with its modern fuel controls has become so complex that many failures may happen. Careful inspection of the total boiler with firing mechanism should be made at the beginning of the firing season. The fuel and water intakes and gauges should be thoroughly inspected by qualified personnel. Further caution should eliminate all extraneous materials in the boiler room.

Elevator Hazards. Elevators, automatic or run by operators, have components that produce many hazards. A thorough knowledge of the proper working of each kind of elevator is basic. This mechanism should not be used unless it has all the necessary safeguards. Elevator manufacturers have manuals for safe operation; the instructions therein should be rigidly followed. The elevator operator should be a trained person.

Miscellaneous Building Hazards. Many hazards occur in various building areas and are dangerous and are often unnoticed. A few common building hazards are:

1. Loose acoustical ceiling tile.
2. Sharp edges in construction.
3. Loose handrails on stairs.
4. Unshielded clothes hooks at eye level height in corridors and other areas.

Local Experiences. Numerous school accidents have occurred during the experience of the author in maintenance operations. These injuries have happened to pupils, teachers, custodians, maintenance personnel, and the public who use the school plants.

Poor housekeeping that may cause these accidents on school premises are:

1. Slipping on greasy, wet, or dirty floors.
2. Tripping over loose objects on floors, stairs, and platforms.
3. Running against projection of piled or misplaced material.
4. Tearing hands or other parts of the body on projecting nails, hooks, or sticks.[6]

Falling objects frequently cause accidents, such as:

1. Leaving tools on ladders in high places which may be knocked off.
2. Tall objects which have a narrow base for a foundation may fall or slide.
3. Parts of the building structure such as cracked plaster on ceilings and parts of the other structure may be loose and fall.

Hand tools frequently are a source of accidents. The accidents may be minor in nature, yet they are a major source of injury. A few of the main precautionary procedures are:

1. Hammer heads should be solidly secured to the handles.
2. Use wrench of the proper size and apply it correctly to the nut or bolt head.
3. Use tools only for the purposes for which they are designed.
4. Never use a wrench when the jaws are sprung.
5. When pushing against a wrench handle in close places, push with an open hand.
6. Use suitable shields to cover dangerous parts of sharp or pointed tools.
7. Be certain that the shells of portable electrical tools are grounded.
8. Use only tools in good condition.

Material handling or storage work is a source of accidents. A few simple precautions should reduce accidents.

1. Wear hand pads or gloves when handling sharp or rough material.
2. Lift by keeping the body upright. Lift with the leg muscles. Lift only such loads that are light and can be easily handled. If load is heavy and/or cumbersome, secure help.
3. Avoid dropping any object, for it may fall on your feet.
4. Protruding nails, wires, and tin on objects or parcels should be removed before handling.

---

6 From *Building Operation and Maintenance* by C. A. March, copyright 1950 (McGraw-Hill Book Co., Inc., New York). Used by permission of McGraw-Hill Book Company, p. 217.

Falling is caused by carelessness on the part of the employee and by certain defects of floor surfaces, stains, ladders, portable steps, scaffolding, and housekeeping. Management may caution employees to be alert by:

1. Barricading floor areas where water or other liquid stands until it is removed.
2. Keeping debris, materials, tools, and supplies placed out of the way of traffic lanes.
3. Keeping floors clean.
4. Providing adequate light.
5. Keeping electric extension cords out of traffic lanes.
6. Keeping stair treads and nosings in good condition.
7. Watching the solidity of portable steps when used.
8. Eliminating turned-up mat, rug and carpet edges.[7]
9. Traveling at safe speed when moving about and performing a task.
10. Noticing the presence of snow on the floors or on surfaces near the task to be performed.

Body protection involves important precautions which the employees must thoroughly understand and perform according to set rules and regulations. Each job or operation has its hazards. Proper clothing should be worn according to job dangers. Each employee needs to take proper precautions in dressing to protect his feet, his limbs, all parts of his hands, his eyes, and his total self in the jobs or operations he performs. Some suggestions include:

1. Wearing proper footwear to protect the feet from dropped objects, acids, alkalis, and slipping.
2. Wearing protective aprons, coats, and jackets of various types to protect the body.
3. Wearing proper gloves to protect the hands when handling acids, glass, and sharp materials of every kind.
4. Wearing goggles to safeguard the eyes when operations or instances involve possibilities of eye injury.
5. Wearing safety belts when they are needed for window washing and pole climbing.

Miscellaneous Practices. These various parctices occur around school plants. They are not deliberate. The worker's mind may be preoccupied causing the worker to proceed thoughtlessly in the operation. Salient precautions are:

1. Put gasoline in a fuel tank only after the engine has been stopped.
2. Never use gasoline for cleaning purposes—use a cleaning solvent.
3. Never inhale the fumes of carbon tetrachloride or allow the liquid to contact the bare skin.
4. Careful disposition of cleaning rags used by painters should be planned.
5. Painters should never stack drop-cloths in a hazardous manner.
6. Never block an exit with equipment when the building is occupied.

STRICT ENFORCEMENT OF RULES

The development of a common code of safety rules for each phase of operations of the maintenance department is a prime responsibility of effective administration. After the rules are formulated, strict enforcement is necessary. Disciplinary procedures must be established to reprimard those who fail to observe the safety rules.

---

[7] From *Building Operation and Maintenance* by C. A. March, copyright 1950. (McGraw-Hill Book Company, Inc., New York). Used by permission of the McGraw-Hill Book Company, p. 225.

SUMMARY

Accidents don't just happen; they are caused by unsafe practices and human error. The school administrator responsible for maintenance operations has definite responsibility to organize the local program of safety. Such a program will tend to prevent a loss of the employee's time, eliminate damage to materials and equipment, and minimize other expenses which may result from accidents.

Chapter 6

MANAGING

MAINTENANCE RECORDS

It is necessary to administer only those records which will answer questions in regard to maintenance. Records which are dreamed up that nobody uses or needs are a false economy. Written communications, with carbon copies for the information of all concerned, are a necessary part of the administration of maintenance services. Well-managed plants no longer use verbal orders and reports. Written reports executing orders give detailed information on the results of the services dealing with such factors as materials and labor. These reports serve to record how the work is performed.

BASIC SCHOOL PLANT RECORDS

Actual experience in making surveys for school districts reveals that the keeping of the basic records of school plants is a most neglected responsibility of administration. The original plans and specifications are rarely preserved. Much time is wasted in redrawing the plans and finding parts for repair in catalogues.

Original Plans and Specifications. These documents should be preserved in a definite place in the school plant whether the school district be large or small. They become extremely valuable for reference as time marches on; also, the approved architects' submittals on separate parts of the building assist maintenance personnel in repair jobs.

As Built Plans. During the construction of school buildings, some features may have to be changed in the plans and specifications. Electrical lines may have to be moved and piping for the sewer may have to be relocated, raised, or lowered. A significant practice is to require the architect to produce one plan which shows the building project as it was constructed. Future economies result when these data are available.

Individual Property Records. The individual property record is important to the school system. Once this record is made, reasonable effort can maintain this document. This document contains a record of the site, building, and equipment (both unit and group control). *Property Accounting for Local and State School Systems*[1] is the best guide in formulating this report. If data processing services are available, the individual plant records can be coded and all the needed information can be consolidated in a brief document. A sample code is found in Appendix B, Note 1. A partial summary of a local plant records system is found in Appendix B, Note 2.

Map of District. A map of the school district showing the location of the various plants gives maintenance personnel a conception of their responsibilities. The map also assists in helping maintenance management in dispatching personnel to save time.

Other Devices. One lined, scaled drawing of the several school sites showing all utility locations bound in book form makes information available for maintenance. Also, one lined, scaled drawing of the floor plans of each building or buildings on a school site in book form is a time saver. Photographs and aerial photographs which show maintenance conditions at various times are helpful.

HELPFUL RECORDS ON PARTS OF SCHOOL PLANTS

As school districts become larger, the problems of replacement become more complex. Frequencies of maintenance services become cumbersome. School administration must have records to back up their decisions in order to be fair to all school plants and give proper budgetary consideration for replacements. Certain parts of the school plant and certain services demand records. The number and kinds of records have to be locally determined. Examples of records which may become necessary are:

Boilers. The insurance company which annually inspects the boilers gives a separate report on the condition of each boiler. The report details the necessary repairs to be made if continued operation is desired. A replacement may be recommended.

Painting. A record of the painting both inside and outside the school buildings is a good device in planning preventative maintenance. This record also insures fairness in making decisions. The kind of paints used should be noted in order to study their durabilities. A record which has been used successfully for twenty-five years is shown in Appendix B, Note 3.

Motors. School plants have become so complex that many electric motors are required. A careful record should be kept of each motor. The location, the date of purchase, the amount of repair, and lubrication dates are basic data.

Plumbing. In the individual school plant record, information on plumbing fixtures is established from the original date. This information on the separate school plants serves as a guide for replacement and modernization.

School Furniture. The inventory of furniture and equipment (both unit and group control) is a very helpful guide in the replacement of furniture. This information when machine processed is easily handled.

Electronic Equipment. Amplifiers, radios, record players, etc., are numbered. The date of purchase, the location, and the costs are recorded. This information when recorded by computer gives up-to-the-minute information on this equipment, the upkeep of which is a maintenance function. A practical coding system for this equipment is found in Appendix B, Note 4. Note 5 which follows shows a partial summary of this equipment.

---

[1] Paul L. Reason and George G. Tankard, Jr., *Property Accounting for Local and State School Systems* (Washington, D.C.: U. S. Department of Health, Education and Welfare, Office of Education, 1959), Bulletin No. 22.

Motorized Equipment. Trucks, cars, mowers, buses, scrapers, trailers, etc., used by the maintenance department must be maintained by the department staff. Their replacement must be scheduled for effective operation. An inventory of this equipment can be coded and machine processed. A helpful code for motorized equipment is given in Appendix B, Note 6. A partial summary of the report is found in Note 7 of Appendix B.

Industrial Arts and Vocational Equipment. The equipment in these areas is costly. In order to keep the equipment modern, an inventory record is necessary. In addition, a study may be made of repairs needed on each item.

RECORDS OF MAINTENANCE OPERATIONS

In school districts of any size certain records are necessary for efficient operation. The records must be simple, easily handled, and easily and conveniently filed. In larger school districts the records become more voluminous; however, the essentials are the same in every district.

Budget. The top maintenance administrator must know the amount of money for labor, materials, and replacements that can be spent for these general items in the fiscal year. He has to plan his work within these limits.

Work Requests. The administrator is confronted with requests for scheduled (preventative) maintenance. The day-by-day requests, those unforeseen problems, must be a part of his consideration.

Scheduled Maintenance. The record of these items is made as a result of the conferences. The record of what needs to be done on the several parts of each school plant is basic for long-range planning. These items may be coded. The computer also writes the work order on scheduled maintenance projects.

Nonscheduled Maintenance. In Chapter 3 a definite plan was established for the disposition of these work requests. The request for approved work is a basic record.

Work Orders. The administrator issues work orders which he schedules to keep his full-time employees busy. The requests for scheduled and nonscheduled work are written. (See Appendix B, Note 8.)

Time Card. Each work order is assigned to the employee whose responsibility it is to keep the time he spends on the assigned project. This executed form is given to the timekeeper. (See Appendix B, Note 9.)

Record of Materials. Each work order requiring materials is assigned to the employee who repairs the assigned project. The costs of materials may be itemized. Unused materials are returned to the warehouse. This executed material cost is given to the timekeeper, when requested. (See Appendix B, Note 10.) A summary of the hours and materials costs on each project in all school plants can be figured. These several projects can be coded, machine processed, and collated into a form easy for handling and study.

Payrolls. The payroll forms are usually furnished by the general administration of the school district. The timekeeper consolidates all time reports of the individual employees at stated intervals for the payroll department to process.

PERSONNEL RECORDS

The personnel records of the maintenance department vary from school to school. Important personal information is needed on each application. Administration has the responsibility of keeping an accurate record of the duration of employment. Clearcut records have two necessary characteristics—readily available and easily understandable.

Application Form. The application may be made on a form. (See Figure 4-1.) This specific form has merit—it seeks information pertinent to maintenance functions.

Absentee Record. A record of absences from the job is very important. Local policies determine sick leave and vacation days. In order for the timekeeper to know how to formulate the time sheets each payroll period, he must know about absences from duty. (See Appendix B, Note 12.)

Employment Form. This form has become a very important instrument of administration because of its data. The social security number, the annual wages the employee receives, and the duration of employment are basic facts in checking the retirement system. (See Appendix B, Note 11.)

ADEQUATE INVENTORY AND STOCK RECORDS

The control of the records of the equipment, apparatus, and tools used by the maintenance department varies. Some school districts direct the supply department to be in control of all maintenance materials and equipment and assign them to the maintenance department. The supply department accounts for all equipment, apparatus, and tools. Other districts purchase these items for the maintenance department and the responsibility for accounting is lodged with this department. In either local procedure, sound administration demands adequate inventory and adequate stock records.

MICROFILMING RECORDS

In the management of maintenance records daily records are received. The difficult decision is to decide the records that will be needed for reference and certification tomorrow or the day after. Decisions must be made as to how long the records are to be kept and how much space is necessary in which to keep them.

Determining factors in record management are (1) how it is needed and used, (2) where it is to be used, (3) who will want it, and (4) how often a record or group of records may be needed.

Efficient administration in each school district studies how best to make copies of records and file them in economical spaces. The use of microfilm may assist management in organizing, classifying, and categorizing information.

SUMMARY

Astute administration plans maintenance work with the minimum number of records, because record keeping is time-consuming and expensive. Unless the record serves a definite purpose, it should be eliminated. When records cost more than they are worth, maintenance administration needs to take a sharp look. The use of the computer provides a means to make periodic reports as desired on the status of the maintenance program. The supervisor of maintenance cooperates with personnel who direct the computer system. The rapidity with which valuable figures can be made readily available is a great asset to the smooth functioning of the organization.

Chapter 7

THE EFFECTIVE USE OF A
CENTRAL SERVICE PLANT

The early one-room schoolhouse with the fuel shed had a resemblance to a maintenance work shop and storeroom. In addition to the protection for the coal, wood, and corn cobs, the shed usually had a specific place for school plant tools and other periodically furnished school plant apparatus. The teacher, acting as a custodian, had a key and performed the ordinary custodial and maintenance functions around the building in addition to his teaching duties. Often volunteer or specific employed people would perform the large jobs, such as occasionally painting the schoolhouse or mowing the school grounds before the school term started.

Consolidation of school districts focused a different picture. The buildings became more complex and a custodian was employed who performed most of the custodial and maintenance work on the school plant. The school district generally made an attempt to employ some person who knew how to make small electrical repairs and care for the maintenance and operation of the building. This kind of school plant signaled expertness in maintenance functions.

The increase in the size and complexity of consolidated and city school plants necessitates skilled personnel. Today, these functions require a work place for the maintenance staff in a maintenance shop. In a small school district the shop may be in an area in the school building. In larger school districts old school buildings may be used for maintenance shops.

School administrators often overlook the undesirability of an old school building or available structures to house maintenance operations. The areas within these buildings are frequently inflexible and are not adaptable to the installation of machinery and equipment needed for efficient maintenance services.

Walls, columns, stairs, and facilities of ingress and egress are not located properly for efficient operation. Unsuitable floors are overloaded and electrical installations are weak. The buildings are usually of insufficient capacity or soon become too small. One or more of these elements hinder efficient maintenance operations. In the long run, the necessary adaption to make these structures functional costs more than a new building or buildings.

Wide experience in inspecting maintenance shops in dozens of districts over the nation for more than twenty-five years discloses that shops built for the local maintenance services are more efficient and more attractive. In practice, the undesirable structure looks dirty, dilapidated, and uninviting. Good plant appearance attracts a better class of workers and assists in selling the importance of the maintenance phase of school administration. Shop areas may be in buildings especially purchased or rented for the administration shop.

This chapter deals with the central maintenance shops for medium to large school districts. The volume and nature of the maintenance work to be performed need a special building, special tools, and special equipment for efficient, prompt, and economical service.[1] Too often the provision for the central maintenance shops is an afterthought in planning.

CENTRAL MAINTENANCE SHOPS

Adequate and efficient facilities are necessary to secure satisfactory operation of the maintenance functions in a centralized service shop. They are the facilities used in performing the actual services. The general problems are: (1) the location of the facility, (2) the capacity of the facilities, (3) the type of production and services employed, (4) the type and design of equipment,. (5) the layouts, and (6) the construction of the buildings.

The shop area layout should provide for: (1) economy in the movement of materials and equipment, (2) economy of space, (3) economy of storage space, (4) allowance for flexibility and expansion, and (5) facility of supervision and the special housing of certain departments.

The building layout entails these problems: (1) cost of construction, (2) the effect in operating costs, (3) maintenance and depreciation expenses, (4) reduction of hazards, (5) expansion possibilities, and (6) appearance.

DESIRABLE REQUIREMENTS

Several general and desirable requirements improve the operation and long-range efficiency of central maintenance shops. They are:

1. The building and plot should be a part of the educational center of the school district. If possible the shops should be located in the central part of a school district.
2. Ample parking space should be provided for the cars and trucks belonging to the shop.
3. Provisions should be made to hide debris by the arrangement of buildings, with wood fences, or by the use of shrubbery.
4. The ingress and egress should be definitely controlled.
5. Provisions should be made for expansion and flexibility in the maintenance shop area.

DETERMINATION OF SUPPLY CONTROL

The administration of the control of supplies and materials differs among districts. This determination is necessary because storage space for a stock of maintenance supplies and materials has to be estimated either in the shops or in the warehouse.

[1] R. N. Finchum, *Organizing the Maintenance Program*, U. S. Office of Education, Bulletin XV (Washington 25, D. C., United States Government Printing Office 1196), p. 57.

Maintenance Control. The policy in some school districts is for the purchasing agent to buy all maintenance supplies and materials. These items are delivered and receipted by the responsible maintenance personnel in maintenance. This practice requires more storage space in the maintenance shops because of the bulk purchasing.

Warehouse Control. The recommended practice is to have all supplies and materials controlled by the supply department. From the warehouse the materials are requested as needed for specific jobs. The materials can also be checked out in particular quantities. Thus, the supply department is responsible for the accounting and inventory of the distribution of maintenance materials to the maintenance department. The maintenance department is then responsible to apply materials to the job for which the requests were made. This kind of control lessens the space requirements in the maintenance shop area.

In the last situation, an effective and economical warehouse-maintenance shop building is highly desirable.

GENERAL BUILDING REQUIREMENTS

Actual experience in the management of maintenance shops for more than twenty-five years suggests several general requirements for the building. These ideas, often overlooked, are important in fostering efficiency and attractiveness.

1. The building should be constructed of fire resistant materials.
2. A standard sprinkler system should be installed.
3. Provision should be made for inclined ramps for loading and/or unloading.
4. Provision should be made for dock offsets with "I" beam and chain hoist extending out over dock.
5. Provision should be made for a freight elevator large enough for a loaded three ton truck (if building has two or more stories).
6. All doors should open out and should have door closers and holders.
7. Panic hardware should be installed on all outside doors.
8. Provide a flag pole on the site.
9. Hose bibs for exterior of the building should be located at intervals not to exceed 150 feet.
10. Provision should be made for electrical and plumbing outlets so the electrically cooled drinking fountains may be distributed throughout the shop area.
11. Gas cutoff valves should be located on outside of the building.
12. Light facilities should include:
    a. Fluorescent and/or mixed artificial lighting should be provided as the separate spaces required.
    b. Outside lighting for the entire project—building and grounds should be provided.
    c. If the building is constructed as a part of the service center, the transformer room would be a part of the electrical layout.
13. The intercommunications system should have:
    a. A switch board, either manual or dial, with lines to the maintenance area.
    b. An intercommunication system installed with controls in the maintenance office.
14. The heating and ventilation system should provide for:
    a. The air conditioning of the main office and certain sub-offices.

  b. Separate heating of the maintenance shop.

  c. Adequate window and mechanical ventilation.

DETERMINING SIZE OF SHOP AREA

Efficiency demands that a school district, regardless of size, should have at least one skilled employee. The greater the number of school plants, the greater the number of skilled employees needed. These employees in small districts are directly responsible to the superintendent. As soon as the number of skilled employees grows to four or five, one person should be designated as the head of the department. This procedure saves the time of the superintendent and allows for better coordination of maintenance services. The volume and nature of the maintenance work in the separate school districts determine the size of this facility.

A good policy is to establish a maintenance shop as soon as the head of maintenance service is designated. *School Plant Management*[2] developed a shop layout the size of which is dictated by need. Check the details in Figure 7-1.

Minimum Shop Areas. The suggested areas in this shop layout include carpentry, machine tools, and power tools. Ample work benches for these areas are planned. Definite places are designated for lumber, pipe, and supply storage with shelving for small materials and packaged supplies. An office, a tool room, and conveniences for the workmen are also included. The plan may be expanded as local needs are determined.

Shop Areas in Large School District. These areas are grouped differently in each district. The size and number of the areas depend on local practices. A convenient grouping of areas for shop spaces include:

Heating and steamfitting	Plastering
Heavy equipment	Plumbing
Landscape	Sheet metal
Refrigeration	Welding
Playground and fence	Electrical & motor shop
Electronics	Masonry
Driver trainers	Machine shop
Clocks and signals	Concrete
Carpentry	Food service equipment repair
Furniture repair	Painting
Shades	Roofing
Glazing	Tile
Drayage and clerk	Other areas

Specific Accommodations Areas. Other areas for efficient operation of maintenance services include:

1. Adequate general office suited to local administrative practices.
2. Office spaces for designated foremen.
3. Tool check room.
4. Combination sample room with adequate food service area for personnel.
5. Adequate toilets conveniently located.
6. Heating and/or cooling room.

---

2 John D. Engman, *School Plant Management for School Administrations* (Gulf School Research Development Association, 3801 Cullen Blvd., Houston 4, Texas, 1962), p. 78.

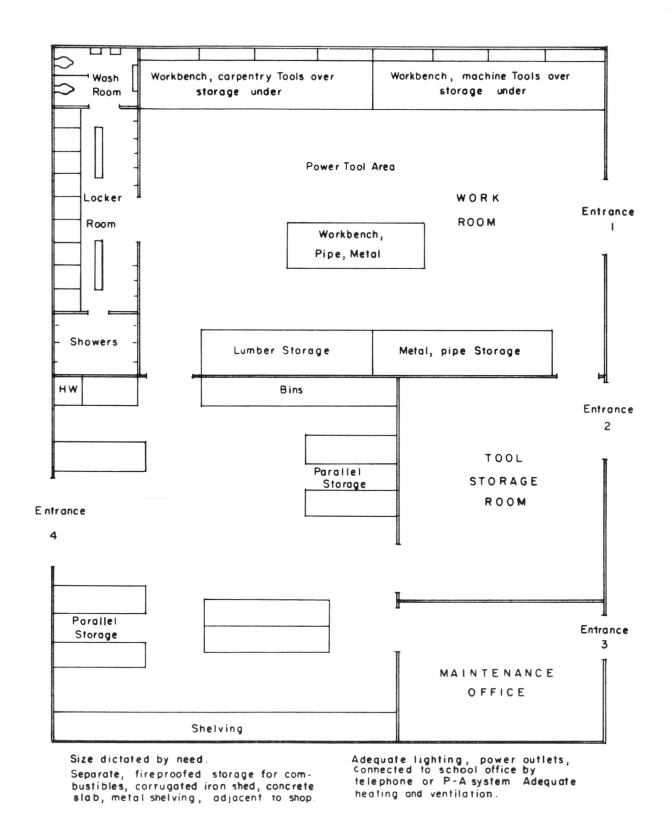

Figure 7–1. Suggested Maintenance Shop Layout.

7. Custodial room with service sink.
8. First aid room.
9. Area for inflammables.

Other Site Areas. Depending on the program of the individual school district, maintenance administration may be more effective by providing definite site areas for:

1. A garage of sufficient size to handle repair to the motorized equipment needs.
2. Filter area adjacent to shop area for care of filters in school system.
3. Filling station adjacent to the garage for cars used in driver training and motorized equipment owned by the school district.
4. Sheds for vehicles.
5. Sheds for dead storage.
6. Open bins for sand and rock.
7. Salvage center with a definite sales area.
8. Incinerator.

Specific Shop Area Requirements. Specific shop area requirements include:

1. Exhaust system in welding area and painting areas.
2. Dust collector system in the furniture and carpentry shop areas.
3. Explosion proof electrical lighting fixtures in the paint room.
4. Overhead exhaust system in the garage.
5. Pits for lubrication and front-end repair in the garage.
6. One large air compressor in the main building so that other units may be attached.
7. One soda acid or water-filled fire extinguisher each 3,000 square feet throughout the building unless otherwise directed.

SERVICE CENTERS

Fortunate indeed is the school district which can arrange to have an adequate service center on an adequate site in a central location in the school district. This center has the space to handle all school supplies and all materials for the operation of the district under the supply division of the business office. The maintenance shop and service areas for the school plants are a part of the total structure of the service center. This division is administered by the buildings and grounds administration.

The size of the service center will vary according to the total maintenance responsibilities of the district. The proximity of the building areas affords a facility which increases efficiency and enhances economies. Figures 7-2 through 7-7 show how one service is arranged to meet local requirements:[3]

Figure 7-2. Outside View of Service Center.
Figure 7-3. Site Layout.
Figure 7-4. Warehouse Floor Layout.
Figure 7-5. Intermediate Floor with Administrative Offices.
Figure 7-6. Maintenance Shops Floor Layout.
Figure 7-7. Elevations of Service Center.

The area components of this service center have been studied and adapted to the local school program employees of the supply and maintenance divisions and the school administration. This planning was performed by extremely well-qualified architects who have planned large warehouses and shops for many government agencies.

---

[3] Oklahoma City, Oklahoma Service Center—under construction.

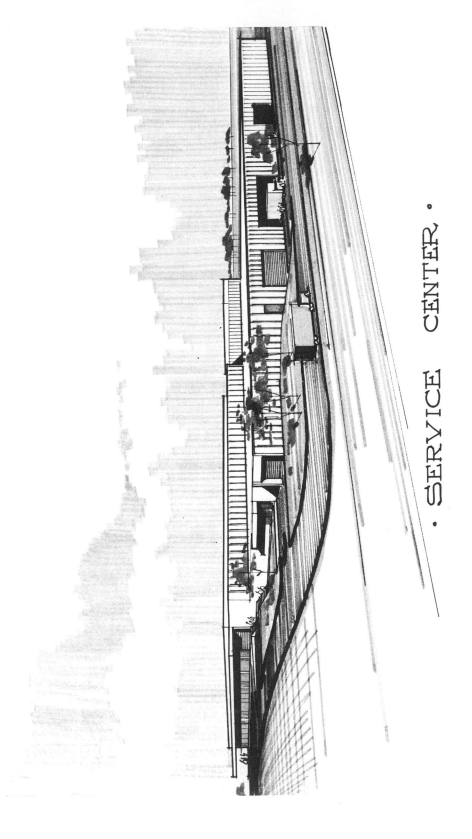

· SERVICE CENTER ·

Figure 7–2. Outside View of Service Center.

Figure 7–3. Site Layout.

73

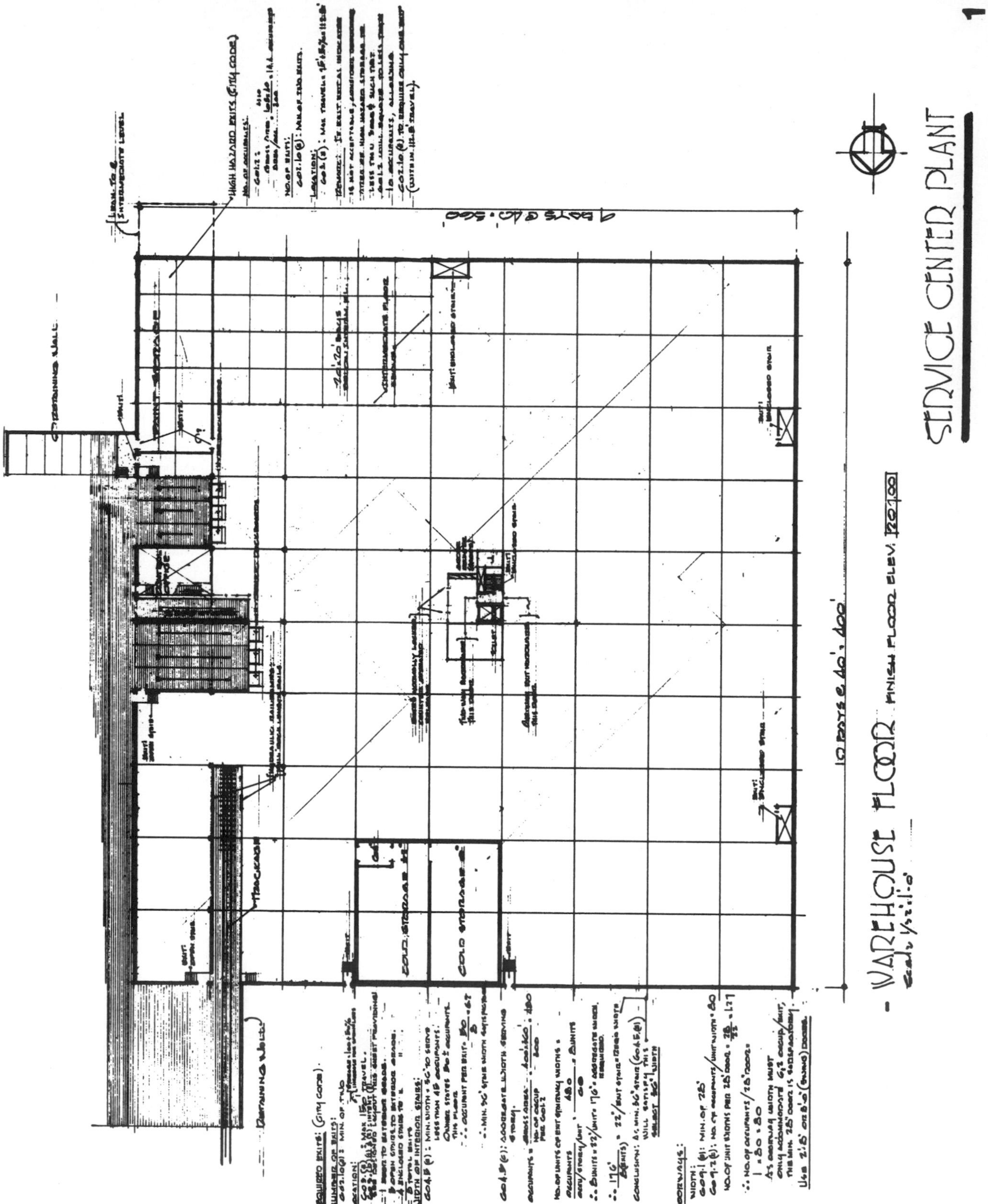

Figure 7-4. Warehouse Floor Layout.

74

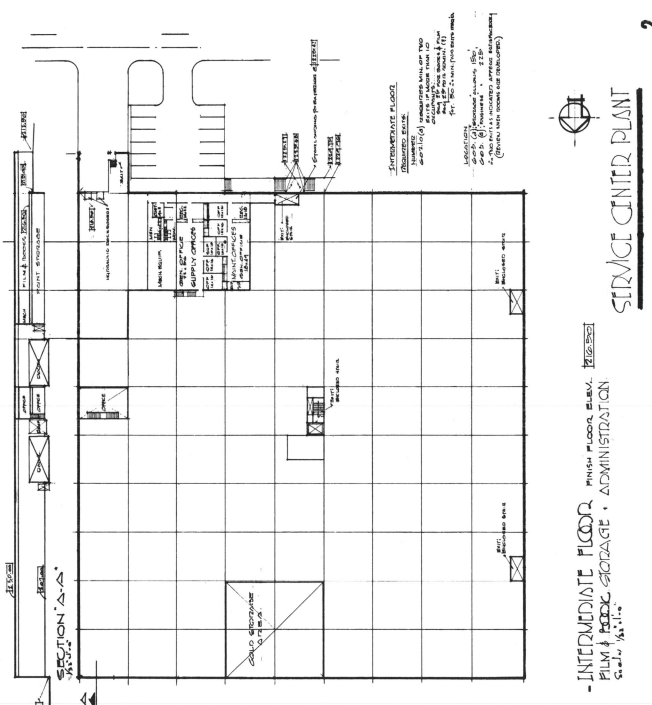

Figure 7-5. Intermediate Floor with Administrative Offices.

75

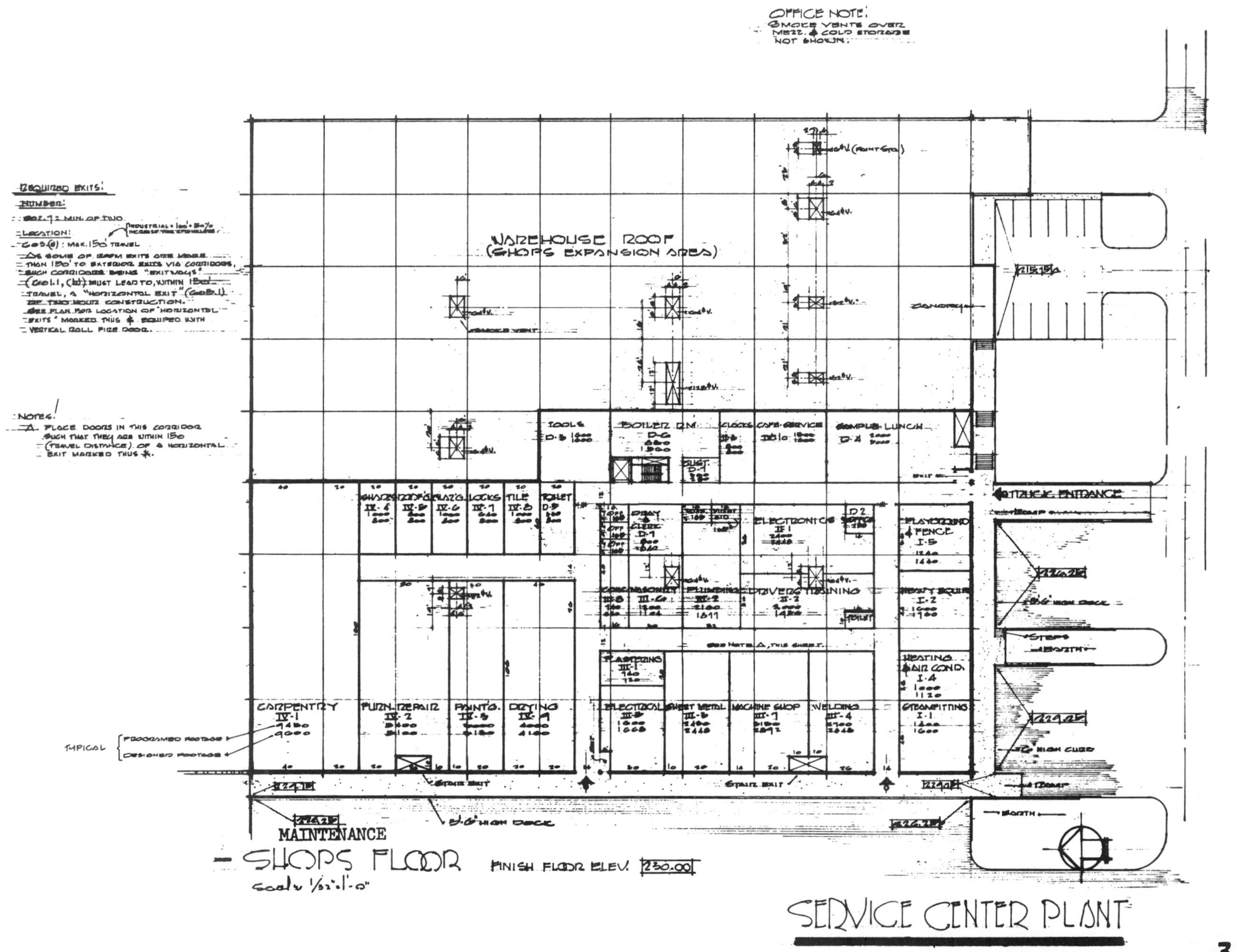

Figure 7-6. Maintenance Shops Floor Layout.

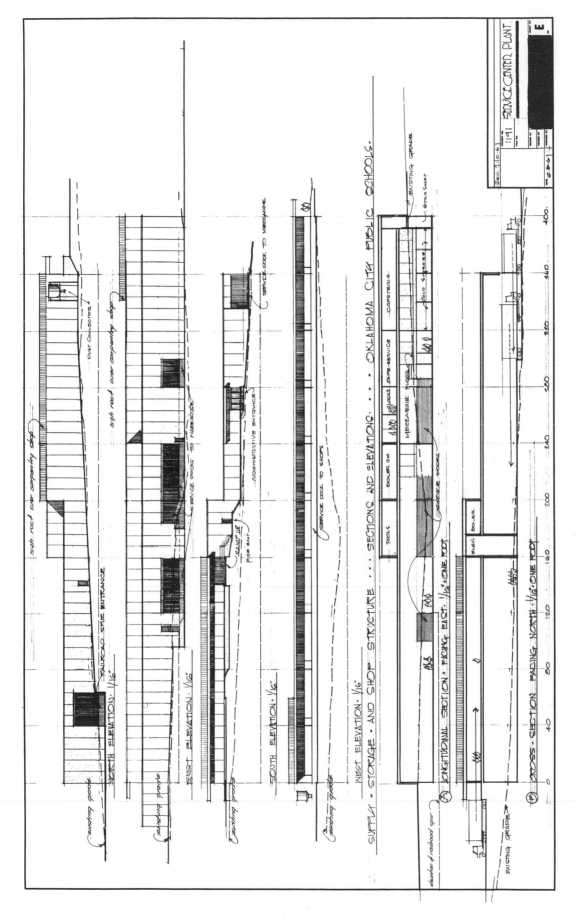

Figure 7-7. Elevations of Service Center.

SHOP EQUIPMENT AND TOOLS

Effective administration provides the proper equipment and tools for each shop area. First class equipment saves manpower and can make the output more efficient. The tools used by skilled workers in field jobs should be the highest quality.

Equipment.

Once proper equipment is installed in the shop, the skilled worker has the responsibility to use the equipment according to the instruction manual prepared by the manufacturer. Only skilled hands should be permitted to use the equipment. In small districts the maintenance personnel may use the vocational industrial equipment. Certain restrictions must be made regarding when the equipment may be used when school is in session. Experience has revealed in the larger school districts that the use of vocational-industrial equipment presents problems which hinder both economy and efficiency. Tools which belong to a particular shop area should have definite places and be kept in those places when not in use. Shop equipment should only be used for school district projects.

Tools.

Skilled workers on diverse maintenance projects throughout the school district need adequate small tools and supplies. The district can afford to furnish these adequate tools and supplies for the assigned jobs to increase economy and efficiency. These tools are fashioned to aid, not replace, the human hand.[4]

Tool Control. Effective administration of tool control demands that one person in the maintenance department or a person in the supply department be accountable for the tools. Each worker must check his tools from this designated person. Once the tools are checked to the workman, he becomes accountable for his tools. If a single tool is broken, or becomes unusable, the worker should present the broken tool to the checker and receive a replacement. Periodically, the tool checker reviews the inventory of tools checked to the worker. The cost of tools lost should be charged to the persons having access to the tools. This practice encourages a better attitude and care of tools and equipment. Continued carelessness in the loss and care of tools is a just reason for severance from the maintenance organization. In no case should tools be loaned to any person other than responsible maintenance personnel, and then a record should be made of the loan.

Care of Tools. High quality tools demand care. Good workmanship requires that the tools be clean, sharp, and rust free. If parts of the tools require oiling, they should be oiled and ready for use. If a workman remembers that every tool not in use has a place and that every tool is in that place in good condition, he will begin to grasp the significance of the proper care of tools.

Tool storage. Each maintenance administrator has definite responsibilities in the method of handling the storage of tools. A uniform system should be adopted throughout the maintenance shop area.

> Many tools can be hung in a locked tool room on a large painted board with spaces sketched in a contrasting color showing the tool belongs in a particular place. This is easily done by tracing the outline with pencil on the board and painting it in with a small brush. Some tools and parts (drill bits, hacksaw blades) must be kept

---

[4] N. L. George, Operation Manual, Oklahoma City Schools (1957), p. 14.

in drawers or boxes. These spaces should be clearly labeled as to contents. Two or three clip boards should be in the tool room, one for the tool check-out forms, one for a short list—items shortly to be needed or replaced—and a third clip board for the tool room inventory.[5]

Records and Inventories. Top maintenance administration is responsible for keeping up-to-date records and inventories of all tools, equipment, and supplies pertaining to maintenance services for which he is responsible. He should also notify the purchasing agent in advance of needed replacement or new purchases.

Necessary Tools and Equipment. The factors which control the amount and kind of tools, equipment, and supplies in a school district are:

1. The magnitude of plants in a school district.
2. The kinds of services assigned to maintenance department.
3. The amount and kinds of work performed by the maintenance services.
4. The skill of employees.
5. The quality of maintenance service desired.
6. The amount of money available for maintenance operations.

Suggested List of Equipment and Tools for a Particular District. A district which has about 200 maintenance employees needs the following equipment and tools to be efficient. The stationary equipment and portable equipment is listed by crafts which follows; the basic hand tools are listed by crafts in Appendix C. The number and size of tools for each craft depend upon the scope of needed work in each craft.

CRAFT	STATIONARY SHOP EQUIPMENT	PORTABLE EQUIPMENT
Carpentry	Air Compressor	Adjustable Scaffold
	Band saw	Air compressor
	Cut off saw	Extension ladder
	Drill press	Floor Tile operator
	Drum sander	Ramset
	Grinder	Roto hammer
	Jointer	Table saw & jointer
	Laminating press	Tank & pump for termite control
	Molding machine	
	Mortise machine	
	Shaper	
	Surface planer	
	Table saw	
	Tenon machine	
Clocks and signals	Bench vise	
	Electric drill press	
	Electric grinder and stand	
	Motor and relay tester	
Concrete		Air compressor
		Aluminum bull float
		Asphalt spreader
		Concrete finishing machine
		Gas cans

---

5 John David Engman, *School Plant Management for School Administrations* (Gulf School Research Development Assoc., Houston 4, Texas, 1962), p. 80.

CRAFT	STATIONARY SHOP EQUIPMENT	PORTABLE EQUIPMENT
		Hand asphalt roller
		Load binders
		Power asphalt roller
		Step jacks and handles
		Step ladders
		Wheelbarrow
Drayage		15 trucks of various sizes equipped for special services.
Driver Training	Bench grinder	
	Bench vise	
	Electric drill press	
	Power probed condensor box	
	Special test boxes	
Electrical		Extension ladders
		Large hydraulic pipe bender
		Step ladder
Filter	Electric fluid mixer	Two wheeled dollies
	Electric hoist	Vacuum cleaners
	Filter cleaning vat	
	Oil spray vat	
Garage	Drum turning machine	Pick-ups for service
	Housing machines	Pick-ups with toch
	Tire breaker	Tow truck
	Valve grinding machine	Welder on trailer
	Welder	Winch truck
Heating and Air Conditioning	Bench vise	Acid flush pump
	Bench vise on roller	Air compressor
	Work bench	Flushing unit
		Freon weight scale
		Hand truck
		High vacuum pump
		Manual boiler retubing equipment
		Pneumatic boiler retubing equipment
		Prestolite set
Heavy Equipment		Back hoe and loader
		Bulldozers
		Cranes
		Diesel tanks
		Dump trucks
		Front end loader
		Gas cans
		Graders
		Ripper
		Roller
		Scrapers
		Tractors

CRAFT	STATIONARY SHOP EQUIPMENT	PORTABLE EQUIPMENT
Instructional Equipment	A.F. generator-sinet Square	Drills
	Bar/dot color generator	Drill hammers
	Bench grinder	Electric drill
	C/R bridge	Extension ladder
	Decade box	Fish tapes
	Drill press	Hand lantern
	High tensity bench lamp	Portable tube tester
	Resistor decode box	Ramset
	Signal tracer	Scooter, four wheeled
	Transistor checker	Set twist drill bits
	Tube tester	Sound powered hand sets
	20,000 OHMS per volt VOM	Step ladder
	Variable supply transistor	Tube testers
	Wide band oscilloscope	Walkee talkee
Landscape		Aluminum irrigation pipe
		Connection hose
		Extension ladders
		Fertilizer spreader
		Grass planter
		Power augers
		Propane fence row burners
		Rotovator
		Sod cutter
		Spray pump
		Step ladders
		Tandem disc harrow
		Tractor graders
		Tractor with mowers
		Water hose
Machine shop	Abrasive grinder	Pumps
	Bandsaw welders	
	Bench grinder	
	Drill-bench	
	Drill-press	
	Large hydraulic press	
	Lawn mower grinder	
	Milling machine	
	Saw grinders	
	Saw set	
	Small hydraulic press	
	Spinning lathe	
	Turret lathe	
Masonry	Brick saw	Brick saw
		Ladder
		Ladder jack
		Mortar box
		Mortar mixer
		Mud jack

CRAFT	STATIONARY SHOP EQUIPMENT	PORTABLE EQUIPMENT
		Sand blast pot
		Scaffold
		Spinning drill
		Staging jacks
		Swinging scaffold
		Wheelbarrow
Motor Winding	Coil winding machine	Paper cutter
		Prestolite kit
		Slot paper cutter and creaser
Paint	Agitator	Air compressor
		Air regulators
		Drop cloths
		Extension ladders
		Ladders
		Ladder jacks
		Scaffolds
		Scaffold boards
		Small swinging scaffold
		Spray guns
		Window jacks
Plastering		Air compressor
		Bench grinder
		Drop cloths
		Ladders
		Mortar boards
		Scaffolding
		Scaffold platform
		Spray guns for acoustical plaster
		Spray vat and pump
		Straight edge
		Water hose
		Wheelbarrow
Playground and Fence	Anvil	Extension ladders
	Bench grinder	Oxygen-acetylene welding rig
	Oxygen-acetylene welding rig	
	Pipe vise	
Plumbing	Pipe threading machine	Backhoe and loader
	Work bench	Electric drills
		Electric hammers
		Electric sewer cleaning machine
		Fire pots
		Power vise
		Prestolite kits
		Rubber boots
		Sewer cleaning gear
		Underground pipe locator

CRAFT	STATIONARY SHOP EQUIPMENT	PORTABLE EQUIPMENT
Roofing		Asphalt kettle
		Asphalt pump
		Gin pole
		Ladders
		Roof scrathers
		Scoop shovels
		Small pitch kettle
		Tar kettle
		Wheelbarrows
Sheet Metal	Bench vice	Drill
	Crimper	Extension ladder
	Leaf brakes—3 sizes	Hand flanger
	Lock machines	Spot welder
	Power shear	Step ladders
	Shear—4 sizes	
	Slip rods—2 sizes	
	Spot welder	
	Surface grinder	
Welding	Acetylene regulator	Goggles
	Anvil	Oxygen-acetylene welding
	Bench vise	rigs
	Cutting torch	Welding helmet
	Metal bender	Welding machine
	Metalizer torch	
	Oxygen regulator	
	Power metal saw	
	300 Amp welding machine	
	Welding table	

HOUSEKEEPING

Effective administration plans and enforces good housekeeping practices in each area of maintenance services. Workers often become careless in housekeeping chores. Shavings, paper cartons, and oily rags are special sources of accidents and fires. The administration must insist that everything have a place and that everything be in its place. Thus accidents are avoided, fires are prevented, and the total shop area evinces efficiency and economy.

Top management has the responsibility of planning attractive plant appearance, which can be created with a small amount of effort and cost. This feature tends to pay off in terms of more output and lower costs, as well as higher morale and a greater appreciation by the public for school administration.

SUMMARY

The efficiency of maintenance services depends greatly on the quality and adequacy of facilities which house these functions. The operation of maintenance services emanating from a functional plant tends to increase efficiency and reduce costs. This concept in the administration of maintenance activities is often overlooked. An adequate maintenance plant for the school district, with provision for adequate equipment and tools and sufficient space for storing tools efficiently, is a coveted ideal. Maintenance employees need a uniform procedure to account for tools and equipment—efficient maintenance administration provides this leadership.

Chapter **8**

IMPERATIVES FOR
EFFICIENT ADMINISTRATION

Effective administration of maintenance services requires continuous scrutiny in the management of all services, since making repairs with your own forces is not always an economy. The very fact that skilled workmen are employed does not necessarily insure that repairs will be performed on the most economical basis. The very nature of maintenance services, especially emergency repairs, demands that these services be performed promptly.

The performance of the little jobs in maintenance accelerates the costs and drains the maintenance budget. These aspects of maintenance operations require constant supervision. Every performance must be efficient in time and effort. The performance of such services necessitates that administration eliminate and focus attention to all forms of waste. Many phases of maintenance operations which need constant review have been mentioned in the first seven chapters of this book. Both efficiency and economy in maintenance services are largely affected by firm management decisions and strict adherence to the maintenance policies of the school district. No attempt is made in this chapter to focus attention on waste in the all the activities of maintenance operations. The same scope of considerations will vary in small districts as well as in large districts. The facets of administration which need continuous evaluation fall into the following topics.

SAVINGS IN THE SELECTION AND ASSIGNMENT OF MANPOWER

Top management has the responsibility of employing the best suited men for the required places in the maintenance program. Low production can only be blamed on management in this case. Management must plan a definite work program each day for each employee. The right man in the right place with a full program tends to insure economy. Maintenance aims to keep things "up to time," making small repairs as rapidly as possible. Management has to study the work flow and attempt to obtain the best performance in each work operation, eliminating as much waste as possible.

Planning the work tests the very ingenuity of management. The right man with the right tools and equipment and with the right methods set for the daily tasks influences greatly the amount of required supervision.

MATERIAL SAVINGS

Savings are possible in the use of salvage material for some maintenance operations, in the selection of the right material, in the pooling of like materials and requesting purchase, in the availability of stock items for repair, and in the standardization of parts.

Salvage Materials. The policy among school districts in using salvage materials for repair and replacement of similar items is a difficult problem to solve. The salvaged materials may cost more than new materials. Economies can only be realized if the labor, transportation, and handling costs in the preparation of making the materials ready for reuse are not excessive. As a rule, salvage materials should not be used if their cost comes within 75 per cent of the cost of similar new materials. Another vital consideration is the predetermination of the cost of the installation of the used materials. If the installation of salvage materials costs more than the installation of new materials, new materials should be purchased.

The Selection of the Right Materials. Top management has the definite responsibility of selecting the correct materials for maintenance activities. The materials should be durable, fire resistive, and attractive if possible, and easy to clean. School districts can follow no hard and fast rules in the selection of materials which will best suit their maintenance operations. Each district is local in nature. Management should work closely with foremen who are the real product and process experts. Materials should be purchased on what they do rather than the appearance the materials possess.

Pooling of Requests for Purchase. Effective administration studies carefully the scheduled yearly program of maintenance activities and plans the work into a schedule. The similar projects will be grouped according to the skilled personnel. The materials needed for the similar projects will be listed and requested for all these projects. A good example is the replacement of lavatories. The number of replacements of lavatories needed for a year will be put in one material request and purchased. This process permits the purchasing department to secure a discount on quantity purchasing. Likewise the plumber may schedule the replacements in a program. Thus, savings are made in two ways.

Availability of Stock Items. In school districts which have a warehouse for stock items, the purchasing of these items becomes automatic. The district records disclose that an approximate number of these items are used each year. As soon as the inventory reveals a minimum number, the supply department re-orders. In school districts without a supply department, effective administration designates some person to check periodically the adequacy of items needed. The needed items are ordered and kept in the maintenance stock for replacement.

Standardization of Parts. Many suggestions have been written on standardizing parts. In school districts which have many plants of varying ages, this performance is a difficult function. Astuteness is required by both engineering and maintenance management. A good example of this situation is where these two parties may help in standardization by agreeing to use fluorescent lamps of four foot length in all installations. Any standardization of parts where efficiency and economies result eliminates waste.

SAVINGS THROUGH BETTER TOOLS AND EQUIPMENT

Top administration in any school district has the responsibility to plan the actual daily execution of the district daily tasks of all maintenance activities. This function entails the provision for facilities, machines, tools, tool setups, fixtures, jigs, controls, and mechanisms in order that the several employers may improve their respective distinct detailed tasks.

Providing proper hand tools is a very important function of top maintenance administration. The cheap tool may be very expensive, and the wrong tools may waste hours every day. The administrator must see that the employees have good tools. Usually good hand tools may be purchased in such numbers that trade discounts are attractive. In addition to the provision of proper tools for each skill, up-to-date management will provide mechanical devices of all sorts which may save indirect time on a project. These gadgets cost very little, yet the provision of such apparatus gives the workmen a feeling of being modern in their techniques.

Technological improvements in machines used in maintenance activities are constantly appearing. In the purchasing of new machines for a repair shop or in replacing or adding machinery, top administration has multiple responsibilities. Will the instrument save time, money, and increase production now? How long will the machine last? Is there a decrease in the school plant materials used in local maintenance functions to justify the normal usage of the machines? Does the administration have up-to-date knowledge of new equipment?

An examination of the literature in the field of machine purchasing does not reveal an infallible guide for selection. Literature discloses that the criteria of (1) suitability, (2) performance and flexibility, (3) accuracy of work, (4) simplicity of construction, (5) reliability of operation, (6) ease of maintenance and repairability, (7) low installation costs and possibility of removal, (8) safety, (9) proper appearance, (10) space, weight, height, and (11) reasonable price and investment are qualities which are desired.[1]

SAVINGS IN METHODS OF OPERATION

Effective administration has the responsibility to familiarize foremen and possibly the workers from time to time about the costs and expenses of the execution of maintenance projects. This information should alert the responsible employers as to the present costs of specific operations and possibly prove to them the need for improvement in the methods of execution to reduce costs if possible.

In attempting to develop and apply the best method for each maintenance operation, administration should aim to obtain by a selected method a truly effective performance. This action has to be taken with available facilities, machines, and manpower provided. Management by the head maintenance personnel and foremen should eliminate unnecessary and weak operations. The fact that a man appears very busy is not a sign that he is producing to the maximum of his capacity.

Administration must keep in mind that the best system of work and operating procedures must be gradually developed. The arm of supervision is difficult and challenging. Men must be alerted as to the best methods to perform certain tasks, and they should be challenged to use the best method or to suggest a better method. Common sense supervision encompasses honesty in teaching, in helping, and in stepping into the act whenever justified. The details

[1] From *Small Plant Management* by W. A. MacCrehan, Jr., copyright 1960 (McGraw-Hill Book Co., Inc., New York). Used by permission of McGraw-Hill Book Company, pp. 146–149.

of each operation must be kept under observation if good, and possibly efficient and economical procedures are obtained.

SAVINGS THROUGH LESS HANDLING AND MECHANIZED TRANSPORTATION

Sagacious administration in maintenance services has double responsibilities. One area of responsibility lies in the handling and transportation of materials within the shop area. The other area of responsibility embraces the transportation of incoming and outgoing materials from the shop and the workers going to and from work.

Within the Shop.

Special attention must be given to material handling in the shop area. Receiving, storage, transporting to the work area, and transporting from one work area to another of materials can be costly. Equipment such as hand trucks, power trucks, simple chutes, simple mechanical movers, belt conveyors, and monorails may assist in internal transportation. Hoists and cranes may also assist. Any such equipment that fits the needs of the particular shop can save costs, speed up flow, and cut idle time. The desired equipment should be purchased from good firms which guarantee their installations.

From Shop to Locations within the District.

The slogan, "Plan your work and work your plans," is appropriate in these operations. The adequacy of both materials and tools must be definitely planned in transporting maintenance materials to job locations to do assigned functions. The omission of one tool or the inadequacy of material often delays completion of the project or extra expense. Much money is spent on drayage unless this function is definitely planned into periodic routes to pick up and deliver to the several school plants of the district. Precaution in routings to and from school plants must be taken by all parties concerned. Sometimes it may be necessary to take a specific piece of equipment to a school plant in order to keep the school in continuous operation. A backlog of parts in stock may eliminate some of these conditions.

Panel type trucks equipped with the most urgent plumbing, electrical, and painting supplies, and materials assigned to responsible personnel can eliminate much travel of the workmen. Some maintenance personnel must of necessity travel among the school plants of the district. These limited personnel should have an adequate allowance for travel expense. The allowance may be set by mileage or by a stipulated monthly amount.

Other personnel travel from their homes to specific maintenance jobs. No allowance is made for this travel.

Probably the most difficult job of the maintenance administrator is the provision of fair and equitable allowances, if any, for the several skilled personnel who perform so many different kinds of tasks at the various school sites. The responsibilities of the skilled personnel are most divergent. The savings in proper organization become significant.

SAVINGS THROUGH A SAFETY PROGRAM

In Chapter 5 the necessity and precautions of safety in the various functions of school maintenance was discussed. Every school maintenance department should have an organized safety program. The safety committee should have the responsibility to detect unsafe practices in the maintenance plant areas and on the assigned projects of the several school plants in the district. Such an organized program will tend to reduce the loss of time and bodily injury of skilled employees. Both factors affect the efficiency of the maintenance program.

SAVINGS IN WORK TIME

The competent administrator maintains and exhibits savings in careful planning and control. In maintenance services, a constant interference exists between the program of scheduled work and the work required to remedy the emergency repairs. In Chapter 3, a lengthy discussion is outlined concerning the elements contained in productive and non-productive work.

In order for the administrator to be effective in planning and executing work time control, he must have the help of capable foremen. These people give as much help as needed in setting up and completing the assigned work. The supervision has to deal with the magnitude and complexities of the assigned tasks. Supervision should be acquainted with the travel time requirements between jobs.

SAVINGS IN IDLE TIME

Probably the most wasteful portion of operating maintenance service is idle time. The employees dispersed among the school plants create situations which challenge the administration. The ratio of idle time in relation to work time in school maintenance is too difficult to calculate. For example, suppose an employee is sent to an assigned task. He finishes the task one hour before the end of the work day. It takes 30 minutes to drive back to his reporting station. How are you going to count the unfilled 30 minutes? Will it be counted as expense of the assigned task that he has finished? How and where is this time charged? How does the employee spend the last 30 minutes of the day?

Administration can really save if proper steps to eliminate idle time are made. Idle times are real cost-creating and time-delaying factors.

SAVINGS IN CLERICAL OR ADMINISTRATIVE PAPER WORK

State laws and local district governing boards require certain reports on maintenance activities. The administrator himself needs the necessary reports to check the efficiency of men, materials, and methods. All paper work cannot be eliminated. However, the administrator should aim to keep this necessary part of his work at a justifiable minimum. Today computing machines are basic equipment in office work to reduce paper work and ticket writing. In maintenance some paper work has to route the projects properly and keep records of costs of projects. The basic records should then be put on carefully selected office machines.

Arranging a minimal paper work system is a task that the administrato must carefully scrutinize. A good rule to follow is to avoid paper work as much as possible. Otherwise, key personnel are burdened with detailed paper work and their proper responsibilities become slighted.

SAVINGS IN FREQUENCY OF GENERAL AND COMMITTEE MEETINGS

Every organization should have meetings of all personnel when a definite need exists. The basis for calling meetings should be to clarify some specific problem. Each person in attendance should be invited to participate. The necessary meetings should give a clear and honest picture of the probelm. Discretion of the number and kinds of meetings held is the responsibility of the administrator.

Well-planned meetings at stated intervals to solve specific problems are positive morale builders. Meetings held only for the purpose of meeting are a wasteful practice.

SUMMARY

No organization can be perfect. As long as men make judgments and school districts have widely dispersed school plant locations, inevitable wastes in efficiency will be created. The whole idea is to reduce waste in as many facets of administrative practices as possible. A small saving in each facet of administration grows into a significant amount of money, and higher efficiency should be the result.

Chapter 9

UPGRADING THE PERSONNEL FOR EFFICIENT ADMINISTRATION

A prime responsibility rests on top management to provide opportunities through which maintenance personnel may grow in knowledge in their respective maintenance tasks. Each capable administrator should study the opportunities in his community which offer such services. He directs the foremen and leadmen to keep alert to community opportunities which they may contact. The competent administrator continually studies the total organization to discover weaknesses in the several groups or skills of the workmen. Upon these findings he establishes training courses for improvement or directs the foreman or certain personnel to study his findings. Helps in upgrading maintenance personnel and maintenance practices take various forms. Districts should maintain and/or encourage their employees to participate in various kinds of training activities.

Maintenance workers may organize to improve their effectiveness. The school administrators provide released time and pay expenses of responsible personnel to attend selected training opportunities.

IN-SERVICE TRAINING

Most in-service training is given on the work time of the employee. Top maintenance administrators in both small and large districts should organize programs of in-service training suitable to the needs of each district. This informal training may use the forms of (1) apprentice training, (2) discussion groups and local workshops, (3) safety committees, and (4) demonstrations.

Apprentice Training. A new employee is assigned to a competent employee, usually as a helper. The competent employee has the task of teaching the new employee the techniques and skills of the particular job. This form of "on the site instruction" has proven to be very beneficial.

Discussion Groups. Many opportunities arise for small discussion groups between the head administrator and foremen, foremen and leadmen, and leadmen and journeymen for discussions pertinent to maintenance activities. In these groups particular techniques can be clarified.

Safety Committee. This essential committee has various opportunities throughout the school year to bring to attention those practices which affect the performance of maintenance personnel. The committee has the responsibility of disseminating the upgrading information.

Demonstrations. This informal training provides a quick and direct way for the maintenance employees to learn about new and different products. Often a factory representative, such as a representative of new insulation products, can meet with the responsible skilled personnel for an hour or so and show how the new products are applied. The demonstration may be for an individual employee or a group of employees. One benefit is the gaining of knowledge of the new product and its application. Second, the demonstration challenges the employee or employees to restudy the products and their applications that they are now using.

Local Workshops. Able administrators periodically plan workshops pertaining to weaknesses they may have discovered in their operations. These workshops need not be lengthy or frequent. The whole idea is to develop an awareness among the employees that improvements can be made if all personnel grasp the problems appertaining to their operation.

Successful workshops can be planned around the ideas relating to all phases of maintenance. Too often, the foreman and employees view the whole district system from their special function. They need to see and understand how each skill is needed and how it fits into the total program.

FORMAL TRAINING

Technological development has recently brought into existence new information and know-how in the fields of electricity, electronics, heating and air-conditioning. Many responsible employees see the need for formal training order to keep up with the advancements in their skills. Some employees grasp chances to take formal training offered by institutions, state departments, and local short courses.

Institutional. A few employees in the maintenance department of a school district take advantage of the college, university, and technical institutes which offer formal courses. The well-prepared employee usually becomes the leader in his craft.

State Departments. The many departments of the several states may offer courses which pertain to the maintenance program. Able administrators plan that the employees interested and responsible for the respective maintenance functions have the opportunity to attend. For example, a state department of agriculture sponsors a program for ornamental pruners and sprayers. The area of study covers (1) safety in tree work, (2) pruning of ornamentals, (3) spraying of ornamentals, (4) lawn maintenance problems, (5) identification of ornamental and tree diseases, (6) identification of trees and shrubs, and (7) identification of ornamental insect problems.

Local Short Courses. One or more school districts may pool their resources and plan a summer program around some maintenance problems. These programs may be in the form of workshops and institutes. Whatever the name or whatever the topic, these courses are planned to provide information and demonstrations pertaining to broad areas of maintenance activities. The district or districts may cooperate with institutions in the local area. This program is effective if well planned.

RECOMMENDED PRACTICES

In the administration of an effective program of maintenance operations, opportunities exist to strengthen the local program. These opportunities do not cost much, yet their effectiveness is often overlooked.

Visitation to Other School Districts.

The able administrator plans for key employees in maintenance to have the opportunity to spend a day or two studying the same work in nearby school districts of similar size. In these cases, the climates and the socioeconomic conditions are similar. The visitor has the opportunity to see how others do similar work, and the employee can evaluate his own work. Perhaps a better method may be suggested as a result of these visits.

Testing.

Experience discloses that much daily time of the top administrators is spent with salesmen who are suggesting new products and new equipment. All of these new products and new equipment do not give the same results if used. The able administrator is interested in using those materials and equipment which fulfill the requirements of the job, and no other.

The top administrator and his foreman will establish a program of testing for the selection of tools and equipment. This testing program must be strictly objective under actual conditions. The testing must follow the printed directions as provided by the manufacturer, be it material or a piece of equipment.

Neither the talk of the salesman nor the printed literature of the manufacturer can give the assurance of a performance test which the administrator directs on the premises of the school district. This task is never completed because of the multiplicity of new products and new equipment.

USING AVAILABLE SCHOOL PLANT INFORMATION

The success of top administration in maintenance operations of a school district depends greatly upon the significance the administration focuses on the continuous change in personnel. The easiest assumption is to hold the viewpoint that the responsible employees know the best school plants in the school district. In a school district which has many school plants of varying size and complexity, the responsible personnel has a cumbersome task.

To avoid costly mistakes, capable leadership refers to the plans and specifications of the initial building with its equipment. The manuals of the manufacturers pertaining to the critical equipment should be catalogued and reviewed often by the personnel responsible. If the manufacturer offers instruction and training for the employee who repairs this equipment, this opportunity should be overlooked.

A competent administrator realizes that the school plants in a school district will continue to operate after the termination of both his services and those of many of his skilled employees. He will plan to keep the school plant information in such a condition that his successor and the successors of his skilled workmen will not be handicapped and thus make as few errors as possible.

SHORT TERM SCHOOLS OF INSTRUCTION

Capable administration has the responsibility to encourage the skilled workmen to improve their qualifications as they work in their respective jobs. The school district likewise has a responsibility to see that the qualified workman continues to increase his knowledge about his assigned responsibility. A good practice for the school district is to pay the expenses of a workman to attend a short term of instruction.

Short Term Schools. The lighting, the driver trainer, the air conditioning, the carpet, the automatic control industries, and others hold periodic short term schools of instruction. The expense of the district would be too great to have the respective employees attend every school. Diligence has to be taken in selection of employees to attend these schools. However, these employees should be sent often enough to keep up on the latest practice, and then these employees should disseminate this information to the other personnel in the craft.

Organization. Probably the best organization for maintenance personnel is the Association of the School Business Officials of the United States and Canada.[1] This organization has about 20 outstanding committees which continuously study the problems of school business. About six of these committees have direct application to maintenance activities. Capable administrators encourage membership and participation in the activities of this organization. The annual volume of proceedings of the yearly meeting should be a *must* in every library for maintenance operations.

Trade Shows. Many trade shows appear in school districts for a day or two. The capable administrator allows workmen to visit these shows. The ideas exhibited often stimulate the worker to evaluate his present assignment.

INSTRUCTIONAL METHODS AND SERVICES

The administration of an efficient maintenance program demands various types of instruction. The types are difficult to select because of the educational backgrounds of the various employees. Many of the employees have only a grammar school education. Others may have a college or technical school record. The able administrator may use several methods and devices to instruct the employees in their respective skills.

Methods.

The selected methods most frequently include those from which all employees may profit. Top administrators should study the craft and adopt the methods suitable to the separate crafts.

Personal Instruction. This kind of instruction ranks high in effectiveness. The man-to-man contact gives good results. A new employee assigned to a task under the guidance of a trained employee eliminates many errors. This method is sometimes called the buddy system. The effectiveness of this system depends on the skill of the assigned trained employee who does the instruction.

Manuals of Operation. Each skilled operation has standard process operations. These operations set forth in a manual stipulate rules to follow and tend to discover and eliminate unnecessary wasteful motions. The employee can do more work in the same time. Also, he can do the same work with less effort. A written procedure for each operation is very useful.

---

[1] A.S.B.O. Headquarters are located at 2424 W. Lawrence Ave., Chicago, Illinois 60625.

Devices.

Short conferences of particular employees with the foremen, leadmen, and top management, as the case demands, are effective. Wherever possible a visual presentation, such as pictures, slides, and charts, assists in stressing a point. Charts posted on bulletin boards create interest in obtaining certain objectives. Carefully prepared exhibits on definite phases of maintenance work are helpful. If the administration can secure pertinent motion pictures on certain phases of maintenance services, these media appear to stimulate interest in the respective performances.

SOURCES OF HELPFUL INFORMATION

Every maintenance center should provide a place for an adequate library for general reading. In addition, the separate shops should have library materials which stimulate improvement in the various areas of performance.

The center shop library should contain catalogues of the various local suppliers of materials and equipment. The separate library corners in the shops should be attractive.

Consult the Bibliography for a list of suggested books, magazines, and periodicals.

SUMMARY

Effective administration of maintenance activities is pursued beyond the performances of day-by-day projects. Alert personnel want to grow in the know-how of their duties.

Employees desire to: (a) improve skills or knowledge required in their present positions, (b) prepare for significant technological changes in their fields, (c) prepare for changes in duties in their present jobs, or (d) prepare for assuming new and different duties as a result of recent promotion.

Definite organization of the means of instruction, the provision of adequate information, and the methods of dissemination are facets for improvement which administration can adapt to its local needs.

PART
II

DAILY MAINTENANCE PROBLEMS

Chapter 10

ESTABLISHING
EFFICIENT SERVICES IN
SCHOOL PLANT AREAS

The efficient administrator makes minor, less important, but necessary decisions concerning the maintenance services in the school system that he supervises. In order to obtain the best performance in every detail of daily action, he has to have at least a general knowledge of the service areas.

The list of services in this chapter deals with the most common areas of the school maintenance program. The correction for the treatment of each problem is the job of the skilled workmen and is not discussed in this book.

PAINTING SERVICES

Outside painting protects from the elements and from wear. Appearance is improved, and the desired color and finish is provided. Inside painting facilitates cleaning and improves the lighting of interiors of buildings.

A most important task of a painter is to prepare the surfaces before the application of paint is made. The next task is to select a paint which is most suitable for the geographical area. Third, the paint must be most suitable for the particular need, that is, art, chemistry, clinics, or swimming pool areas. Fourth, the care of brushes and equipment must be efficient.

Often paints chalk, blister, alligator, check, crack, spot, wrinkle, scale, stain, and sag. The skilled painter will determine whether these conditions are present on account of improper preparation of the surfaces, the quality of paint, improper application, or paint not applied according to instructions.

Outside Painting.

Special attention should be given to (1) moisture penetrating surfaces, (2) painting over damp surfaces, and (3) areas with little or no ventilation and excessive recoat thickness. Also the responsible painters should inspect the paint on the south side of the buildings to see if the sun has affected this area and the paint on the north side to see if excessive moisture has impaired that area. In some localities these exposures need paint more often than the others.

Interior Painting.

Authorities agree that the ceilings should be refinished with an 85 per cent reflection factor, flat white paint. The upper walls from the ceiling line to door or wainscot should be finished with a minimum of 60 per cent reflection factor paint. The lower walls from top of dado or wainscot, including the baseboard, should be finished with a 40 per cent reflection factor paint. A minimum of 60 per cent reflection factor paint is considered good practice when the entire wall areas from ceiling to floor are finished in one color. The trim should be stained with a 40–60 per cent reflection factor varnish. Experience has disclosed that painting wood trim is very expensive because objects hitting the paint break the paint and unsightliness soon results.

All areas painted should be recorded with date, brand name, and kind of paint used. A record also should be kept of the method of application. The usual application methods are brush, dipping in vats, roller, and spray.

Contract Painting.

Should the district seek to have the painting performed by contract instead of using their own skilled labor, careful components should be placed in the specifications. The instructions to bidders should define the scope, the exceptions, workmanship expected, preparation of surfaces, materials to be used, protection of property inspection, the removal of materials, and clean-up.

Glazing.

Closely allied to the skill of painting is that of glazing. Replacing building glass from accidental breakage and from vandalism, caulking and puttying are the primary functions of glazing. Other assigned tasks may include replacing mirrors, replacing glass in vehicles and heavy equipment, and replacing plastic domes and skylights.

Problems arise on account of glass breakage in excessive vandalism and the widespread travel on account of the small jobs scattered among the many school buildings in a district. Many glasses are broken by shots from guns and from heavy objects thrown against glass surfaces.

This expensive function can be aided by the proper choice of materials and skilled workmen.

ROOFING SERVICES

The maintenance of roofs on school buildings is probably the greatest problem in many school districts. Expensive repairs to school buildings occur because of leaky roofs. The water which gathers on the roofs seeks lower levels. If water does not pass through the channels as constructed, water penetrates the interior of the building through ceilings and down the walls which damages plaster, paint, and often the floor materials and furnishings. Each roof is a specific problem and requires periodic inspection by skilled workmen to catch failures in their incipient stages.

Causes for Failure.

Roofs are affected by the extreme temperatures of cold and hot weather which expand and contract the materials used for covering. Hail, wind, ice and snow, and faulty application are also factors affecting the efficiency of roofing materials. Unwarranted foot traffic on roof surfaces has become a major problem. Leaks appear on good roofs weeks later on account of this unknown damage.

In general, roof failures may be attributed to:

> Insufficient or improper specifications
> Inferior materials
> Faulty installation
> Inadequate inspection and lack of preventive maintenance
> Insufficient materials (particularly in built-up roofs)
> Use of unseasoned lumber for framing and substructure
> Application of improper materials
> Weather (wind, hail, snow, etc.)
> Structural failure
> Related failures affecting roof service.[1]

Additional failures in roofing on school buildings occur because:

1. Leaks occur frequently on buildings where additions abut, whether the addition is of the same or different elevation.

2. Leaks occur in roofs where the custodian gives inadequate inspection and attention to the roof. Often he fails to report the unsatisfactory condition he finds. His failure to keep debris off the roof and the scuppers cleaned causes roof damage.

3. Lax or no supervision during the construction or replacement of roofs produces potentially poor roofs.

4. Structural failures in buildings often cause the roofs to crack. This includes expansion of the structural roof system components.

5. Responsible skilled personnel often overlook the fact that anything that comes through or penetrates the roof is a prospective failure point.

This discussion omits the kinds of roofs and the different component parts thereof. The treatment for failures of the different kinds of roofs is also omitted.

More than one skilled craft is involved in checking and repairing roofs. The portions of building adjacent to the roof must be checked and repaired.

Other areas which involve other skills include: end walls, party walls, fire walls, parapets, chimneys, hips, pent houses, skylights, and bulkheads. Inspection of adjacent areas to roofs is made periodically to find defects in materials that cause leaks.

Roofers repair flashing, coping, downspouts (both inner and outer), underground and splash block drainage, gutters, scuppers, cant strips, gravel guards, and roofing materials.

Other miscellaneous items, if present on the structure, may cause leaks. These include antennae, cooling towers, vent pipes, and stacks.

---

[1] R. N. Finchum, *School Building Maintenance Procedures* (Washington, D. C.: U. S. Department of Health, Education, and Welfare, Office of Education, 1964), p. 12.

Methods of Repair.

Effective administration plans to repair the small leaks in roofs by the maintenance personnel. The replacement of entire roofs and large areas of roofs on school buildings should be contracted. Otherwise, the roofing personnel will be spending all their time on large jobs and not be available to repair small leaks. Small leaks increase in magnitude and create maintenance problems which become very expensive.

ELECTRICAL SERVICES

Electrical services in a school plant are basic to the efficient functioning of modern schools. The first installation usually meets the standards of the National Electric Code and is installed by a licensed electrician.

The techniques and special skills required for maintaining electrical systems are the responsibility of qualified electricians. These services are so complex that dangers are constantly present in repairing the parts of the electrical system. Some safety features are listed in Chapter 5, page 58 of this book.

Scope.

The electrical systems supply energy for light, heat (where electricity is used for this purpose), heating and cooling controls, power for programming systems, signaling or warning devices, instructional media, and intercommunication systems.

The various parts of the system are overhead and/or underground service lines, wiring controls, service entrances, transformers, main feeders, distribution panels, branch circuits, fuses, circuit breakers, convenience outlets, switches, and grounds.

The scope of responsibility usually includes the inspection and repair of all electrical motors, controls, pumps, blowers, compressors, elevators, and other electrical equipment.

Expert Services Needed. These necessary services are very important:

a. Periodic inspection by diligent employees is basic to efficient operation.

b. A careful division of the responsibilities among the building service employees as to who is to do the repair work.

c. Immediate repair when defects occur.

d. All safety precautions should be understood by all responsible people performing the repair work.

Common Problems.

In the administration of school district programs experience reveals that most of the problems in electrical services occur because of the human factor.

1. *Overloaded circuits.* Teachers in classrooms and school administrators usually do not have the knowledge of the capacity of the present wiring systems, and they unconsciously add to the electrical load. The size of the installation should be carefully checked to avoid dangerous conditions.

2. Sometimes school building service personnel are not careful enough when they check the amount of oil in motors.

3. Vandals break outside lights on school premises including lighting fixtures. This continuous practice adds greatly to the repair work of the electrician. Building

mounted and/or pole mounted fixtures are less convenient for the vandals to damage.

Lighting.

The goal of the maintenance department is to keep the lighting system operating at efficient lighting levels. In schools the most common lamps are incandescent, fluorescent, mercury vapor, and cold cathode. Custodial care is responsible for keeping the lamps and surfaces clean. The maintenance personnel are concerned with sockets, luminaries, reflectors, shades, louvers, starters, shafts, ballasts, and the controls in the many designs of light fixtures and/or lighting facilities. The maintenance personnel also has a responsibility to keep the surfaces painted with the proper light-reflection paint.

Many suggestions are available from the electrical industry of school lighting as to how to handle fluorescent luminaries for an effective lighting maintenance program. The incandescent, mercury vapor, and cold cathode lamps are easily replaced with a minimal amount of maintenance.

Effective administration should study the group replacement of fluorescent lamps. Each installation should be considered separately. The factors of lamps and replacement costs are the only basis for comparison of individual or group replacement cost. The cost of replacing lamps where scaffolding or large extension ladders are needed is a significant item.

Significant practices which effective administration of electrical service follow are:

1. All major electrical repairs are performed by a licensed electrician if the school district employs this type of skilled workman.
2. If a licensed person is not on the maintenance staff, the major repair work should be done by local commercial firms engaged in this type of work.
3. Some small electrical jobs can be done by diligent workmen without a license if the jobs are carefully outlined and the workmen are trained in procedure.
4. Sufficient electrical parts are kept in stock in order to perform immediate repairs by the assigned personnel.
5. School districts without licensed electricians should probably maintain or repair program systems, electric clocks, and complicated electrical instruments by the employment of factory trained mechanics and technicians. These kinds of services may be purchased under a service contract.

HEATING AND VENTILATION SERVICES

These two environmental conditions are very closely related in maintaining the comfort conditions for school children and school personnel. Both conditions are necessary for comfort in a school building. Heat is necessary when dictated by weather conditions. Ventilation is necessary throughout the year.

Heating.

The system which supplies heat to the school building must be sufficient to cover all heat losses. Heat losses occur by radiation, conduction, and convection. Air also enters the building through cracks and ventilating ducts.

Systems. A treatment of the advantages and disadvantages of the different heating systems is not a subject for discussion in this chapter.

Boilers. Many repairs are needed on steam or hot water boilers to keep them safe and operating. Tables must be replaced, valves must be repaired or replaced, and automatic water feeder equipment must be kept in prime condition. Other items which require constant attention are: burners, water legs, boiler stay bolts, manhole and handhole, and their plates and gaskets. Pumps, steam lines, drainage, insulation, condensate traps, air lines, radiators, and univents have possible malfunctioning parts.

Fuels. Generally coal, oil, natural and L-P gas are the fuels used in firing boilers. Each type requires special equipment for firing.

Boiler Controls. The skilled personnel maintain controls and repair or replace electric and pneumatic controls on boilers, air compressors, vacuum pumps, and hot water circulating pumps which are necessary to keep the proper supply of heat in the school buildings. Room thermostats are repaired, replaced, and calibrated to keep schools in a comfortable and healthy condition.

ı *Filters.* The cleaning and repairing of the filters in unit ventilators are maintenance staff functions. A definite program should be planned in order to schedule these services in all the schools. Oil bath filters also come under this heading.

Water Treatment. The water used in boilers usually has chemicals which cause rust, corrosion, and pitting. In some school districts water sometimes is taken from several sources. Efficient administration provides a schedule for testing the water used in each boiler of the school system. Additional chemicals are provided to adjust the variations of test results to a proper level, thus minimizing rust, corrosion, and pitting of the boilers.

Ventilation.

Proper ventilation in every occupied space of a school plant is mandatory for efficient learning conditions. The air the occupants breathe determines their comfort, health, and efficiency.

"Good ventilation is of vital importance for several reasons:

1. It removes odors.
2. It provides air circulation so necessary in diffusing heat to all parts of the room, preventing air and heat stratification, with hot air at the top and cold air at the bottom of the room.
3. It is a factor in temperature control.
4. It helps regulate relative humidity.
5. It provides a supply of oxygen.
6. It adds to the comfort of room occupants."[2]

Gravity and mechanical systems of ventilation are found in most school buildings. A few school buildings may have forced ventilation. Regardless of the system, efficient administration strives to keep the ventilating systems functioning to full capacity.

Year Around Control of Ventilation. Good maintenance procedures become very important on complicated air conditioning equipment. This equipment controls the humidity of the air and cools, filters, and circulates the air. The smallest room type of air conditioner requires a periodic air filter change or cleaning. The typical installation in a large building demands proper maintenance.

Many types of equipment are involved. The goal of maintenance is to provide trouble-free operation and assure minimum downtime for repairs. To achieve this goal, the operator

---

2 R. N. Finchum, *School Building Maintenance Procedures,* p. 134.

or building engineer must have a working knowledge of the principle of operation of all air conditioning equipment. This information is available from the equipment manufacturers and it should be studied thoroughly.

The maintenance of this equipment is a highly specialized field. A service contract for a particular system may be an economical procedure. In larger systems where several types of equipment are in operation, special personnel in the maintenance department assist the building engineers. These people must have adequate knowledge and training in the maintenance of all types of this complicated equipment.

MECHANICAL SERVICES

The scope of work in this department is very extensive. School buildings constructed over a long period of time have gas and water lines which run from the main supply line to the meters and from the meters to the utilities as piped to specific areas throughout the building. Steam lines also run from the boiler room to specific areas of the building. Sanitary lines run from the sanitary facilities to the main sanitary collection line, and the storm pipe runs from roof drains to the main collection storm sewer line. In locations where gas and/or oil are used for fuels, gas supply lines also exist. In the areas in which coal is used, the handling equipment must be kept in first class shape.

Other responsibilities include the maintenance of water lines for the lawn sprinkler system and of septic tanks, disposal systems, and lateral lines. General repair and replacing of piping to food service equipment, grease traps, domestic hot water systems, water coolers, aquariums, dressing room fixtures, swimming pool pumps, heaters, and filters are added responsibilities. Special service lines to cosmetology, art, homemaking, vocational equipment, and science instructional areas are added responsibilities. The repairing or replacing of frost proof sill cocks is necessary for economy.

Sanitary Facilities.

Plumbing fixtures which include water closets, urinals, lavatories, classroom sinks, and drinking fountains are scattered throughout the school buildings. The major repairs and replacements are definitely a part of the maintenance program.

Aims of Mechanical Services.

Aims of service of this department are: (1) to see that all schools be provided with a supply of pure, wholesome water, neither connected with unsafe water supply nor subject to the hazards of backflow or back siphonage, (2) to adjust all plumbing to use the minimum quantity of water consistent with proper performance and cleaning, (3) to keep the drainage systems maintained in order to guard against fouling, deposit of solids, and clogging, and (4) to see that all piping of the plumbing and utility systems is repaired or replaced with durable material, free from defective workmanship, and constructed to give satisfactory service for its reasonable expected life.

Common Problems.

A school district with many school plants constructed over a long span of time has the following administrative problems:

1. A large size of stock of varied material is necessary in order to repair the emergency situations caused by the breaking of pipes. Pipes for utility and heating lines break frequently and have to be repaired or replaced immediately.
2. Tree roots often cause fractures in pipes.
3. Plumbing fixture trim in old structures cannot be replaced with modern fixtures. Thus, a large supply of plumbing fixture parts is necessary.
4. Individual building service employees should be alerted to use the proper tools on plumbing fixtures and sill cocks to avoid unnecessary replacement.
5. The importance of standardization on as many parts of plumbing fixtures as possible should be considered seriously.
6. The quality of the parts for replacement should be watched very closely. Often a cheap part will cause replacement at an earlier date. The long term cost thus becomes greater. The saving in the cost of parts is overcome by the cost of double labor.
7. The utility lines, such as water, gas, and electric conduits in many relatively new schools, leak before normal expectation. Close scrutiny of these leaks often reveals that the quick deterioration is on account of electrolysis. If such a condition exists, the responsible maintenance personnel should take advantage of qualified consultative services before replacing the lines.

CARPENTER SERVICES

The personnel who perform repair work are divided into at least two areas, viz., the carpenter shop in the central service center and in the several school plants of the school districts. These services encompass the construction and repair of structural woodwork and equipment in all school plants of the district. The work is performed from blueprints, drawings, approved work orders, and oral instructions.

The scope of carpenter services may best be described by dividing these services as outside the school building, the outside surfaces of the school building, the inside parts of the school building, and assigned services.

Outside of the School Building.

Entry ways, covered patios, canopies, wood fences, stadia, and bleachers which are made of wood must be kept in condition.

Outside Surfaces of the School Building.

The major items in this classification which need repair are soffits, fascia, cornices, doors, windows, and fly and protective screens (both wood and metal). If the outside walk of the building is wood, this element is included.

Inside Parts of School Building.

Numerous items of the building interiors need the services of the carpenter. Maintenance repair carpenters build, repair, or install the following items:

Ceilings	Bleachers	Weatherstripping
Doors	Thresholds	Folding gates
Door transoms	Curtains	Counters

Trim and sash	Stairs & stair railing	Cabinets
Window sash	Floors, repair	Benches
Window sills	Floors, sanding	Partitions
Building framework	Shelves	Display cases
Display board	Chalkboard	Tackboards
Bulletin boards	Map rail	Auditorium seats
Science tables	Home economics fixtures	Shop equipment
Ceiling tile	Floor tile	Sheet plastic wall coverings
Window shades	Venetian blinds	Curtain rods
Wall fans	Finish hardware	Building insulation
Kick plates	Ventilators	

This department often has the responsibility for pest control, such as termites, ants, rats, mice, and other rodents throughout and around all properties of the school district.

Goals.

First, personnel constantly seek to find small defects and make small repairs, thus preventing expensive replacements in the future. Second, the personnel use quality materials in repair and/or replacement projects which prevent repetitive repair work.

The repair work in this department is so extensive that effective administration must plan the program in detail. Otherwise, the performance of many small repairs throughout all the buildings in a school district becomes very expensive.

FURNITURE REPAIR SERVICES

Attractive, well-maintained furniture and movable equipment give the proper aesthetic appearance to instructional and office areas in schools. The children and school staff use these items every day.

Effective administration of the program of repair entails the establishment of a definite method of periodic inspection and identification of the furniture needing repair. The building principal, the building custodian, and the responsible maintenance personnel share in these procedures.

Building custodial help should keep furniture and equipment in good condition. Should a piece of furniture be broken, immediate removal from the area is a mandatory safety precaution.

Practices in school districts differ as to the specific areas where the furniture and equipment is repaired. Some districts repair the furniture in the custodial work room. A separate room in a school building, the industrial shops, and the central repair shop areas are used by other districts.

Scope.

The scope of these services includes repairing desks, chairs, tables, drafting tables, bookcases, cafeteria tables and benches, surfaces of pianos, replacing glides on chairs and desks, sandblasting metal furniture, and refinishing the surfaces.

Common Problems.

The responsibility of keeping the furniture and equipment clean belongs to the custodial personnel. The responsibility of keeping the surfaces of desks, chairs, and tables in such condition that custodial personnel can keep these surfaces clean belongs to the local school staff and the maintenance personnel. Many surfaces on desks, arms on chairs, and tables become marred, filthy, and unusable.

The critical problem in furniture repair services is the determination of the factors to include in the policy of discarding furniture. The most crucial considerations appear to be:

1. Will this piece of furniture or equipment have use for continued educational purposes if repaired?
2. Can replacement be made as inexpensively as the cost of repair?
3. What percentage of replacement cost should be spent in repair?
4. In considering the repair cost, the labor item is most significant. If the repair work is performed in a central repair shop, the costs of loading the furniture at the individual school, trucking same to the central shop, unloading the furniture, reloading the furniture after repair, and unloading back at the individual school site must be added to the cost of repairing.

The solution as to the costs is the problem of each individual school district. The answer is easily determined when the adequacy of the maintenance budget is examined.

Materials.

The common procedure is to sand, shellac, and varnish. Recently new materials on the market have changed procedures. These tough, durable, and attractive materials are not easily cut or marred. These materials give permanency to surfaces, are colorful, facilitate cleaning, and are pleasing in appearance.

Effective administration of this phase of the maintenance program demands a continuous evaluation of all costs and procedures.

MASONRY SERVICES

These skilled workers usually deal with artificial stone, brick, concrete, and stone. Their services extend from the foundation to the top of the highest chimney and to all parts of the school site.

Responsibilities.

The specific responsibilities of this craft of skilled workmen include these assignments:

1. Repair and waterproof masonry and stone exterior walls.
2. Repair and point interior masonry walls.
3. Repair and replace glass block.
4. Repair brick chimneys, stacks, and towers.
5. Keep fire boxes in boilers and incinerators in good condition.
6. Repair quarry and ceramic tile floors.
7. Repair marble window sills and marble toilet partitions.
8. Construct masonry in small remodeling projects.
9. Repair foundations.

Other assignments may include:

1. Sandblast stone and brick.
2. Operate mud jack to raise sidewalks and concrete floors.
3. Build and repair manholes.

4. Construct area inlets.
5. Caulk around exterior openings.

Methods of Repair.

The repair work performed by the craft ranks among the most costly in maintenance services. In school districts of any size, effective administration periodically inspects the elements listed above throughout the school district. Determining the immediacy of repair is a most important decision. In a small system the repair work may best be performed by contract. In larger systems the amount of work usually requires continuous employment of this skilled personnel.

Problems.

Water penetrates defective masonry walls. Water saturating a masonry wall freezes and thaws. The wall cracks, crazes, spalls, disrupts, and disintegrates. Partially filled or imperfect mortar joints are the most common cause of leaks.

Efflorescence may appear on outside walls and detract from the appearance of the building. Exterior masonry walls become dirty. Then this cleaning becomes necessary.

Leaks are stopped by tuck pointing, dampproofing, and waterproofing of exterior masonry walls. The repair of adjacent flashing, if defective, is a must. Cement-based paints and silicones may be used to repel water. Experience discloses that a concave tooled joint of proper materials deters leaks. Also, coatings may trap water as well as repel it.

Cleaning exterior masonry may be performed by high-pressure steam, sandblasting, hand washing, high-pressure cold water, and by chemicals and steam.

Effective administration in this expensive area of maintenance services seeks expert information about the methods of correction. If the defects are not corrected quickly and properly, costs of repairs accelerate, greater operational costs appear, damages to interior surfaces continue to occur, rusting and disintegration of metal anchors and steel skeletons take place, the rotting of the wood elements of the school plant continues, and the loosened pieces of masonry of the deteriorating wall may be a source of danger.

PLASTERING SERVICES

Many old and some new school buildings have plaster applied on walls, ceilings, partitions, masonry, furred spaces, and concrete. The partitions have metal lath or wood lath or gypsum tile to which the plaster is applied.

This construction is fire-retardant and produces a good sound barrier. Acoustical plaster is applied to ceilings for sound control. Sound deadening can be a product of proper insulation and acoustical plaster. In previous years decorative textures were applied to certain surfaces, and molds and ornamental features were formed by skilled plasterers.

Causes of Repair.

Plaster deteriorates with years of use. Cracks occur on account of stress caused by the movement of parts of buildings. Indentations in plaster are make by the careless shoving of heavy objects against it. Often nails for hanging articles on the wall make holes and small cracks appear. In places of improper ventilation mildew appears which affects its solidity. Moisture from leaking roofs and improper curing affect its solidness. Plaster becomes loose from the bond on walls and ceilings.

Effective administration has the responsibility to determine the extent of dangers occurring from the above list of possible defects. The repairing and patching of plaster surfaces is a continuous process which is costly and messy. Successful interior painting depends much on the planned program of plaster repair.

Administration may find after careful analysis of each building condition that the deteriorated surfaces may be treated with wood paneling, fiber glass paneling, tile, or other materials more economically than with replastering.

GROUNDS AND LANDSCAPING SERVICES

School and civic pride are enhanced by good maintenance procedures applied to the school campus or campuses. A well-maintained campus for each school is a desired goal of effective administration. Responsibility for the upkeep of school campuses ranges from the superintendent in a small school to director of the physical plant in the larger schools. Between these limits of responsibility the principal and his custodial engineer have assigned responsibilities.

Plant Life.

A primary responsibility of maintenance of grounds lies in the preparation of the soil, the planting of the grass indigenous to the community, and the care and maintenance of the sodded areas.

The next line of responsibilities includes subsurface and surface drainage, irrigation, fertilizing, aeration, mowing, and weed control.

Landscaping functions comprise the planting and replanting and the care of choice shade trees, flowering trees, shrubs, perennials and annual flowers, hedges, and vines. These additions necessitate the expenditure for permanent maintenance.

In addition, disease and insect control of lawns, shrubbery, and trees requires definite maintenance attention.

These functions activate other services, viz., the removing of dead trees or limbs and shrubs, the timely trimming of trees and shrubs, and the systematic removal of this debris from the site. The control of the growth of grass in fences and vine growth becomes an important function.

Site Improvements.

The responsibilities in this area are (1) the upkeep of fence and gates, (2) the repair of sidewalks, drives, and pickup areas, (3) the upkeep of parking areas including the striping, and sign painting, (4) the upkeep of flagpoles, foot scrapers, and safety guards around gas meters, and (5) the repair of outside benches, patios, courts, screens and walls, and other features. Other responsibilities include the correcting of drainage on old sites and fertilizing the grounds where needed.

Outside Instructional Areas.

Tennis courts, baseball and softball fields, football fields, tracks, sodded play areas, asphalt play areas, and school gardens are the common areas on school campuses which require maintenance functions.

Play Equipment.

The play equipment the local district provides on school grounds is also a responsibility which requires continuous periodic attention. Accidents are frequent on play equipment which is not kept in good condition. Unrepaired equipment may add to the frequency of accidents.

This part of the school plant is often visited by the public when little or no supervision is present. Consequently, many things may happen which hinder the proper upkeep of the grounds. Flowers are plucked and pulled, branches on trees are broken, irresponsible vehicular traffic hits fences, and all sorts of debris are dumped on the grounds. The last described conditions add much to the costs of the upkeep of school sites.

Properly maintained school campuses add greatly in providing stimulating educational environments for both the children and the public. This aesthetic consideration should not be overlooked in school plant administration. School campuses may be overdeveloped and increase costs. Prudent judgment in the campus development and good administrative maintenance practices can be economical aids to attractive campuses.

SUMMARY

The services mentioned in this chapter comprise the most visible functions of maintenance. These basic elements of the school building demand programmed upkeep. If any of these ten services become lax or unattended for a period of time, the negative aspect creates inefficient, unattractive, uneconomical, and probably unhealthful conditions. The many items in the ten services vary with the quality of materials in the original construction and with the annual upkeep the building has been given. The school district maintenance administration has the responsibility for a planned maintenance program for each plant in each of these ten areas.

Chapter 11

MANAGING ALLIED
MAINTENANCE SERVICES

Several maintenance functions may or may not be organized in separate areas in school districts of varying sizes. Larger school districts with enough year around repair work to keep crews busy may have allied maintenance areas. In the smaller district these may be assigned to other crafts or may be contracted.

CONCRETE SERVICES

The scope of these services includes repairing foundations, concrete planter boxes, concrete steps, concrete porches, concrete loading platforms, concrete ramps, and concrete fixtures in patios.

Other areas of concrete repair work are present in repairing, pouring and finishing concrete floors, sidewalks, retaining walls, drains, curbs, parking lots, leader lines from downspouts to curbs, and repairing and resurfacing play areas. Pouring concrete bottoms for sanitary and storm sewer manholes is another responsibility.

The personnel may construct piers for portable and demountable buildings which will be discussed in Chapter 12.

The common problems are the replacing of wood floors with concrete in multiple buildings, working in freezing or rainy weather, and the observance of safety in all concrete operations.

These personnel strive to maintain a high level of workmanship and coordinate their work with the individual crafts.

SHEET METAL SERVICES

The mechanics in this craft fabricate, assemble, install, and repair sheet metal products and equipment. Using the hammer, (1) they shape metal over anvils, blocks, or forms, (2) they set up and operate soldering and welding equipment to join together sheet metal parts, and (3) they make smooth seams, joints, or burred surfaces.

Sheet metal mechanics make air ducts, downspouts and headers; they repair roof ventilators, soffits and fascias. They also make metal cabinets, make and install range hoods, gutters, flashing, gravel stops, scuppers and appliance vents, and vent water heaters and space heaters. In addition this craft makes containers of all sizes and shapes and metal clad doors.

The treatment which the students give to corridor and dressing rooms is the biggest problem for this craft. Doors are kicked in and sprung. Lockers are loosened from braces in the wall. Some members of this craft are continuously repairing student lockers.

WELDING SERVICES

The maintenance welder is a versatile craftsman around school plants, but his work is not so easily seen as that of other crafts. The repair of metal parts of worn or damaged machines and the repair of fabricated, cast, forged, or welded metal parts are the general responsibilities of this craft.

The services this craft performs in a school district are welding, boiler tubing, replacing water legs in boilers, remodeling and repairing incinerators, welding gas lines, welding breeching of stacks, and welding metal parts for all schools and crafts.

In addition this craft does special welding on boiler plates, motorized equipment, and structural steel. The craft is adept in repairing and making bicycle racks, playground apparatus and equipment, trash can racks, and ground soaking equipment.

Other assigned duties may include installing heating coils, assisting the garage personnel in rebuilding surplus property for an adapted maintenance use, and welding on parts of heavy ground equipment.

The personnel of this craft work in the designated shop area, in all parts of the school building from the basement to the roof, and in every school plant of the district. The very nature of the welding process demands that the personnel in this craft follow all safety precautions. Special attention to fire prevention precautions is an important part of the required training and qualifications.

DRAYAGE SERVICES

Each school district organizes these services differently. Many large schools do not provide mail and film delivery services to the schools. In such cases, some designated person in each attendance unit picks up and brings the mail to a specific location in the administration building. These designated people do likewise with the films.

Scope.

A program of drayage services which has proved been effective involves these services:
1. Deliver and pick up mail and films on stated days each week.
2. Deliver textbooks from warehouse or central library to all schools as demand requires.
3. Pick up printed materials from print shop and deliver to warehouse.
4. Deliver groceries and supplies for the food service department. Also deliver new equipment which is to be installed in cafeteria kitchens.
5. Deliver vocational-industrial arts materials, such as scrap material, large lathes, power saws, and drill presses.

6. Pick up and deliver benches and risers for school events as needed.
7. Pick up and deliver folding chairs, music racks, musical instruments, and live plants for stated programs.
8. Pick up and deliver tables, chairs, and equipment for summer playground programs and for fun nights.
9. Pick up and deliver pianos, organs, and equipment for special programs. Return the same after the performances.
10. Pick up and dispose of trash on the scheduled program.
11. Haul dirt to designated places in the school district.
12. Pick up and haul sand and gravel for playgrounds and the various maintenance crafts.
13. Pick up and haul light materials to and from maintenance projects.
14. Also haul heavy equipment—bulldozers, tractors, and ditching machines—to and from maintenance projects.
15. Pick up equipment that has to be repaired in the shops and deliver the same after repairs are made.
16. During mowing season deliver gasoline and oil to schools operating their own grass cutting equipment.

Aims.

The personnel in this area of services plan to:

1. Expedite the movement of materials and equipment for the educational and maintenance programs.
2. Assist the custodial and maintenance department in the removal of trash and scrap materials left from the repair work in the individual schools.
3. Make emergency deliveries as quickly as possible.
4. Promote safety in driving habits and the handling of heavy materials.

Common Problems.

These services are often handicapped by retention of incompetent and undependable personnel.

1. The wage rate is so low that the personnel turnover is frequent. About the time a drayage person becomes proficient, he resigns or seeks a position which has better remuneration. The new employee must then be oriented to his duties.
2. The requests for pickup and delivery are not received in time to work into the daily schedule. Often special deliveries may be costly.

The services performed in this area are menial, but efficiency in drayage services is necessary. The time and the travel costs of school administrators are saved. Maintenance personnel also have supplies and materials on hand when needed. Effective administration of school maintenance must not overlook the function of this phase of operation.

GARAGE SERVICES

Authorities agree that a central garage is economical when the school district operates six or more motorized vehicles. Experience indicates that economies are forthcoming when many school buses and many pieces of motorized equipment are district operated.

This area of maintenance operations services trucks, school buses, automobiles, and other motorized equipment in a school district. The equipment is inspected to ascertain the need for gasoline, oil, water, and supplies. Batteries and tires are tested. Oil is changed and the motorized equipment is lubricated. The personnel keeps a record of the gas and oil supplied to each piece of motorized equipment. Road test is a recommended procedure.

Scope.

The services in a school system may:

1. Keep mobile units in service by performing major and minor motor overhaul. Specific services are given to engine tune-up, electrical wiring systems, carburization, starters, generators, batteries, transmission and differentials, water pumps and radiators, brakes, turn signals, marker lights, head lights, springs, axles, clutches, and other critical parts.
2. Service separate equipment which includes tune-ups and repairs on air-compressor engines, concrete mixer engines, and starting motors on heavy equipment.
3. Dispense gasoline and oil for school buses, driver trainer cars, tractors, and similar motorized equipment.
4. Grease chassis and engines and give complete lubrication to motors and chassis transmission differentials on all motor equipment. Also lubricate all motorized nonmobile equipment.
5. Convert motors to desired equipment and install surplus motors in equipment which have motors beyond repair.
6. Give complete service to heavy equipment (diesel), lubricate, do minor and major repairs, repair clutches, cables, hydraulic power systems, replace filters, and make oil changes.
7. Service, lubricate, do motor overhaul and tune-up, and repair hydraulic systems on small tractors.
8. Inflate, repair, and replace tires on all rubber tired equipment.
9. Repair and replace bearings as needed, straighten axles, frames, etc., on tractor pulled mowers.
10. Repair or replace winches, and replace cables on cranes and winch trucks.
11. Repair gasoline motor and repair power welding machines.
12. Clean windshields and wash vehicles as the occasions demand.

Aims of Services.

The employees strive to maintain these standards of services:

1. Keep equipment in safe operating condition.
2. Evaluate the need of repair or replacement on the equipment brought in for repairs and expedite the repair of the same.
3. Keep appearances of the equipment as attractive as possible with the cooperation of the paint shop.
4. Keep equipment up to standards required by city and state laws.
5. Keep the garage as clean and presentable as possible.

Common Problems.

Ubiquitous problems are:

1. Shortage of space to handle work load.

2. Difficulty in finding and keeping parts for the varied types and makes of equipment.

These cumbersome duties keep the garage personnel fully occupied. Careful planning is necessary for efficient garage administration.

THE MACHINE SHOP SERVICES

Skilled personnel in a school district which has school plants of all ages save many a shutdown. The school plants of various ages have machinery parts which have been discontinued by the manufacturer or parts which are obsolete. The well-equipped shop has lathes, drill presses, and broaching, milling and screw machines, power tools, and precision measuring instruments. These tools are used by the skilled mechanic to replace worn or defective parts. The number of duties will vary according to the size of the district. Small districts may have commercial shops in the communities perform the services.

Scope of Services.

Skilled workmen in machine shops may perform these services:

1. Sharpen tools for maintenance workers. Some districts also sharpen tools and make band saw blades for the vocational and industrial arts shops.
2. Sharpen handsaws and power saw blades for the school district.
3. Make parts for all kinds of machinery.
4. Rewind and repair electric motors for all school machinery and equipment.
5. Repair air handling units and pumps for the heating department.
6. Repair power hand tools for vocational-industrial departments such as drills, skill saws, and belt sanders.
7. Repair power equipment in shops in vocational-industrial departments.
8. Repair floor machines and vacuum sweepers.
9. Sharpen, repair, and overhaul lawn mowers, edgers, and rototillers.
10. Repair laundry equipment.

The lack of standardization of power tools, lawn mowers, and circulating and other pumps forbids the stocking of supply parts. This maintenance area makes the parts for these tools and equipment in addition to the other duties.

SNOW REMOVAL SERVICES

School districts located in regions where snow often falls usually have tools and machines to remove snow readily from sidewalks and entrances. A few districts have buildings with snow melting systems in main sidewalks and entrances which melt the snow as it falls.

School districts located in regions where the snow rarely falls have a definite removal problem. Tools are used so rarely that they are often misplaced. The custodial employees have the responsibility to free the sidewalks of snow and ice to prevent accidents caused by falling on hard ice.

Snow falls on roofs, melts, and freezes during the night. Additional snow falls. Experience has revealed that an accumulation of snow and ice becomes heavy and causes roof failures. Maintenance employees must know the various roofs of the school system to the extent that they can watch roofs where this condition may become dangerous under these special weather conditions.

KEY SHOP SERVICES

Each school district has a different method of controlling keys. The key control and hardware repair and installation function efficiently in a separate maintenance area. This central administration keeps a duplicate key for every door and gate which has locks in the school system. A uniform key system cuts down the number of keys as they are numbered for each plant. The keys to the older plants are numbered on an adopted system. The keys are checked from the central system to the head custodian of a school plant.

Regulations concerning distribution of keys are:

1. The head custodian is responsible for all keys to his building.
2. A complete record of all keys must be kept on file by the custodian. All keys not in use are to remain locked in key cabinet and are properly labeled.
3. A fee of a stated amount for classroom keys and a higher amount for master keys is charged for all keys taken out and not returned at the close of each semester. This fee is collected by the head building custodian and a record is kept of same by him. He sends the money to the designated person in the central business office.
4. Outside door and gate keys, also pass keys, are given to principals only. Keys to inside doors of classrooms are given to teachers and other responsible employees of the system.
5. All keys are checked and reassigned at the beginning of each semester or school year.
6. After the keys have been assigned to teachers by the custodian, they may be kept in the office of the principal for the convenience of the teachers.
7. At the close of the school year all teachers and employees are to check keys in to the head custodian and receive a receipt for same from him.
8. A complete report of keys not returned on the afternoon of the last day of school is made to the head maintenance key man and to the security department at once—by telephone if necessary.
9. Any conditions not covered by the above regulations are referred to the maintenance office.

All keys are numbered to correspond to the serial number of the building and to the floor and door number if the uniform system is not used. All keys of the uniform key system are numbered according to the number made by the manufacturer.

The principal jobs the personnel of this area perform are:

1. Make keys to replace lost or broken keys.
2. Open filing cases in school plant when key is lost and replace key.
3. Keep the key records of all school plants up to date.

The one problem in key control is the duplication of keys. Experience reveals that the inscription, "It is unlawful to duplicate this key," imprinted on each key is a strong deterrent to duplication.

Additional responsibilities of the personnel in this department are:

1. Repair or replace all parts of hardware.
2. Repair or replace regular and exit door closers.
3. Install master keys in remodeling jobs.
4. Key remodeling jobs.
5. Repair all locks.

The equipment for the combination key-hardware shop includes a bench with a vise, a duplicating machine, a combinating machine, and a combination buffer-grinder. Special hand tools are needed for the many kinds of door closers.

VANDALISM RESTORATION SERVICES

The unpredictable and numerous break-ins in the school plants in a school district are an enigma. These incidents occur in single events and in group occurrences. The damages to the building often affect security and the parts of the building have to be restored immediately.

Protective screens are cut, window glass is broken, the glass on doors is broken, the outside doors are pried open which scars the outside door finishes, and hardware on outside doors is damaged by vandals.

The interior of the building is marred by the vandals in various ways. The door glass is broken, doors are pried open, locks are damaged, and the veneer is ruined on the surface of the doors. Vandals ransack pupils' and teachers' desks and scatter contents over the floors. Fire extinguishers are damaged. They pry open vending machines and refrigerators and scatter contents. Eggs and liquids found in the vending machine are often thrown on the ceilings and wall surfaces. Pencils, crayons, and magic markers are used on walls and surfaces. These markings are very difficult to remove from the surfaces.

The vandals seem to be in search of money and equipment which can be sold. Professional vandals usually have tools which really ruin different parts of the building. Sometimes the vandals are children who attend the school and desire to seek revenge in order to get even with members of the local school staff.

Cleaning after an entry by vandals becomes the responsibility of custodial personnel. The immediate restoration is the responsibility of the maintenance departments.

FIRE PROTECTION SERVICES

All custodial and all maintenance personnel who work in a school district have responsibilities in fire prevention and protection. The manner of detecting, warning, and extinguishing fires is different in school districts, and these factors may differ among buildings in the same district. These types of fire protection may be installed in separate systems or in a complete coordinated system.

The critical information employees should know includes:

1. The upkeep of detective-warning devices which should be assigned to qualified personnel who have complete knowledge about their components and how they operate. These devices are electronic or at least transmit electric impulses which activate bells, horns, or other such warning signals.
2. Fire exit procedure of the school district.
3. How to use portable fire extinguishers. (Chemical solution, water, loaded stream, foam, vaporizing liquid, dry chemical, and water agents.)[1]
4. How to operate the fixed fire protection systems within buildings if a system is part of the building. (High pressure carbon dioxide extinguisher systems, fixed-foam systems, standpipe and inside hose systems, and sprinkler systems.)

---

[1] National Fire Protection Association, *Maintenance and Use of Portable Fire Extinguishers,* Standard No. 10A, 1967, Boston, Massachusetts.

5. Minimal extinguisher ratings such as one size 2A approved extinguisher is required to protect 6,000 square feet of floor space in a normal classroom or 3,000 square feet in a shop classroom. The maximum travel distances to extinguishers is 75 feet. Directional signs assist in locating the extinguishers.[2]

Other responsibilities in this area include keeping the normal means of ingress and egress in working condition and keeping fire doors with panic locks functioning at all times. In cases where open fire escapes must pass windows, such windows must be wire glass set in metal sash. The employees should be especially alert to the condition of the fire extinguishers in the area where they work.

The maintenance personnel should recognize that some special processes create special fire hazards. These processes are spray painting, welding, plastic, motion picture projection, and air conditioning. The employees who have anything to do with the storage and handling of inflammable liquids have a special responsibility because these liquids ignite with such speed and burn so fast that first-aid fire fighting is practically impossible.

SUMMARY

The maintenance services which are briefly treated in this chapter are not the services that the school staff and public can easily observe. Each of the hundreds of small details which pertain to these services are very important. One small detail unattended may shut down an individual school plant. These detailed services are concerns that keep the school plant in operation. Fire safety, life and limb safety, pupil and adult transportation, services for the instructional program, administrative communication, and plant operation are basic items for efficient school administration.

Since maintenance services mentioned in this chapter are present in a school district regardless of its size, the performance of these services will vary. Some services may be performed by contract while others may be performed by seasonal labor.

---

[2] National Fire Protection Association, *Installation of Portable Fire Extinguishers*, Standard No. 10, 1967, Boston, Massachusetts, Chapter 4.

Chapter 12

MANAGING ASSIGNED
MAINTENANCE TASKS

Some maintenance services do not pertain to the functioning of the plant itself and some do not seem to be maintenance problems. The former class is the maintenance on instructional equipment and the latter class pertains to phases of maintenance which may belong to other employees or to special plant operations. These services which belong to other building service employees become so large that executing the services in the individual school plants is not economical or feasible.

This chapter treats the maintenance services classified under instructional equipment and other services.

INSTRUCTIONAL EQUIPMENT SERVICES

Practices of repair of this equipment vary in school districts. The smaller districts may have service contracts to keep the equipment in good repair. Those districts which have enough equipment to keep a man or more busy on each type of instructional equipment employ full-time employees. The use of school plants at nights and for summer schools often hinders the immediate repair of instructional equipment.

Drivotrainers.

This equipment is used as auxiliary equipment to train the youth to be safe automobile drivers. The author has had experience in a school district which operates 134 drivotrainers and eleven recorders. Experience reveals that two men are required for proper maintenance of this equipment with other local assignments. The maintenance personnel for drivotrainer repair has to be highly specialized. They should:

1. Attend the factory where the equipment is built.

2. Make regular inspections to avoid possible breakdowns.
3. Make emergency repairs.
4. Assist other maintenance personnel in the installation of new equipment.
5. Keep the records of the purchase equipment up to date.
6. Work closely with the safety education departments.

Athletic scoring equipment has complexities similar to the drivotraining equipment. Experience dictates that these personnel are able to maintain and repair scoring equipment for baseball, football, basketball, and wrestling.

Electronics.

This area of local maintenance services may perform tasks pertaining to television sets. Two television channels may broadcast daily lessons in school subjects to 75,000 children of the district through almost 2,000 television sets. The maintenance on the sets is a tremendous responsibility. If the set is not in good or excellent condition, the class instruction loses its supplemental instructional material. The goal of the personnel is to provide maximum use with minimum outages.

Other duties of this department are:

1. Repair language laboratory equipment.
2. Repair speech laboratory equipment.
3. Repair typing laboratory equipment.
4. Repair shorthand laboratory equipment.
5. Repair audiometers.
6. Repair master tape duplicating equipment.
7. Repair automatic film inspection machines.
8. Install and repair antenna system for all schools.
9. Install closed circuit TV co-axial systems for indoor graduation exercises.

The common problems in this maintenance area are equipment breakdowns because of the misuse of the equipment and student vandalism of parts of the equipment.

Each piece of equipment is numbered, stamped, and coded. The data processing equipment can publish a list of equipment in a few minutes.

The personnel who work in electronics are highly trained and the supply of local trained personnel for this area is very small. In small school districts the necessary repair to the electronic equipment may best be performed by service contracts.

Instructional Media Equipment.

This phase of instructional equipment has increased the last few years by leaps and bounds. Full-time employees have become necessary to keep the equipment in repair.

For example: A school district with 3,000 instructional areas has 800 16 mm projectors made by five different manufacturers, 2,000 record players of 80 varieties, 700 tape recorders of five varieties, 500 overhead projectors of four varieties, 100 electronic microscopes of three varieties, 30 lecturnettes of two varieties, 500 filmstrip slide projectors of five varieties, 500 jack boxes, and 3,000 head sets of listening center equipment.

This volume of similar media equipment scattered among the many school plants demands a program of maintenance. Administration has the challenge to provide a central office repair area, central office management, and field crews to keep the equipment in proper condition for use.

The responsibilities of this department are to provide a schedule of preventative maintenance, to keep records of lubricating, to clean equipment, and eliminate excessive operating failures.

The problems connected with the services in this area are vandalism in the classroom, the instruction of personnel on proper operating procedures, and keeping the critical parts of this equipment in stock to avoid operating failures.

The repair services in smaller districts may best be performed by service contracts.

Sound Systems.

These facilities are a part of the building which require special skills to function properly. New construction details installation of these systems. Older plants present many hearing problems. In large schools the repair and conditioning of these sound systems become a burdensome task for maintenance. In smaller school districts the repair services in this area may best be performed by service contracts.

The extent of the repair work in a large system involves the repairing of consoles (a complex instrument), wiring, and individual sound outlets. The skilled people in this area of maintenance may assist in relocating equipment when buildings are remodeled, additions added, and alterations are made in school buildings. They may also establish a maintenance program updating the sound systems in the individual buildings of the district.

The problems connected with sound systems are:

1. Detailing operational procedures to new school personnel each year.
2. Correcting improper usage of microphones.
3. Replacing microphones, cords, and plugs when necessary because these elements have a high casualty rating.
4. Planning the updating of equipment as soon as the equipment ages twenty years.

The aims of the service of the repairmen in this area are:

1. Provide near continuous and instantaneous coverage of building areas containing students for emergency and general announcements.
2. Expedite the handling of emergencies which arise in classrooms.
3. Eliminate loss of time in communication between the office and any school personnel.
4. Provide FM (school station) programming to any/all classrooms from the central sound console.

The skilled personnel in this area add needed equipment to designated facilities for graduation exercises and other special affairs. Their knowledge is very helpful in advising on acoustical problems which occur in auditoriums and gymnasiums.

SCHOOL SITE MOWING SERVICES

The management of mowing school sites in small districts is usually delegated to custodial personnel, especially if the school sites are small. In large school districts with many campuses of various sizes, the responsibility of mowing the sodded areas is usually divided between the custodial and maintenance personnel. Large site areas where large mowing machines can be operated are the responsibility of the maintenance department. Smaller site areas are the responsibility of the custodial personnel. A good plan is to draw definite areas for each class of building service employees on a plot of each site.

The intensity of sunlight and the climate govern the choice of grass. Some grasses grow faster than others, therefore the mowing program has local adaption.

School lawns require a specific mowing schedule. These areas cannot be mowed during rain or when the land is muddy. Efficient administration of mowing services desires to keep the school lawns as attractive as possible.

Mowing football fields is another responsibility which has to be programmed. These areas are fertilized at stated intervals, and water is applied by the watering system or by rainfall. Experience reveals that these fields should be mowed at least once a week. In the early part of the season the first and second cuttings should be close to the ground and all cuttings removed.

The appearance of the school sites is an important asset to the total appeal of the importance of education. Proper appearance demands adequate mowing equipment and manpower to operate this equipment.

RELOCATING PORTABLE CLASSROOM SERVICES

School districts of all sizes may have crowded conditions. In both small school districts and in large districts, portable buildings are used to house pupils. These structures may be one room buildings which are commonly called annexes or buildings which house two or more instructional areas, called demountables. The name is given to the latter structure because the building is moved in sections.

Both portable and demountable buildings are placed near the permanent school building. Insurance is cheaper on both the permanent and the portable buildings if there is 30 to 40 feet between them and the main building.

Small districts may employ house movers to move portables. Larger districts have tools to move the portables with a small amount of additional equipment other than the equipment which the large district owns.

The problems incurred in moving portables in a large district include:

1. Seeking a building permit from the municipality or municipalities through which the movement of the portable is routed.
2. Paying for a police escort.
3. Locating the building on the site where proper accessibility to the permanent structure is located and yet be close to gas lines, electrical lines, water lines, and connection with the sanitary sewer.
4. Removing trees and shrubs in order to locate the portable at a desired location.
5. Placing the portable in the best location often requires installation of additional paved play area and sidewalks.
6. Removing and replacing fences on sites where portables are moved from one site and placed on another site.

The task of moving portables, an added responsibility of the maintenance services, becomes routine and time-consuming. Effective administration must procure the necessary equipment to move these structures. Sequential moving of portables is preferred as many crafts are involved and the movement can be planned to provide as many economies as possible.

In congested areas the routing of the movement of portable buildings is lengthened by low underpasses, low utility lines, hanging traffic signals, and narrow streets and bridges.

The installation of concrete sidewalks and canopies completes the job of moving portables.

ELEVATOR REPAIR SERVICES

An elevator is a complicated machine which is subject to wear and general deterioration. A school district may have a few elevators to transport handicapped children and school equipment and supplies from floor to floor.

The repair services are so technical that service contracts for the maintenance of the elevators are recommended, if available, even in a large school district. The paucity of trained elevator repairmen in a community almost dictates this procedure.

Should a school district decide to maintain elevators, top management must establish definite procedures. They must:

1. Set up a complete system of periodic inspection on all parts of the elevator.
2. Set up a positive schedule for lubrication with a chart on which the date of the lubrication is recorded.
3. Set a definite period periodically to take the elevator out of service and give a complete examination.

Items which should be included in the complete examination include:

1. Cleaning of all parts of the elevator.
2. Hoist way enclosures and protection.
3. Car and car equipment.
4. Signal systems, hoisting machines, and brakes.
5. Wire ropes and mechanical safety devices.

The proper operation of an elevator, be it hand or automatically operated, with scheduled preventive maintenance almost insures satisfactory services.

LAUNDRY REPAIR SERVICES

In school districts which operate their own laundries, a definite maintenance program must be established to assist the laundry management. Good equipment of adequate size and proper design properly operated and maintained should help keep the cost of laundry services economical.

The maintenance services are very important. Effective administration will establish a system of preventative maintenance by periodic inspection and repairs when the laundry plant is shut down. The critical points are:

1. An adequate water supply is maintained.
2. The suitable water must be at the correct temperature to activate proper cleaning.
3. The electric washers, tumblers, centrifugal dryers, extractors, mangles, and other labor saving devices are kept in good repair.
4. All pipes, fittings, bearings, valves, and gaskets are kept in repair.
5. All running machinery must be lubricated according to a planned schedule.

PEST CONTROL

The control of pests was mentioned in Chapter 10 as an assigned responsibility of carpentry services. In a large school district many environmental conditions exist.

Insects.

Domestic flies, mosquitoes, cockroaches, lice, bed bugs, fleas, ticks, mites, scorpions, spiders, and centipedes may be a problem in one or more attendance areas. The local community surroundings may contribute to conditions which abet the presence of any one of these insects. Poor housekeeping in the school or the home may provide beds for the presence of these insects. The U.S. Department of Health, Education and Welfare, Washington, D.C., has bulletins dealing with these problems.

Termites.

Maintenance services to control the work of termites in school buildings are necessary. An eagle eye at least once a year should survey all buildings to see if termites are present. Structural changes may be made to block the termites from the building. The soils next to the building may be treated to stop destruction. Chemical treatment of several kinds can be applied to wood to control the infestation.

If any termites exist on school sites, the administration of maintenance has the responsibility to treat soils and build protection equipment on the outside and inside of the building to eliminate the presence of these insects. Small districts need to exercise extreme precaution in contracting for eradication of termites.

Domestic Rodents.

The control of rodents is a prime responsibility of maintenance administration. The control is both a housekeeping chore and maintenance function. Cracks or crevices around pipes and other outside openings can be closed with gratings to keep the rats out. Rats may also enter buildings in shipments of supplies. The proper storage of food supply is the first precaution in rat control. After maintenance personnel close all holes and rats cannot enter, types of poisons may be used to kill the rats contained in the area.

Birds and Flying Insects.

Sparrows, starlings, and pigeons deface buildings, sidewalks, trees, and shrubs. The birds may bring mites and lice to the building. Top management has the responsibility of constructive contrivances and screens on buildings to prevent a roost if possible. Experience with chemicals reveals that chemical treatment is only effective for a few days. Administration has to work with public authorities and existing laws with whatever solution is desired.

The control of flying insects on the outside and entrances of the building is also a problem which has both custodial and maintenance responsibilities. Maintenance personnel construct the panels and install the black lights. Custodial personnel keep the pans clean into which the dead insects fall.

Miscellaneous Pests.

During the school experience of the author the lack of upkeep of outside grates in foundations and floors has caused much concern. Skunks, opossums, badgers, and rats have entered the ruptured grates. Often these animals die under the building and the school has to be dismissed until the carcass is removed and the area under the building is deodorized and fumigated. The importance of the control of all pests in, around, or under school buildings cannot be overemphasized. Diseases are carried by pests. Pests bring unpleasant and obnoxious odors if trapped and left unattended. Custodial personnel must be alert to all small openings in floors and lower walls of a building. Maintenance personnel is responsible for minute inspections of these critical areas.

CARPET SERVICES

Several years ago, schools began to use carpet, and it is now a growing field. Carpet care is largely the responsibility of the custodial personnel in a building. The tools and equipment to keep the carpet clean are also largely custodial.

The maintenance employees are beginning to be confronted with these problems:

1. Acquiring the know-how to patch carpet where the materials may be torn.
2. Installing carpets on bare floors will probably become a responsibility of this department.

In addition the maintenance employees will be saddled with the responsibility of keeping the grounds and entrances in excellent condition in order to prevent tracking in dirt.

SUMMARY

School districts are locally administered. The assigning of functions of the maintenance department will therefore vary. The size of the school district also largely determines the number of assigned functions.

Chapter 13

MANAGING SERVICES
FOR ANCILLARY AREAS

School districts have varying ancillary areas. Some districts have data processing rooms, mobile laboratories, school stadia, swimming pools, greenhouses, and television studios. Most all school districts have central administration plant areas, food facilities, and federal projects.

DATA PROCESSING ROOM SERVICES

Comparatively new in the administration of school districts is the provision for data processing rooms. Often these rooms are provided in existing buildings. In new construction the architectural knowledge of this area is forthcoming. In existing buildings, whether the modification is made by maintenance personnel or contract, maintenance personnel should be knowledgeable about the basic elements.

The desired location of these rooms is the ground floor to reduce the vibration problem. If located on upper floors, the floors have to be checked for load requirements. A floating or raised floor is preferred in order to locate the power cables and conceal the pertinent facilities. Access to the facilities is made by lifting any of the panels which are equipped with leveling devices. In addition, the noise levels in this area are a primary consideration. The surfaces of the ceiling and sometimes the walls will need acoustical treatment. Careful attention has to be given to the noises which may travel through ducts.

The lighting in the area is zoned according to the critical work areas. Electrical power requirements are critical. The entire electrical power layout must have equipment such as separate feeders, separate breakers, power for air conditioning, and lighting requirements with proper controls. Independent air conditioning is recommended. The desired temperature must be between 65 and 90 degrees. The humidity must be between 20 and 80 per cent.

The custodial personnel have the responsibility for the care of this area. Maintenance services should entail the changing of filters in the air-handling units. Doors should have automatic door closers. Windows should be caulked in order to prevent the entrance of dirt and dust. The maintenance personnel should keep the elements of the building in superior working condition to prevent injury to the complicated, costly equipment in this area.

MOBILE LABORATORY SERVICES

School districts which have mobile laboratories have the responsibility of keeping these units in repair. In addition to keeping the chassis and engines in good repair and serviced, maintenance personnel has the responsibility of keeping the interior of the laboratories in first class working condition.

These units are purchased with or without air conditioning. If these units are purchased with air conditioning, the scope of the elements to be kept in repair include:

1. Wiring	7. Carpets
2. Lighting	8. Chalkboard
3. Electrical power supply	9. Carrels
4. Heating	10. Screens
5. Ventilation	11. Curtains
6. Cabinets	12. Shelving
	13. Tables and chairs

This type of school equipment is so new to school maintenance activities that the problems have not been carefully delineated. Maintenance problems are bound to appear. The degree and number of defects will depend largely on the quality of the elements contained in the original purchase.

SCHOOL STADIA SERVICES

The upkeep of school stadia is often a responsibility of the maintenance department. Sometimes the proceeds from the gate receipts pay for the maintenance costs. A definite procedure for maintenance is necessary in a school district where the department is responsible regardless of the manner in which the repair expenses are paid. This facility should be inspected periodically and a preventive maintenance program should be established.

Many kinds of stadia exist. Some schools have adequate seating with adequate lockers and shower rooms constructed of good materials. Other districts have limited facilities of lesser quality. Astute administration of maintenance services demands careful analysis of the costs, because a large percentage of the maintenance budget can be spent on this facility.

The elements of the stadia which need careful checking are: the seats, framework, aisles, entrances and exits, stairways, ramps, expansion joints, walks, railings, gates, and fences. Experience has revealed that the drainage, sidewalks, and drives are also important elements.

Other important elements of this facility which demand maintenance attention are the dressing rooms, shower rooms, toilets, attendant's room, first-aid station, mechanical equipment area, storage space, and the concessions areas.

The above areas must be well ventilated. The construction should be of fire-resistant durable materials. The care of the plumbing during slack periods is important. Local administration delegates the responsibility for plumbing care to either custodial or maintenance personnel.

The maintenance of electrical facilities at a stadium is often a troublesome responsibility. This facility only has seasonal use and is often left unsupervised during the slack season. Many defects develop during the slack season. Periodic inspection of electrical facilities is a

must. The replacing of light bulbs in the high light poles is a definite problem. Most maintenance departments are not equipped to replace bulbs on tall poles, so utility companies often
help perform these services. Flood lights, flag poles, scoreboards, clocks, public address systems,
and field telephones are items which need periodic attention.

Press boxes have to be painted, masonry repairs made, and roof repairs are necessary.
Door locks and fence repairs must be scheduled. The replacement of sod, shrubs, and landscaping must be planned and performed to keep the structure attractive. Periodic safety inspections must be made to seating facilities, stairways, and entrances. Incinerators must be kept
in repair.

Most of the public probably use the stadium as much or more than any other segment of
the total school plant. Maintenance is responsible for keeping all the many elements in prime
condition in order that the facility can be easily cleaned.

The stadium and its equipment is probably the most intermediate part of the school plant
of a district. Job allocations of the operation and maintenance personnel must be carefully
delineated. Constant safety vigilance by both classes of personnel is necessary to remove any
conditions which are unsafe, unsanitary, or undesirable.

SWIMMING POOL SERVICES

The maintenance of swimming pools is a most important function. Local health authorities have definite regulations governing the operation of swimming pools. Some form of water
purification is required. The equipment which controls the purification is intricate and must
be kept in first class condition. Maintenance services in the swimming pool areas are costly.

Many different types of equipment are manufactured both as units and as complete
systems. Maintenance services include care of the following items:

1. Inlets and outlets
2. Overflow gutters
3. Steps, ladders and step holes
4. Runways
5. Dressing rooms
6. Visitors' galleries
7. Showers, toilets, lavatories
8. Lighting, ventilation, heating
9. Recirculation system
10. Hair and lint traps
11. Water heater
12. Suction cleaner
13. Piping system
14. Thermometer
15. Filtration system
16. Diving boards
17. Chemical feeder
18. All valves
19. Heating facilities
20. Chlorination or iodine systems
21. Surfaces (ceramic tile, etc.)

The indoor swimming pools must have adequate ventilation. Experience reveals that
interior metal rusts, wood decays, and paint disintegrates because proper ventilation has not
been installed or the pools are used without operating the ventilation system. Keeping these
facilities clean and in a sanitary condition is a custodial responsibility. The keeping of the
elements in repair in order that this facility may function as the health regulations demand is
the job of maintenance.

GREENHOUSE SERVICES

In school districts which have greenhouses for propagation of plants for instructional
purposes or for the plantings on the several school plants, the maintenance thereof is an exact-
ing problem. The outside surfaces are glass and/or plastic with various other materials.

The maintenance problems consist of replacing broken glass, repositioning slipped glass, and caulking all places through which air can leak. The exhaust fans, shutters, automatic controls, and motor-operated inlet shutters need constant attention. The humidistats and/or thermostats are critical items for maintaining cooling and ventilating as the weather conditions demand.

In addition the wall mounted fans, the roof mounted fans, the sump pump, the pumps, and piping are elements which need periodic inspection and repair. The painting of the superstructure, if wood, is a periodic service for efficient maintenance.

Maintenance personnel must realize that heating, ventilation, cooling, and humidification are necessary in all kinds of these facilities. The kinds of materials and the different elements may vary, but these four processes must be in operating order at all times to protect the plant life.

Outside plant areas or gardens served by irrigation line or ditches of water entail constant upkeep.

TELEVISION STUDIO SERVICES

Educational television is becoming a part of the modern school. The master switching console and the stationary components of the system are in one room. Generally this room in the modern school is a part of the instructional communications center. Other school systems have regular broadcasting centers.[1]

The communications equipment is so complex that only experts who furnish this equipment have the know-how of repairing when defects occur.

This facility demands exact electrical power for operation. Experience has shown that the facility has to be maintained at a high level of efficiency. Problems in acoustical treatment of the surfaces is an important maintenance function. The area has to be air condtioned in most geographical areas because of the heat from the klieg lights. The maintenance of this equipment is a basic function. In adapting present classroom areas for a T. V. Studio, the major problem has been to provide enough storage space for the materials used in broadcasting. The second major problem has been in sound control. Often doors have to be sound treated as well as other room surfaces.

CENTRAL ADMINISTRATION PLANT SERVICES

The central administration is housed in various ways. Usually the central administration offices are housed in a separate area of a school building, a separate structure (school building or residence) which may be adapted, or a structure especially planned for the administrative offices of the school district. The supply department may be housed in an abandoned school building, an adapted building, or a structure constructed for supply administration. The maintenance department likewise may have housing similar to the supply department. Occasionally the supply department and maintenance shops and headquarters are housed in one building constructed for the individual school district. (See Chapter 7.)

These important facilities of the school system must be maintained regardless of the manner in which housing is provided. The degree of proper maintenance of these structures assists greatly in selling the importance of education in a community. Often proper maintenance is difficult in plants in which the site is too small and the buildings are old.

---

1 *Audio-Visual Roundup.* American School and University, April, 1967, pp. 28, 29, 30, and 75.

The custodial care of these structures is very important. The responsibility of the maintenance department must be clearly defined as to the placement of materials and general appearance. Cooperation of all personnel is necessary.

The responsibilities of the maintenance personnel are to inspect these properties periodically
and put adequate amounts in the proposed budget for proper maintenance. The supervisor of
maintenance must be alert to proper maintenance of these facilities. Thus he helps to keep the
proper image of the importance of education in the school district.

FOOD FACILITY SERVICES

School food service is recognized as a definite part of general school administration. Building spaces are provided as an integral part of the building or in a separate building on or
near the site. Some school districts have central kitchens where the food is prepared and dis-
pensed by trucks to the several attendance area buildings in the district.

The method of financing varies. Some districts provide the building spaces and the original
equipment and furniture, and the proceeds from the sale of foods are used to operate the
kitchen and replace the equipment and furniture. The upkeep of interior and exterior surfaces
of both areas is usually the responsibility of the maintenance department of the school district.
A few districts provide the spaces for school food services and the proceeds from food sales
pay all expenses except the maintenance of the interior and exterior surfaces.

A good policy to follow is for the district to provide the original spaces and original equipment for the kitchen and dining area. The district also pays all utility bills. The repair and
replacement of kitchen equipment is made from the proceeds from food sales. The food service personnel is responsible for the cleanliness of the kitchen and equipment. The local school
custodial staff is responsible for the cleanliness of the dining area. The maintenance department is responsible for the upkeep of the interior and exterior surfaces of both spaces and the
furniture in the dining area.

Food service centers must be kept clean and attractive. These areas are used often by the
public, in addition to the school use.

The special elements which require periodic inspection and regular upkeep may be grouped
as follows:

1. Exterior items are fly and protective screens, outside doors, outside lighting, and
   locks on outside doors.
2. Interior items are floors, walls, ceilings in cafeteria, kitchen furniture in dining
   areas, utility lines and connections, screen doors and/or garbage or waste disposal
   area, insect and rodent control, grease traps, and adequate hot water which the
   state laws prescribe.

Regardless of the manner of the financial arrangement of operating food facility centers,
the maintenance of these facilities becomes a part of maintenance services.

FEDERAL PROJECTS SERVICES

An average school district probably receives monies under at least five or six titles of the
various Federal Education Acts. The monies from these acts make changes in the educational
program and purchase the appurtenances necessary to implement the program.

Room sizes are altered, different utility services are needed, instructional equipment has
to be installed, and additional book shelves are needed. In addition the new equipment and

the books have to be delivered to the several schools. Experience in developing these areas to implement these programs reveals that these building and equipment jobs are small. Expedient adaption and installation have been best performed by the maintenance personnel.

The problems encountered are in providing the necessary adaptations according to a schedule. Equipment and books are purchased when monies are available. These often arrive at a time when the maintenance personnel are busy with assigned projects. This action causes either delay in installation or delay in the execution of the assigned project. Following a schedule for planned maintenance and emergency repairs has become more difficult.

This extra assignment for maintenance personnel is necessary for expediency of immediate use of the equipment and books. Capable leadership in maintenance services meets its problems presented in this area as these problems occur. Maintenance leadership trusts that better scheduling of purchasing and deliveries will be possible.

OTHER ANCILLARY SERVICES

School districts in different areas of this nation have various other regional functions which require maintenance services. Some districts have natural skating rinks. Others construct artificial skating rinks. A few districts have ocean beach fronts. A few districts have school camps of varying sizes. Golf courses are present on some campuses.

Each of these facilities has elements which are the concern of the maintenance department. The specific maintenance problems of each facility appear to be of minor significance, because literature in the field has little to offer. If such a facility is present in a school district, periodic inspection and budget planning are necessary for effective maintenance.

SUMMARY

The advancement in technology as it is applied to school administration and operation has hurled a challenge to effective maintenance administration. The new services, the new machines, and the new spaces in the school plant require specific knowledge.

Many of the promising practices are so localized that they are not readily published. A special technology is required for adequate services in the ancillary areas. Each local maintenance program must be thoroughly examined and analyzed to make the program as inclusive as possible.

Chapter 14

UPGRADING EXISTING
SCHOOL PLANTS

Upgrading existing school plants has a direct relationship to guidelines for construction of new school plants. The relationship is like two halves of a round-trip ticket: "Not good if detached." No one way exists to perform the upgrading. The problem is a complexity of new creations and/or reconstructing superior environments for the educational program. Upgrading the school plant may entail remodeling, rehabilitation, modernization, and repairs.

Look at the life cycle of a school plant as far as adequacy and upkeeping are concerned. The cycle falls into about three phases.

First Phase. During the first twenty years the repairs and modernization items are likely to be few and far between.

Second Phase. During the second twenty years these items become more frequent. Individual items in the building have started to deteriorate. Annual maintenance costs increase. The fixed equipment wears out. Heating and operating become more expensive. Educational programs change space requirements.

Third Phase. During the third twenty years the equipment wears out and defects become marked. Alterations become necessary to adapt the building to the current educational program. The problems generally point to a need for complete overhaul.

School plant's age.

Unless each plant is periodically adapted to the changing needs of education, it becomes less desirable as a home for the children of the community, less effective in protecting the safety of children and adults, and less valuable as a learning laboratory.

The problems of keeping the physical environment, excluding the educational features of a school plant, in a state of adequacy require a course of action.

Each school plant is a distinct problem. If a school district has a well-planned school building constructed of durable materials, then the approaching problem is not extensive.

132

Another school district builds the cheapest school possible at the time of erection. This district disregards the annual cost figure which is a composite of the costs of operation, upkeep, finance, and adequacy. Other school districts have school plants which have qualities that fall between these two extremes.

The three major factors of upgrading physical facilities of a school plant are (1) the projected length of service expected of a structure, (2) its adequacy for contributing to the educational program and its objectives, and (3) the economic feasibility.

"Guide lines to assist school districts in proceeding wisely in determining whether or not they are making a wise investment of public funds are practically non-existent."[1] This complex problem is ever present in school districts which have many school plants of varying dates of construction.

A school building may be structurally sound, while the school plant is inefficient or obsolete. The upgrading of standards, passage of time, or maintenance neglect contribute to obsolescence. Other factors include educational changes, improvement of design, construction techniques and patterns, and new materials. Local officials have the responsibility to plan a continuous upgrading program for the several school plants of their district.

Most state departments have minimum standards for construction. Any school district which has plans for school plants must use these minimum standards as a basic plan in construction.

EDUCATIONAL RESPONSIBILITY

The superintendent of schools and his staff have the responsibility of determining the adequacy of present plants for the present educational program. The methods used to study present plants will vary. School plant literature has many score cards which may be used. School plant authorities have developed master lists of items to use in checking the functionalism of the present plant. Faculties often make their own lists. No score cards, no faculty list, and no master list is a panacea. Yet each device, if intelligently used, may become a guide for decision making.

THE USE OF SPECIALISTS

Astute school administrative personnel rely on reports of the structural engineer, architect, mechanical engineer, electrical engineer, fire marshall, and health agency personnel. The acoustical engineer, if employed separately, should study the sound absorption factors. These reports are helpful to the chief school administrator as he studies the educational adequacy and the estimates of the cost of upgrading. Equipment specialists (science, art, homemaking) should be given opportunity to make suggestions for modern furniture and equipment.

THE USE OF IMAGINATION

Many old school plants may be upgraded for modern educational programs by the use of a vivid imagination. Such ideas as the re-arrangement and enlargement of educational building service areas by installing, removing, and altering partitions are basic to upgrading.

---

[1] Louis Bruno, *Modernization of School Building—A Feasibility Study* (A report to the 1963 Washington State Legislature—State Department of Public Instruction; Research Report No. 09–01, February, 1963), p. 2.

The exchange of building areas for different educational programs is also a possibility. Another good idea is the selection of color and of materials which add attractiveness to the new environment.

CRITERIA FOR JUDGING EXISTING PLANT

The site, the building, the building equipment, and the furniture and furnishings must be judged separately. This chapter treats the many points of all components as a specific senior high school is studied. The scope is extensive. Each item needs consideration. Can a specific building be upgraded to meet adequately the educational need? The physical fitness of the structure has to be examined and the adequacies of specific facilities in the upgraded plant have to be determined. "The problems must be answered by someone representing the school administration when a specific building is being considered."[2]

Criteria for Site.

An adequate site embraces the educational program. Its location and accessibility are important. The important questions which need definite answers are:

1. Is the site properly located in respect to the area it serves?
2. Can the site be reached by good highways, streets, and walks?
3. Are the grounds adequate for conducting a senior high physical education program?
4. Is the site adequate for facilities such as stadium with a fully developed track?
5. Is additional area available? Where?
6. Is it possible to expand the present site at a reasonable cost?
7. Is the site free of traffic hazards?
8. Is the site reasonably free from disturbing or interfering noises?
9. Is the site remote from business establishments having undesirable influences on youth?
10. Is ample off-street parking available for normal automobile concentration?
11. Are service drives properly located for student safety?
12. What is the condition of the site?
    a. Is the site well drained?
    b. Are sidewalks and approaches present?
    c. Is the site sodded?
    d. Is the site suitably landscaped?
    e. Are athletic fields properly fenced?

Supplemental Site Criteria.

A high school plant is never finished because of the ever changing educational program. The basic question is, will the site readily accommodate all the activities required in the present and future program? Other questions include:

1. Is additional space available for parking when athletic events are held? Are the parking areas lighted?

---

2 E. B. Sessions, *Rehabilitation of Existing School Buildings or the Construction of New Buildings?* (Research Bulletin No. 2, Research Corp. of Assoc. of School Business Officials, Chicago, Illinois, 1963), p. 2.

2. Is space available for loading and unloading buses, delivery trucks, and fire equipment?
3. Is provision made for a good student traffic flow pattern?
4. Are ingresses and egresses adequate for the present and future loads?
5. Are play areas for high school grades present? These areas include provision for football, soccer, field hockey, basketball, soft ball, track, tennis, and archery. The play areas for boys and girls must not conflict. Certain areas may overlap: areas used for soccer and field hockey may be baseball outfields, softball fields, or archery ranges in the spring. Outdoor paved areas for basketball may be flooded for hockey or used for overflow parking. A practice football field is necessary in addition to the regular football field. Suitable stands for spectators are necessary.

Criteria for the Building.

A study of all usable space in the present high school building is necessary. Specified spaces may be altered, enlarged, or made smaller to meet modern allocations for definite instructional areas. Answers to the following questions are very important:

1. Do the existing facilities have adequate space for a senior high school program?
2. Can adequate space be constructed by rearranging space or additions?
3. After upgrading, what will be the normal pupil capacity?
4. Can the existing subject areas be increased in size without extensive structural changes? Mechanical changes?

The local administration must study the total building area to see if adequate space is available for any or all of the following instructional areas:

General classrooms	Home economic classrooms
Physical education	Commercial classrooms
Service rooms	Arts and crafts rooms
Science laboratories	Music rooms
Mechanical drawing room	Dramatic classrooms
Electric shops	Shop classrooms
Wood shops	Drivotrainer rooms
Metal shops	Auto shops
General shops	Printing shops
Farm shops	Cosmetology rooms

Other shop areas are determined by local school administration.

Other areas which need definite study are those which pertain to the pupil activities.

1. Is the gymnasium adequate for the indoor physical education program?
2. Are the shower and locker rooms adequate?
3. Is the seating space adequate for the normal number of spectators?
4. Is the library adequate for the size of the school?
5. Does the size of the cafeteria affect the proper functioning of the school?
6. Is the auditorium facility adequate?

Pupil accommodation areas are important in modern high schools.

1. Can adequate space be provided for a student lounge?
2. Can adequate space be provided for a student store?
3. Can a room be provided for student government headquarters?

The administrative area of a high school plant is the focal point where all activities start.

1. Can space be provided for an ample office site?
2. Can definite space be allotted for the number of counselors?
3. Can space be provided for a clinic?

Teacher accommodation areas are important for the morale of the teaching staff.

1. Is space available for lounging areas with sanitary facilities for each sex?
2. Is space available for a teacher conference room?
3. Is space available for a faculty dining room?

Special service rooms are the spaces needed for custodial personnel and storage for all the school instructional areas of the school plant.

1. Are custodial rooms separate from the boiler room?
2. Are they ample in size and properly constructed?
3. Are storage rooms provided for books, instructional supplies, and equipment for the whole school and for each department?

Custodial storerooms	Auditorium equipment
School supplies	Fuel storage
School books	Custodial workshop
Educational equipment and teaching accessories	Yard tools
	Out of doors play equipment
Storage in instructional rooms	Lost and found articles
Audio visual materials	School patrol equipment
Gymnasium equipment	Receiving and shipping

4. Is space available for the storage of surplus furniture and equipment?

Supplemental Educational Requirement Criteria.

The existing spaces must be studied in relation to the methods of modern grouping, location of spaces for safety, and adequate size.

1. Can the building space be arranged to accommodate the use of individual study carrels, rooms of 10, 15, 25, and larger groups?
2. Is it possible, if the present structure has areas for numbers of students on the upper floors, to relocate these areas on the ground level? (Many old structures have libraries, administrative suites, gyms, cafeterias, and auditoriums on the second floor or higher. Modern administration constructs these areas on the first floor for ease of ingress and egress and for safety of each occupant).
3. Does the size of a regular classroom approximate 800 square feet?
4. Do the sizes of specialized classrooms meet the functional needs of the designated instructional areas?

Criteria for Existing Construction.

The type of construction of the high school building is an important determination. If upgraded, how safe is the updated structure? The foundations and footings, the outside walls, the roof, and the outside openings are definite building elements which need careful scrutiny.

1. Is the building fire-resistive or semi-resistive? (Buildings predominately of masonry, concrete or similar non-combustible wall, floor, and roof construction.)
2. Is the building of masonry construction? (Buildings of masonry, concrete or

similar non-combustible wall construction, but with floors or roof of non-combustible construction.)

3. Is the building of frame construction? (Buildings of combustible wall, floor, and roof construction. Frame brick-veneered walls are classed as combustible.)
4. Are any foundation walls out of alignment?
5. Are defects in foundations of settling, cracking, tilting out of plumb, and leaking present?
6. Are foundation walls leaking on account of water pressure from the outside soil?
7. Are drains present to carry downspout water away from the building?
8. Are provisions made for the ventilation of foundations?
9. Is seepage of water evident around windows, door openings, or masonry joints?
10. Are wall cracks present because of foundation failures?
11. Are wall cracks present because of expansion and contraction?
12. What is the condition of the mortar in the surface joint openings?
13. Does the exterior trim need repairing?
14. Does the paintable part need repainting?
15. What is the condition of caulking materials around outside openings?
16. Is efflorescence present?
17. What is the condition of downspouts?
18. Are obsolete exterior elements present which should be removed?
19. Do the outside walls, if brick or stone, need cleaning?
20. What is the condition of the roof and roofing surfaces, roof drains, and sky lights?
21. Are steeples, domes, belfries, and dormers present which should be removed?
22. Could the roof be replaced with a different type of roof?
23. What is the condition of flashings, gutters, and downspouts?
24. Are the parapet walls in good condition?
25. Does the present roof have adequate insulation?
26. What is the condition of the entrances?
27. Do any parts need repair or replacement?
28. Does the entrance need paint?
29. What is the condition of the windows?
30. Do any parts need repair or replacing?
31. Is the caulking tight around windows?
32. Do the windows need paint?
33. What is the condition of the protective and fly screens?
34. What is the condition of all outside doors?
35. Do any need repair or replacing-wood door frames, or ornamental trim?
36. Is the caulking tight around doors?
37. Do the doors need paint?
38. Is the hardware in good condition—door closers and panic devices?

Supplemental Type of Construction Criteria.

Further important questions which need expert examination to avoid overlooking appear minor. Experience has revealed that each question needs a definite answer.

1. Are structural steel members adequate?
2. Are there signs of rusting in crawl and attic spaces?
3. Are wood floor joists adequate?
4. Does dry rot or termite damage appear anywhere?

5. Is there evidence of any cutting or altering of floor joists or additional loads imposed?

6. What is the possibility of eliminating some of the window area in the classroom?

Criteria for Interior Building Elements.

The surfaces of the circulation areas, all instructional areas, and large meeting areas (gymnasium, auditorium, lunchroom, and library) should be inspected for appropriateness and physical condition. Electrical facilities are closely connected with the adequacy of these spaces. This list of questions is important.

1. Are the ceilings in the circulation spaces acoustically treated?
2. Are the floors in good condition?
3. What is the condition of the walls?
4. Are there adequate exits?
5. Are adequate lockers installed?
6. Does the circulation space need repainting?
7. What is the condition of the floors?
8. Are corridors and stairways adequate and properly located?
9. Are there any areas not adequately served by corridors or fire exits?
10. Are the ceilings in the classrooms acoustically treated?
11. Do the walls and partitions show defects?
12. Do these areas need decoration?
13. What is the condition of floors?
14. Is built-in equipment in good repair?
15. Are the provisions for chalk and tackboards adequate?
16. Do any of these areas have incidents of overloading the floor?
17. Do the exit facilities meet the requirements of the building code?
18. Are adequate sinks and cabinets provided in these areas?
19. What is the condition of shades and blinds?
20. Does the woodworking area have a dust collector system?
21. Has provision been made for the floor mats at the entrances?
22. Are these areas acoustically treated?
23. What is the condition of the ceilings?
24. What is the condition of walls?
25. What is the condition of the floors?
26. Are exit facilities in good condition?
27. Does the wiring meet the standards of the current building and fire safety codes?
28. Is the wiring in old portions fire safe?
29. Do the lighting fixtures provide adequate viewing in each area of the building?
30. Are ample electrical receptacles provided in each area of the building?
31. Is the emergency and exit lighting functional?
32. Are provisions for sound, fire-alarm, and program systems effective?
33. Is wiring provided for electric kilns and spot air conditioning?
34. Are floodlights installed on the building or on the site?

Plumbing, heating, ventilating, and disposal facilities are basic to good health and comfort in high school. The adequacy and conditions of these elements should be checked by these questions:

1. Is an ample supply of potable water provided?
2. What is the condition of the water line?

3. Is extensive pipe replacement necessary for altered or added spaces?
4. Does the hot water piping system need extension?
5. Does the location, number, type, and condition of plumbing fixtures meet standards?
6. What is the condition of the plumbing fixtures as to appearance?
7. What is the condition of the shower room facilities?
8. Do the toilet rooms have impervious materials on the floors and walls?
9. Are outside faucets adequate for community use?
10. What is the condition of the present boilers?
11. Will an additional boiler be needed?
12. What is the condition of the chimney?
13. Are efficient controls installed on the heating equipment?
14. Is the present system adequate to provide economy of operation and room comfort?
15. Is the boiler located in a fire-resistive room?
16. Is the fuel storage room, if coal is used, adequate?
17. What is the condition of the domestic hot water boiler?
18. Is the ventilation system adequate to provide proper air changes in winter? In summer?
19. Does the ventilating system have proper controls?
20. What is the provision for protection against fire in the vertical vent flues?
21. Is adequate ventilation provided in the auditorium, gymnasium, shops, storage rooms, kitchen, cafeteria, and dressing room areas?
22. Is the inside incinerator large enough for its purposes now and in the future?

Other facets of this study include the fire safety of the present high school building and the use of basement areas, if any.

1. Does the location of the boiler room, auditorium, balcony of auditorium, gymnasium, cafeteria, kitchen, and eating areas present any problem to fire safety?
2. What is the condition of the fire alarm and intercommunication systems?
3. Is the portable fire extinguisher equipment adequate?
4. If sprinkler system exists, is this system in operating condition at all times?
5. Is the basement necessary for classroom areas?
6. Are basement areas clean, dry, and free from hazardous conditions?

Supplemental Building Interior Criteria.

A high school building has many features which may easily be overlooked in an evaluation. Some features which need careful checking are:

1. If a multiple story building, are the outside fire stairs in good condition?
2. Are the stairs constructed of fire-resistant materials?
3. Are adequate stairwells present for safety purposes?
4. Is all glass in doors of the correct type and located properly for safety?
5. Is the provision for chilled drinking water present?

Criteria for Furniture and Equipment.

A high school with an adequate size site and adequate plant space should have up-to-date furniture and equipment. The replacement and repair must be periodically performed. Some pertinent questions regarding these elements are:

1. Is it economical to rehabilitate the school and office furniture?
2. Does the present furniture facilitate flexibility?
3. Does the equipment in the following areas meet the requirements for the modern school programs?

Home economics	Shower and dressing rooms
Business areas	Auditorium
Art department	Library
Science areas	

4. Will the old or new furniture fit the decor of the area for the purpose for which it is planned?

MASTER PLAN

The best way to avoid short-sighted upgrading of the school plant is through the use of a master layout for every project. This scheme is important whether the job involves an entire master plan or a home economics area. Master plans tend to eliminate space which may be useless. This plan may also consolidate duplicate functions or improve operating efficiency.

PLANNING THE BUDGET

No one set plan of establishing costs and budgeting for upgrading exists. Architects and engineers may give estimates of costs on specific items. Responsible maintenance management may give estimates of costs of specific items. Often contractors assist in establishing estimates of cost. Once the items in the program for each building are defined, a tabulation of the estimates on each item is necessary to ascertain the total approximate cost.

SETTING UPGRADING PROGRAM

Once a decision is made to proceed with the program of upgrading, the methods of performing the work must be determined. All the work may be contracted, a part of the work contracted and a part performed by maintenance employees, or all the work may be performed by maintenance employees. Unless the specific items are large and time-consuming, top maintenance administration may employ skilled personnel or use present employees to do the upgrading. In the latter case the district purchases the materials. Careful bookkeeping and competent supervision become necessary.

SUMMARY

Upgrading a school plant is a cooperative undertaking of educators, school plant architects, specialists, and maintenance personnel. The process is time-consuming and harrowing. After all decisions are made and a master plan is formulated, top maintenance administration has the responsibility of performing the work assigned to this department.

Chapter **15**

PROMISING PREPLANNED
MAINTENANCE POINTERS

The effective administrator of school plant maintenance realizes that the new school plant will be his responsibility to keep in repair as soon as the warranty period expires.

In new construction the architect rarely works directly with the supervisor of maintenance. He relays his findings to his superior officers. His experience in maintaining older school plants is invaluable. He knows the kinds of materials which are durable in the local situation. The climatic regions of countries vary in humidity and dryness, coldness and heat, and sunshine and cloudiness. These conditions limit the use of some materials in school construction in some geographical areas. Certain geographical areas demand sturdier and more costly materials. Thus, the architect works as a member of a team in selecting materials for construction.

Regardless of the quality of materials, the final building depends upon the quality of craftsmanship. Good workmanship insures good quality and also acts as a guarantee against maintenance trouble and costs. Operation costs are also less. Poor craftsmanship results in a botched-up piece of work which, in turn, results in dissatisfaction and usually trouble for the maintenance department. The architect has the responsibility of checking the quality of craftsmanship.

The supervisor of maintenance recognizes that each state has laws and building codes and may also have local codes which govern the construction of new schools or additions thereto. These regulations also pertain to remodeled or reconstructed schools.

General regulations are that all school buildings of more than one story must be of fire-resistant construction (a basement is considered to be a story). The heating plant may not be located beneath any portion of a school building and must also be of fire-resisting construction.

The architect assumes complete responsibility for a building project from its conception to completion as the owner's agent and counselor. Every project has its problems, and the architect must have knowledge of these conditions and problems as they arise. A good practice is to employ a clerk of the works or inspector. He acts as the eyes of the school board and architect in every step of the building process. He inspects materials delivered to the site to determine whether they comply with specifications as well as each phase of construction. Carefully prepared plans and specifications for materials and services adequately supervised during construction insure less maintenance.

The supervisor of maintenance services who has a concept of the major items of a modern school plant has advantages in planning maintenance work. This chapter treats these concepts in capsule form. These concepts are also good ideas to use in a repair or modernization program.

TOTAL SITE LAYOUT POINTERS

The first step is the planning of the use of a total site. The soils must be tested, and a definite subsoil exploration is fundamental in selecting suitable foundations. The setting of the floor level is a primary consideration for drainage and safety. The drainage of the first 20 feet adjacent to a building is necessary. The location of the school building near the corner of a school site assists in the total site development and enhances access to the site. The school building should be located at least 100 feet from the streets. The layout of the drives, sidewalks, play areas, lighted parking areas for cars and bicycles, and flag pole must be carefully planned. Proper drainage for the entire site, sod areas, play areas, and drives is a proper consideration. Turf areas should have a 2 per cent slope. The concrete walks and steps should have a rough finish. Sidewalks which abut the building are a long term economy. Lower elementary pupils require site areas for special playground equipment. Upper elementary pupils require site areas suited to their particular needs, interests, and abilities. Some 200 different kinds of recreation activities can be planned on school sites. Adequate site planning prevents many costly maintenance problems.

In planning the different play areas on the sites, the planning should permit the extensive use of mechanized equipment for maintaining lawns and planting. It is wise to plant only trees, shrubs, and grasses which are indigenous to the community. Caution is needed in planning the number of trees and shrubs. Too many school sites have too many trees and shrubs for proper maintenance.

TOTAL BUILDING POINTERS

The school building is an architectural expression of an educational philosophy which implements the program of education for a specific community. This important educational tool should be a learning laboratory for all the people of a community. This building should be beautiful—every part of the building, such as covered walks and entrances, should relate to the total building.

The expansibility of the building should be detailed in the master plan. This concept is especially important in secondary schools, for a secondary school is never finished.

The appearance of the building should be attractive. Competent architects can design attractive schools without the use of arched openings, dormers, belfries, fake chimneys, Greek columns, and cupolas. The avoidance of designing the building to make it look like an institution is a challenge to the architect. Better school buildings appear as homelike as possible. All areas commonly used by large groups are placed at or near grade level.

Special precautions for territories which are subject to termite damage include (1) the treatment of the entire building site for the prevention of termites (this treatment is an economical long term expenditure), (2) all wood forms used on building construction be removed before a building is occupied, (3) loose or casual wood not be stored in direct contact with the ground under any part of the building, and (4) the use of pressure-treated wood where the use of lumber is required.

EXTERIOR FINISH POINTERS

Poor security control of a building is caused by inherent faults in design. Eliminate outside protrusions to the roof, adequately insulate the roof, eliminate parapet walls where possible, use extreme care in the selection of materials used on the soffits and fascia, and use only approved skylight installations. Four to six feet wide overhangs protect the sides of buildings and are a long-range economy.

Provide adequate scuppers as a part of the roof structure. Install inside downspouts with adequate cleanouts. If outside downspouts are used, the pipe or iron boot should be a minimum of five feet above the ground. If splash blocks are used, the process of anchoring to the building determines the required maintenance. Lightning protection should be provided on chimneys. The use of brick for outside walls is economical. Only tooled joints should be used. Provide weep holes in the lower course of brick.

Install only quality window walls so that they will be kept tight. An economical design is to place the name of the school in cast stone letters set in an outside wall. The outside doors should be hollow metal set in a hollow metal frame. These doors should be without glass inserts and have antipanic hardware.[1] Use a maximum of two windows per classroom. Single and double-hung aluminum windows are economical. Buildings move on account of soil conditions. Aluminum insect screens for toilet and food serving areas and protective screens have durability and relatively good weather resistance. Expansion and slip joints are needed in buildings. The number and kind depend on the size of the building and soil conditions.[2]

The construction of foundations based on soil tests is a paramount consideration. Insist on the best materials and superior installation of roofing materials.

POINTERS FOR BUILDING SPACES

All educational space should be above the ground in a one story or multiple story structure. These spaces within the structure should be constructed as flexibly as possible in order to provide variable grouping of students. Flexibility may be provided in spaces with or without partitions and folding partitions. Dividers, articles, folding screens, demountable panels, and movable storage units are useful devices. The key element in equipment flexibility is seating.

Adequate spaces for toilets, storage, heating, ventilation, and/or air conditioning equipment, custodial help, and teacher lounges are some of the necessary spaces to make a modern school function. An inside incinerator is required in many communities. Space is also needed in the building for yard tools.

POINTERS FOR INTERIOR FINISHES

The type of floor gives a personality to an instructional space. The materials for the classroom floors should be resilient. Many systems prefer vinyl asbestos with not more than 50 per cent reflection. A few schools are installing carpet for covering floors and controlling noise.

---

[1] N. L. George, *Tips for Preplanned Maintenance* (Milwaukee, Wisconsin: School Board Journal, April 1966), p. 26. Copyrighted by the National School Board Association.

[2] N. L. George, *Tips for Replanned Maintenance*, p. 26.

The floors of corridors should be terrazzo or a good resilient material. Tile floors are economical in shower areas. Floors in toilet rooms should be ceramic or quarry tile.

Brick or pre-faced concrete masonry units or structural tile should be used on the walls in the instructional areas to the height of the lower edge of chalkboard. This practice eliminates frequent cleaning and frequent painting of the lower surface. If concrete haydite or cinder block is used on the walls, the joints should be tooled. A special precaution is necessary to carry all classroom walls to the roofs to eliminate the transfer of sound. The use of structural tile or pre-faced masonry units as a base is economical. If the base can have a cove on the floor, cleaning is made easier. A window sill of synthetic marble saves frequent varnishing. If wood is used as trim, it should be stained and kept natural in tone. The walls of corridors with brick or structural or pre-faced tile to a height of five feet four inches and tool jointed are economical. The walls of a cafeteria kitchen should be structural tile or pre-faced tile to full height. The walls of gang toilets with structural glazed tile mosaic or other tile type to a minimum of five feet four inches are easily cleaned. No painting is required. Full height walls of these materials are recommended if money is available. The walls of both the boiler and mechanical rooms may be concrete block with a tooled joint. The walls of the gym should be of impervious material to the top of the doors.

The quality of chalkboards, tackboards, bulletin boards, and tack strips determines the amount of maintenance on these appurtenances. Use sloping tops on lockers in corridors and elsewhere to eliminate furring and facilitate the ease of cleaning. All lockers should be installed on tile bases.

Ceilings.

Ceilings in instructional areas should be five-eighths inch thick acoustical mineral tile. The use of one inch tectum for the ceiling in the corridors is practical. A white insulated metal for ceiling is easy to clean in a cafeteria kitchen. Ceilings of plaster in toilet rooms are economical. Ceilings in shower rooms of cement plaster or ceramic or mosaic tile are easily cleaned.

Doors.

Interior doors with metal frames eliminate termite treatment. Solid wood doors equipped with one way hardware for instructional areas with small rectangular vision strip (except where classroom vision area is adjacent to door) are economical. Door holders on classroom doors can be eliminated. Kick plates installed on the inside of all entrance and classroom doors eliminate early maintenance problems. Operable doors or partitions should be constructed of the desired decibel rating for the intended use or they are not economical.

Safety.

Every school building of more than two classrooms shall be equipped with a suitable fire alarm. A centrally located mechanical system may be used only in one story buildings of not more than eight classrooms. Closed circuit, supervised, or break-glass electrical systems shall be installed in schools of more than eight rooms or more than one story. The fire alarm signal shall be distinct from other call systems. The signal system may be an audio call system. The system installed shall be approved by the Underwriters Laboratories and stations shall be located in shops, chemistry laboratories, food laboratories, kitchens, auditoriums, stages, and in the office of the principal.

Other requirements to promote safety include:

1. Approved fire doors equipped with automatic self-closing devices in openings leading to heating plant rooms, required stair enclosures, projection booths, attics, fan rooms, transformer rooms, and vertical shafts.

2. Wire glass in metal sash in heater and fuel room windows, in the interior windows of high fire hazard areas.

3. Stairs, incombustible in all cases; enclosed if serving more than two stories; no closets located under stairs.

4. Master gas shutoff valves should be installed for groups of three or more outlets.

5. Install electrical pilot lights on outlets for electrically heated devices such as flatirons and gluepots.

6 Exit lights should be installed and kept in operation when the building is occupied.

Color.

The choice of color for interior surfaces is important. The *1964 Guide for Planning School Plants*[3] lists the recommended reflectances of surfaces for schools as follows: ceilings 70–90 per cent, walls 40–60 per cent, chalkboards up to 20 per cent, desks 35–50 per cent, and floors 30–50 per cent. Experience reveals that attractive instructional areas are possible when the painters use these recommendations.

POINTERS FOR CONSTRUCTION

Avoid sharp corners, recesses, and indentations too small for the ordinary cleaning equipment to reach. Provide keys alike and locks master-keyed. Corridor corners where considerable hand truck traffic is expected should be of steel. Allow ample space for storage of supplies and equipment. A need exists for stronger and more durable entrance doors and hinges to cut the cost of repair and replacement; hydraulic hinges are a constant source of trouble. Avoid large unbroken areas of materials with joints which make partial repair or replacement impossible without showing a patch. Install recesses in corridor areas so that drinking fountains and other objects do not protrude over eight inches in the passageways. Omit thresholds at the inner doors on classroom floors.

The building is placed at least 100 feet from the street to prevent the noise of traffic from being a disturbance. Specific noisy areas are isolated. Acoustical considerations are important in administrative areas, corridors, classrooms, libraries, shops, laboratories, and mechanical rooms. Sound control is necessary in gymnasiums, cafeterias, toilets, and music rooms and is especially critical in auditoriums. Special consideration in the planning stage of the acoustical problems in these areas is a basic responsibility. Special consideration must be given to noise following ducts.

POINTERS FOR ELECTRICAL SERVICES

The main service to the building should be underground. Plan ample service capacity for the ultimate building plus 50 per cent expansion. Electrical systems including all wiring, panels, services, feeders, and circuits should be designed to allow for additional loads of at least 15 per cent. Twist-lock receptacles with grounded terminals shall be installed in corridors for custodial cleaning equipment. In corridors electric outlets should be provided on all floors, main lobby,

---

3 *Guide for Planning School Plants* (East Lansing, Michigan: National Council on Schoolhouse Construction, 1964), p. 126.

and basement floor. Adequate floodlights for public use should be mounted on the building. Wiring, ducts, and pipe can be located in corridor walls; overhead installation is preferred. All grounding media should be bonded together. All chimneys should be grounded. Major transformers are best located outside the building.

Panels in halls should be flush type and equipped with locks. Safety lighting and alarm circuits are better taken off the line ahead of the main service switches. The main distribution panel, all secondary panels, and all branch circuits deserve protection by automatic circuit breakers. Panel boxes of the dead-front, metal clad type are preferred. Wiring for 110 volts and 220 volts three phase should be arranged. Astronomical switches should be planned for lighting the exterior of the building and school.

Wiring for bells, program systems, public address systems, and motion picture speakers should be in separate conduits.

Ample duplex outlets must be located in classrooms. At no place in this area should it be necessary to use equipment with an extension cord over six feet long. Avoid the use of extension cords. Duplex outlets in corridors should be 75 feet apart. Strategically located, all-weather electrical outlets are desirable in certain outside locations. Electrical equipment for the maintenance of the site may be attached at these points.

The design of lighting should follow the standards listed in the 1964 Council on Schoolhouse Construction Guide.[4] Winches should be provided for lowering lights in areas with high ceilings.

Lighting maintenance is difficult, so fixtures should be easy to clean, and air circulation is needed around recessed lighting fixtures. Bad starters happen on lighting installations and plastic lighting diffusers discolor. Avoid placing shutoff disconnect switches and valves which are not adjacent to electrical and mechanical equipment. Avoid placing electrical lines and conduits in inaccessible spaces. Telephone and electric floor ducts should be installed in all store and basement areas that could be used as offices.

POINTERS FOR MECHANICAL SERVICES

These vital services of a school plant contain many elements that require meticulous study and careful planning. A few important considerations are listed under the topics of (1) water systems, (2) sanitary facilities, (3) heating facilities, and (4) ventilating facilities. The provision of these elements of adequate size and quality forestalls many maintenance problems.

Water Systems.

A potable water supply of from 10 to 30 gallons per day per student (depending on total building facilities) has to be distributed to appropriate locations. An adequate system for the disposal of human and other wastes is essential. Work sinks require hot and cold water. A swivel faucet detailed to serve as a hose bib, high enough for a 14 quart pail in the sink, is good equipment in a custodial room. Sill cocks on the outside of the building every 100 feet for garden hose connections are a long term economy. Extreme care has to be exercised to avoid cross connections between potable and non-potable supplies of water.

Cooling systems which provide 190 gallons of drinking water per hour per 1,000 students are adequate. The drinking fountain bowl should be vitreous china or stainless steel. The water should issue from the jet at an angle of 45 degrees.

---

4 *Guide for Planning School Plants* (National Council on Schoolhouse Construction), p. 126.

Each hot and cold water riser shall be separately valved with drains and valves at the bottom of each one. All risers shall be properly valved. In the case of toilet risers, valves should be installed for branches at each floor so that all toilets will not have to be shut down in case of the failure of one fixture control valve. Automatic flow control devices will eliminate guessing as to proper pipe sizes, make it possible to figure accurately peak requirements, and conserve on overall costs of water, particularly heating of water.

Sanitary Facilities.

Separate gang toilet facilities should be located for each sex on each floor and placed not more than 150 feet from the most distant instructional station. Floor drains and hose bibs are basic elements for ease of cleaning. Mirrors should not be placed over lavatories. Soap dispensers, hand-drying facilities, bookshelves, and waste containers are minimum equipment. Toilet room windows should be fly screened and have colored glass. Wall hung urinals and wall hung closets have long term economy. Lavatories may or may not be supplied with hot water.

Heating Facilities.

The central boiler should not contain any batteries. Heating should be fully automatic with burners of the highest efficiency. Blower motors, controls, fans, dampers, and filters should be so installed as to be easily accessible for servicing.

Avoid the location of a boiler in a basement area. Plan this room large enough to replace tubes without removing a wall or cutting tubes. The heating plant should be designed for failsafe operation. Install the master gas valve outside the building for the use of the local fire department. Classrooms and/or administration areas should be served by centralized heating or cooling equipment constructed with the fewest possible parts which require periodical maintenance.

Specialized areas such as gymnasiums, auditoriums, and cafeterias should have zoned heating. The only extra expense is the installation of valves. This provision is an economical operating expenditure as the total building will not have to be heated when only one part or parts of the building are used.

Ventilating Facilities.

Positive mechanical exhaust ventilation should be provided for these areas: (1) toilet rooms, (2) food service rooms, (3) science rooms, and (4) locker rooms.

POINTERS ON EQUIPMENT AND FURNITURE

The equipment and furniture in each instructional area are sized to fit their users. At least five categories of equipment exist: (1) fixed equipment incorporated in the building contract, (2) fixed equipment other than the integral parts of the building requiring utility connections, (3) built-in equipment not requiring utility connections but a part of the building, (4) stationary equipment which is fastened to floor, and (5) movable equipment and furniture.

All equipment and furniture should be attractive and colorful. The classroom furniture should be free from sharp corners, leg interferences, awkward shapes, and bulkiness. Safety is a prime factor. If possible, some of the seating should be stackable. The surfaces of furniture and equipment should have a matte finish. Stainless steel glides on the chairs should be a minimum of one and one-fourth inches in diameter.

SUMMARY

The considerations that pertain to a school building and its equipment number into the hundreds. Forethought in the selection of the proper materials and equipment for each space is necessary to make the school plant adequate. The failure to apply the best current practices soon necessitates an extra expenditure of money. This expense may be a capital outlay or a maintenance expenditure which will be greater than the prescription in the original plans and specifications of the school plant.

APPENDICES

Appendix A.

NOTES FOR CHAPTER 2.

These materials are given as aids to responsible maintenance personnel who make decisions concerning the maintenance of school plants. These instruments assist in identifying defects in the several school plants of the district.

NOTE   PAGE

1.   School Site - Master Checklist........................... 150

2.   Exterior of Building - Master Checklist............... 151-153

3.   Circulation areas-Interior of Building-Master Check-
     list.. 154-155

4.   Sanitary Facilities-Interior of Building-Master Check-
     list.. 156

5.   Boiler Rooms-Interior of Building-Master Checklist........ 157

6.   General Classroom-Interior of Building-Master Check-
     list.. 158-159

7.   Special Classrooms-Interior of Building-Master Check-
     list..160-161

8.   Large Meeting Areas-Interior of Building-Master Check-
     list.. 162

9.   Custodial Quarters-Interior of Building-Master Checklist.. 163

10. Administrative and Health Areas,Interior of Building,
     Master Checklist.. 164

11. Electrical Services-Master Checklist..................... 165

12. Inspection Checklist..................................... 166

13. Principal's Annual Request for Maintenance............ 167-168

NOTE 1. SCHOOL SITE – MASTER CHECKLIST

_____
Name of School

_____
Date

	Good	Bad	Remarks
I. Drainage:			
Entire area			
New buildings			
II. Soil:			
Top soil			
III. Special Areas:			
Play areas			
Apparatus			
Hard surfaced			
Loading areas			
Foot scrapers			
IV. Service Areas:			
Parking			
Bicycles			
Cars			
Drivers			
Lighting – night			
Sidewalks			
On grade			
Off grade			
V. Landscaping			
VI. Fencing:			
Fence			
Gates			
Posts (barrier)			
VII. Miscellaneous:			
Flag pole			
Retaining walls			
VIII. Other			

_____
Employee Checking

NOTE 2. EXTERIOR OF BUILDING – MASTER CHECKLIST

Name of School

Date

The most vulnerable of all exterior
surfaces to the effects of the weather
is the roof. Every roof is a separate
problem and should receive regular
inspection.

	Good	Bad	Remarks
I. Roof:			
A. Condition of roof			
Blisters			
Seams			
Cracked ridges			
Hollows			
Drains			
Coping			
B. Miscellaneous			
Condition of cornices			
Gutters			
Headers			
Flashings			
Downspouts			
Drains			
Parapet walls			
Copings			
Attic (vented)			
Dormers			
Chimney			
Condition			
Spark arrestors			
Skylights			
II. Walls:			
Plumb			
Settlement cracks			
Seepage			
Lintals			
Exposed surfaces painted			
Waterproofing			
Dampproofing			

	Good	Bad	Remarks
III. Foundation:			
Condition			
Drainage			
Need for underpinning			
IV. Openings			
A. Windows and Transoms			
Condition of paint			
Condition of panes			
Condition of Sills			
Caulking			
Glazing			
Operation			
Weatherstripping			
Screens			
Protective			
Fly			
Ledges			
B. Doors			
Condition of paint			
Condition of doors			
Frames			
Glass			
Weatherstripping			
Checks			
Holders			
Anti-panic hardware			
Kick plates			
Thresholds			
C. Entrances and Porches			
Condition of paint			
Steps			
Stonework			
Ramps			
Platform			
Overhang			
Lamp posts			
D. Fire Escapes			
Condition of paint			
Solidity			
V. Fire Hydrants			
Condition			
VI. Signal Devices			

MASTER CHECKLIST - NOTE 2 (Cont'd.)

		Good	Bad	Remarks
VII.	Lighting			
VIII.	Hose Bibs - 100' apart			
IX.	Other			

———————————————————
Employee checking

NOTE 3 – INTERIOR OF BUILDING CIRCULATION AREAS – MASTER CHECKLIST

	Name of School

_____

Date

	Good	Bad	Remarks
I. Walls			
II. Stairs			
Treads			
Handrails			
Stair lighting			
III. Exit Facilities			
Marked			
IV. Floors			
Condition			
Baseboards			
Floor mats			
V. Traffic signs			
Marked			
VI. Lockers			
Condition			
VII. Fire Apparatus			
Extinguishers			
Other			
VIII. Trim in corridors			
Condition			
IX. Bulletin Board			
X. Display areas			
XI. Trophy cases			
XII. Duplex receptacles			
XIII. Lighting			
XIV. Heating			

154

MASTER CHECKLIST - NOTE 3 (Cont'd.)

		Good	Bad	Remarks
XV.	Drinking fountains (one for each 75 students)			
	Side mounting bi-level			
	usage			
XVI.	Dispensers			
	Condition			
XVII.	Adjacent floor area			
XVIII.	Doors			
	Kick plates			
	Knobs			
	Glass below panic bar			
	Panic lock			
XIX.	Miscellaneous			
	Shoe cleaners			
	Divider			
	Gates			
XX.	Other			

_____
Employee Checking

155

NOTE 4.   INTERIOR OF BUILDING SANITARY FACILITIES – MASTER CHECKLIST

_____

Name of School

_____

Date

	Good	Bad	Remarks
I. Toilets			
Floor			
Walls			
Ceiling			
Windows			
Doors			
Partitions – Toilet stall			
Ventilation			
II. Lights			
III. Heating			
IV. Fixtures			
Stools			
Adequacy			
Siphon breaker			
Open front seats			
Lavatories			
Urinals			
Mirrors			
Tissue holders			
Towel holders			
Towel receptacles			
V. Metal handles on faucets			
VI. Other			

_____

Employee checking

NOTE 5.   INTERIOR OF BUILDING BOILER ROOMS — MASTER CHECKLIST.
          AND APPURTENANCES

		Name of School

		Date

	Good	Bad	Remarks
I. Fire resistant materials			
II. Condition of doors			
Interior			
Exterior			
III. Floor			
IV. Condition of paint			
V. Cleanliness			
VI. Incinerator			
VII. Apparatus			
Boilers, condition			
Sump pumps			
Re-circulating pumps			
Hot water heaters			
Breeching and/or chimney			
VIII. Radiators			
IX. Valves			
X. Thermostats			
XI. Pipe covering			
XII. Unit ventilators			
XIII. Other			

Employee checking

NOTE 6.   INTERIOR OF BUILDING GENERAL CLASSROOMS - MASTER CHECKLIST

Name of School

Date

		Good	Bad	Remarks
I.	Floors			
II.	Walls			
	Paint			
	Plaster			
III.	Ceiling			
	Paint			
	Acoustical			
IV.	Windows			
	Panes			
	Sills			
	Shades			
	Drapes, if any			
	Curtains			
	Venetian blinds			
V.	Chalkboard			
VI.	Tackboard			
VII.	Map Holder			
VIII.	Flag Holder			
IX.	Lighting			
X.	Heating			
XI.	Ventilation			
XII.	Built-ins			
	Storage			
	Lockers			
XIII.	Electrical Receptacles			
XIV.	Shelving			

158

MASTER CHECKLIST - NOTE 6 (Cont'd)

		Good	Bad	Remarks
XV.	Bookcases			
XVI.	Sink Tops			
	Faucets			
	Drinking fountains			
XVII.	Hardware			
	Locks on doors			
	Locks on cabinets			
	Locks on windows			
	Window lifts			
	Door holders			
	Push plates			
	Kick plates			
	Door butts			
XVIII.	Trim - wood			
	Evidence of termites			
XIX.	Other			

_____

Employee checking

NOTE 7.   INTERIOR OF BUILDING SPECIAL ROOMS — MASTER CHECKLIST

Name of School
_____

Date

(Special classrooms; science, home training, business, art, shops)

	Good	Bad	Remarks
I. Floors			
II. Ceilings			
III. Walls			
IV. Windows			
Panes			
Sills			
Shades			
Drapes, if any			
Curtains			
Venetian blinds			
V. Chalkboard			
VI. Tackboard			
VII. Flag Holders			
VIII. Chart Holders			
IX. Lighting			
X. Heating			
XI. Ventilation			
General area			
Storage areas			
XII. Condition of storage rooms			
XIII. Equipment			
XIV. Electrical receptacles			

MASTER CHECKLIST - NOTE 7 (Cont'd)

		Good	Bad	Remarks
XV.	Shelving			
XVI.	Bookcases			
XVII.	Other			

Employee checking

NOTE 8.   INTERIOR OF BUILDING LARGE MEETING AREAS – MASTER CHECKLIST

	Name of School

Date

	Good	Bad	Remarks
I. Auditorium			
All items in Note 7			
Seating			
Curtains			
Stage			
Cleanliness			
Storage			
II. Gymnasium			
All items in Note 7			
Bleachers			
Folding			
Permanent			
Dressing rooms			
Cleanliness			
Lockers			
Showers			
Toilets			
Drains			
Storage areas			
III. Food Service			
All areas in Note 7			
Social areas			
Kitchen			
Storage			
Apparatus			
Teachers' dining area			
Grease traps			
IV. Other			

Employee checking

NOTE 9.   INTERIOR OF BUILDING CUSTODIAL QUARTERS – MASTER CHECKLIST
         LIST

_____
Name of School

_____
Date

		Good	Bad	Remarks
(Custodial quarters, storage spaces, and workrooms)				
I.	Storage of supplies			
II.	Cleanliness			
III.	Service sinks (hot and cold water)			
IV.	Shelving			
V.	Electrical outlets			
VI.	Lighting			
VII.	Other			

_____
Employee checking

NOTE 10. INTERIOR OF BUILDING ADMINISTRATIVE AND HEALTH AREAS-
MASTER CHECKLIST

_____
Name of School

_____
Date

	Good	Bad	Remarks
I. Floors			
II. Wall			
III. Ceiling			
IV. Lighting			
V. Paint			
VI. Toilets			
VII. Sinks			
VIII. Other			

_____
Employee checking

NOTE 11. ELECTRICAL SERVICES - MASTER CHECKLIST

_____
Name of School

_____
Date

	Good	Bad	Remarks
I. Lighting			
II. Underground service			
III. Services			
Audio visual			
Bell and signal system			
Outside signal system			
Program clocks			
Public address system			
Telephone			
Television			
Fire alarm system			
IV. Flood lighting entrances			
V. Electric ranges			
VI. Electric refrigerators			
VII. Electric dishwashers			
VIII. Lightning protection			
IX. Duplex outlets			
X. Other			

_____
Employee checking

NOTE 12-INSPECTION CHECKLIST

1. Ceiling

    A. Plastered
    B. Tile
    C. Lay-in
    D. Acoustical

        (1) Paint peeling
        (2) Needs painting
        (3) Loose
        (4) Missing
        (5) Damaged
        (6) Needs patching
        (7) Stained

2. Walls *Wainscot
    **Above Wainscot

    A. Block
    B. Plastered
    C. Brick
    D. Tile
    E. Concrete
    F. Wood
    G. Plasterboard or
       Cement Asbestos

        (1) Paint peeling
        (2) Needs painting
        (3) Stained by water
        (4) Cracked
        (5) Needs patching
        (6) Dirty
        (7) Chipped or damaged

3. Floors

    A. Tile-Asphalt or vinyl
    B. Concrete
    C. Wooden
    D. Terrazzo
    E. Ceramic tile
    F. Quarry tile

        (1) Needs replacing
        (2) Missing
        (3) Damaged or worn
        (4) Evidence of termites
        (5) Needs sanding
        (6) Cracked
        (7) Mastic appears through
            cracks
        (8) Uneven

4. Light Fixtures

    A. Incandescent
    B. Fluorescent

        (1) Bulb or tubes
            missing
        (2) Fixtures damaged
        (3) Fixture missing
        (4) Bulb or tube not
            working
        (5) Insufficient
            lighting
        (6) Needs refasten-
            ing
        (7) Fixtures dirty

5. Doors

    A. Wooden
    B. Metal clad
    C. Fiberglass clad
    D. Aluminum
    E. Overhead or
       rolling

        (1) Need painting
        (2) Scratched or
            damaged
        (3) Door closer
            damaged
        (4) Glass needs re-
            placing

        (5) Needs replacing
        (6) Closes improperly
        (7) Faded

6. Windows

    A. Wooden
    B. Steel
    C. Aluminum
    D. Glass
    E. Shades

        (1) Needs Painting
        (2) Needs replacing
        (3) Needs glazing
        (4) Needs weatherstrip
        (5) Painted shut
        (6) Hardware missing
        (7) Need repairing
        (8) Need sash cord
        (9) BB holes

7. Lavatories

    A. Partitions
    B. Urinals
    C. Other fixtures
    D. Floor
    E. Ventilation

        (1) Corroded
        (2) Needs paint-
            ing
        (3) Needs re-
            placing
        (4) Not working
        (5) Mechanical
            needed
        (6) Not being
            used
        (7) Dirty

8. Roofs
        (1) Leaks
        (2) Tar dripping
            into room

9. Stairs

    A. Concrete
    B. Tiled
    C. Wooden
    D. Terrazzo
    E. Guard rails

        (1) Spawling
        (2) Slick
        (3) Broken
        (4) Loose
        (5) Cracked
        (6) Needed
        (7) Worn

10. Skylights

    A. Plastic
    B. Glass

        (1) Dirty
        (2) Leaking
        (3) Needs re-
            placing
        (4) Eliminate
        (5) Need shades
            repaired
        (6) Needs shades
        (7) Cracked

NOTE 13 – PRINCIPAL'S ANNUAL REQUEST FOR MAINTENANCE

SCHOOL CODE_____   SCHOOL NAME_____

(Please fill out three copies and return all three to this office)

Modifications and Repairs

LOCATION OR ROOM NUMBER	EXACT DESCRIPTION OF WORK TO BE DONE	YOUR PRIORITY
B-207	Replace Blackboard	1
	Display case on cabinet on west end of room needs to be torn out and a large bulletin board placed on the wall. (Display case was marked by vandalism and it takes up too much needed room)	3
	Cabinet door to be repaired (Southwest corner of room)	2
	Tile in floor to be replaced (west end)	3
	Formica needs to be replaced around	2
	sink also leak around faucet	1
B-206	Replace window glass	2
	Supply cabinet in northeast corner is in bad condition as a result of leakage during rain.	3
	Drainboard needs change due to chemical stains.	2
A-201	Replace mirror above sink in S.E. corner	3
	Replace glass in 3 windows	2
	Repair six screens	1
	Repair doors on cabinet in S.W. corner	2
A-100	Replace window glass in 4 windows	1
A-101	Paint part of north wall	2
	Replace window glass in 1 window	1
A-108	Replace tile on wall by door S.W. corner	2
	Replace window glass in 4 windows	1
	Tile needs to be replaced on bottom of cabinet located in N.W. corner of room	3
B-204	Repair ceiling (roof leaks in spots)	2

LOCATION OR ROOM NUMBER	EXACT DESCRIPTION OF WORK TO BE DONE	YOUR PRIORITY
	Repair hot water faucet	1
	Also cold water faucet	
	Replace linoleum around sink	2
	Replace mirror over sink	2
	Replace bulletin board on south wall	1
	Repair lock on room door	1

Appendix B

NOTES FOR CHAPTER 6.

This material is given as an aid to the school administrators for the formulation of a report of all the school plants in a district. The coding systems should assist in the preparation of the first records as to the number of items for a local report and as to how these items may be coded. Similar codes may be applied to each class of equipment classifications in the local district.

NOTE   PAGE

1. School Plant Record Coding System and Definitions..... 170-184

2. Partial Summary of Individual Plant Records............... 185

3. Painting Records.. 186

4. Coding System – Electronics........................... 187-190

5. Partial Summary Electronics Equipment and Maintenance
    Record.. 191

6. Code for Motorized Equipment.......................... 192-195

7. Partial Summary – Motorized Equipment..................... 196

8. Work Order..197-198

9. Time Card... 199

10. Stock Requisition... 200

11. Maintenance Personnel Information......................... 201

12. Absentee Record.. 202

Note 1. SCHOOL PLANT RECORD CODING SYSTEM

AND DEFINITIONS

CARD NUMBER 1 - LAND FACILITIES

Total Site ....Area in square acres to the nearest hundredth.

Year Acquired ....Last two digits of year in which original
site was purchased.

Year Additions ....Last two digits of year in which addition
Acquired   up to the third was acquired.

Last Addition ....The number of the last addition and the
last two digits of the year in which it was
purchased.

Reversion ....0 - Reversionary clause on original site.
1 -   "   "   "   1st addition to
site
2 -   "   "   "   2nd   "   "
site
3 -   "   "   "   3rd   "   "
site
9 -   "   "   to original and sub-
sequent additions
to site.

Total Cost of Original Site and Additions - Total cost of site at
the time it was purchased. Costs are re-
corded to the nearest dollar.

Cost of Parking and Pickup Area - All costs connected with the
initial construction or extension of
parking areas and drives for vehicular
traffic, including curbs and gutters. Costs
are recorded to the nearest dollar.

Total Cost of Water and Sewage System - All costs connected with
the initial installation or extension of
outdoor water and sewer systems for the
site, involving such work as installation
of pipes, pumps, drinking fountains, sewers,
septic tanks and wells that are not part of
a building's service system. Costs are
recorded to the nearest dollar.

Total Cost of Instruction or Play Areas on Site - Outdoor instruction or play areas are those site improvements developed and equipped for instructional or play activities such as playgrounds, athletic fields, and outdoor swimming pools. Costs are recorded to the nearest dollar.

Total Cost Of Fences and Retaining Walls on Site - All costs connected with the initial construction or extension of fences and retaining walls on any part of the site. Costs recorded to the nearest dollar.

Total Cost of Landscaping Site - Landscaping includes such work as preparing landscape plans, soil analysis, preparing the grounds for planting, planting grass, shrubs, or trees, and general grading that is not specifically for outdoors service systems, play areas, fences and retaining walls, or construction of buildings. Costs recorded to the nearest dollar.

Total Cost of Miscellaneous Improvements - All costs connected with the initial or additional installation of miscellaneous site improvements, such as flagpoles, outdoor rifle ranges, drainage ditches, signs, and firebreaks. Also included are any off-site improvements such as roads or sidewalks that are not part of some specific improvements to a site. Costs recorded to the nearest dollar.

CARD NUMBER 2 - GENERAL BUILDING DATA

TYPE OF CONSTRUCTION

Code

1 - Fire Resistive

A building constructed entirely of fire-resistive materials; or a building with fire-resistive walls and partitions, floors, stairways, and ceiling. A building of this type may have wood finish, wood or composition floor surfaces, and wood roof construction over a fire-resistive ceiling.

2 - Semi Fire-Resistive

A building with fire-resistive exterior and bearing walls and fire-resistive corridor and stairway, walls, floors, and ceilings, but with ordinary construction otherwise, such as combustible floors, partitions, roofs, and finish.

3 - Combustible

An all-frame building; a building with fire-resistive veneer on wood frame; or one with fire-resistive bearing walls, but otherwise of combustible material.

4 - Mixed Construction

A building with one or more sections of one type of construction and one or more sections of another type of construction.

RATED CAPACITY

Elementary Schools - Thirty students per regular classroom plus fifty students per kindergarten room.

Secondary Schools - Thirty students per teaching station. Large areas such as gymnasiums are counted as two teaching stations.

CARD NUMBER 2 - GENERAL BUILDING DATA

NUMBER OF ROOMS - Total number of rooms available for instruction including special areas such as shops, gymnasiums, kindergartens, and science rooms but excluding such areas as libraries, auditoriums, and cafetoriums.

GROSS FLOOR AREA - The gross floor area of a building is the sum of the areas at each floor level included within the principal outside faces of the exterior walls, neglecting architectural setbacks or projections.

YEAR OF ORIGINAL BUILDING - The last two digits of the year in which the school district became the owner of the building. For a building constructed by school district employees, it is the date construction was completely acceptable.

YEAR OF ADDITIONS - Last two digits of the year in which each addition, up to a total of three additions, became the property of the school board.

LAST ADDITION - The number of the last addition to the building and the last two digits of the year in which the addition became the property of the school board.

BUILDING SIZE

Basement - The net area in square feet of any floor that is below grade level on all sides and has clear standing head room of at least 6 feet 6 inches.

Area of First Floor - The net area in square feet of the first floor, beginning at the bottom of the building, that is at or above grade level along at least one entire side and has clear standing head room of at least 6 feet 6 inches.

Area of Each Additional Floor - The net area in square feet of each floor above the first floor with clear standing head room of at least 6 feet 6 inches.

COST OF BUILDING - The cost of the building is the actual cost
to the school board in acquiring the building, regardless of how the building may have been acquired. Costs
are listed to the nearest dollar.

CONTRACT COST - The cost for the actual erection of the building
including built-in equipment. Listed to the nearest
dollar.

ARCHITECTURAL-ENGINEERING COSTS - The cost for architectural and
engineering services or plans, drawings, specifications, and consultative services rendered in connection
with the construction of the building. Listed to the
nearest dollar.

CONSULTANT-LEGAL COSTS - The costs for legal services and educational consultive services rendered in connection with
the construction of a building. Listed to the nearest
dollar.

INSPECTION COSTS - The cost of inspection services rendered by
the board of education. Listed to the nearest dollar.

CARD NUMBER 3 - SERVICE SYSTEMS

TYPE OF CONSTRUCTION

Code

    1 - Fire Resistive

    2 - Semi Fire Resistive

    3 - Combustible

    4 - Mixed Construction

Use Code

    00 - Kindergarten

    01 - First Grade

    06 - Sixth Grade

    07 - Seventh Grade

    08 - Eighth Grade

    09 - Ninth Grade

    10 - Tenth Grade

    12 - Twelfth Grade

    13 - Manpower and/or
         other adult classes

Kind Code

    01 - Instruction

    02 - Stadium

    03 - Central Administration

    04 - Pupil Transportation
         Building

    05 - Maintenance Building

    06 - Warehouse

    07 - Library Services

Availability Code

    1 - For Complete Occupancy

    2 - For Partial Occupancy

    3 - Abandoned for Occupancy

Mobility Code

    1 - Permanent

    2 - Portable

    3 - Demountable

    4 - Mobile

Heating System - Central

    A central heating system is a heating system whereby the heat is conveyed to various parts of a building through pipes or ducts leading from a central source.

Code

    1 - Radiators or Convectors

    2 - Unit Ventilators

    3 - Warm Air Furnace

    4 - Fan Blast or Forced Air

    5 - Radiant Pump

    6 - Heat Pump

    7 - Combination of Above

Heating System - Local Zone

    A local zone heating system is a heating system whereby a building's heat is supplied by two or more heating units each of which is designed and installed to function independently of the other units as a central heating unit for a given part of the building only.

Code

    1 - Radiators and Convectors

    2 - Unit Ventilators

    3 - Gravity Warm Air Furnace

    4 - Fan Blast or Forced Air

    5 - Radiant Panel

    6 - Heat Pump

    7 - Split System. A heating system that combines a forced air system with in-the-room radiation.

8 - Room-fired heaters

9 - Combination of the above

Source of Heat

Code

1 - Wood

2 - Coal

3 - Natural gas

4 - Oil

5 - Electricity

6 - Manufactured gas

7 - Liquified petroleum gas

Cooling Systems

Code

1 - Central cooling system whole building

2 - Central cooling system part of building

3 - Local zone cooling system whole building

4 - Local zone cooling system part of building

5 - Individual cooling units whole building

6 - Individual cooling units part of building

Ventilating Systems

Code

1 - Window ventilator

2 - Gravity ventilator

3 - Mechanical exhaust

4 - Mechanical supply

5 - Combination of above

CARD NUMBER 3 – SERVICE SYSTEMS (Continued)

Water Supply

   Code

     1 – Municipal

     2 – Drilled well

     3 – Dug well

     4 – Other

     5 – Disaster water supply

Sewage Disposal

   Code

     1 – Municipal

     2 – Septic tank

     3 – Filter-sludge bed

     4 – Aeration

     5 – Other

Electrical System

   Code

     1 – Completely wired

     2 – Partially wired

     3 – Auxiliary lighting system

Communications System

   Telephone Code

     1 – Completely

     2 – Partially

Speaker System Code

     1 – Completely

     2 – Partially

Program System Code

     1 – Completely

     2 – Partially

CARD NUMBER 3 - SERVICE SYSTEMS (Continued)

Television System Code

1 - T.V. Receiving System

2 - Program originator provision

3 - Both of the above

Fire Protection

Number of fire alarm boxes

Number of sprinkler heads

Number of fire hose cabinets

Number of fire extinguisher stations

Elevator Code

1 - Primarily passenger

2 - Primarily freight

Fire and Security Signal Systems

Code

0 - None

1 - Tone on speaker system

2 - Manually operated electric program bells

3 - Manually operated mechanical single stroke gong

4 - Electrically operated fire alarm bells

5 - Manually operated electric noise making device

6 - Voice on speaker system

Number of Refrigerated Fountains - The total number of refrigeration units in a building. Some units will cool water for more than one bubbler head whereas others have a single bubbler.

Number of Classroom Sinks - The total number of sinks installed in rooms including those in special areas such as art, homemaking, and shops.

Number of Custodial Sinks - The total number of sinks located in maintenance and operation rooms in a building.

Number of Bubbler Heads - The total number of bubblers in a building including those located on classroom sinks.

Number of Lavatories - The total number of lavatories located in a building including those in food service areas.

Number of Stools - The total number of toilet stools located in a building including those in adjunct toilets.

Number of Urinals - The total number of urinals located in a building including those in adjunct toilets. Trough urinals will be counted as three regular urinals.

Shower Heads - The total number of shower heads located in a building including those in adjunct shower rooms.

Enclosed Circulation Area - The total area in square feet of all circulation areas inside a building, consisting of such areas as corridors, including extensions into deep recessed doors or entryways; equivalent floor opening area at each floor level for stairs, elevators, ramps, and escalators, and foyer and vestibule areas, including any recessed entrance described as part of the gross area.

Outside Passageways - The total area in square feet of enclosed or unenclosed covered passageways which are connected to the building but lie outside the principal exterior walls. This area is not included in the gross floor area of the building.

Number and Area of Maintenance and Operation Rooms

A maintenance and operation area is an area designed, or adapted, for use in making repairs to a school plant and keeping it open and ready for use. They include such areas as furnace rooms, pump rooms, fan rooms, and other mechanical service areas; and fuel storage rooms, custodial quarters, receiving areas, building work or repair shops, custodial service closets, and other similar building service areas.

Number and Area of Separate Toilet Rooms

Number of separate toilet rooms - the total number of toilet rooms in a building that do not open into and serve as adjuncts to other facilities in the building.

Area of separate toilet rooms - the total area in square feet of toilet rooms in a building that do not serve as adjuncts to other facilities.

CARD NUMBER 4 - BUILDING FACILITIES

Number and Area of Regular Classrooms

A regular classroom is a classroom designed, or adapted, in such a manner that it can be used to house any class that does not require special built-in equipment tailored to its specific needs.

The total area in square feet of all regular classrooms in a building including any storage and other service areas opening into, and serving as adjuncts to, particular classrooms. The area is measured between the principal wall faces at or near floor level plus wall case or alcove spaces, or both, opening into and designed to serve the activity carried on in that area.

Number and Area of Kindergarten Rooms

A kindergarten room is a special classroom designed, or provided with special built-in equipment, for use by a group or class that is organized to provide educational experiences for children for the years preceding the first grade.

The total area in sqaure feet includes any storage and other service areas opening into, and serving as adjuncts to, particular kindergarten rooms.

Number and Area of Science Rooms

A science room is a special classroom designed or provided with special built-in equipment for pupil participation in learning activities involving scientific experimentation and other experiences.

The total area in square feet includes any storage and other service areas opening into and serving as adjuncts to particular laboratories.

Number and Area of Industrial Arts and Vocational Education Rooms

Industrial arts and vocational education rooms are special classrooms designed or provided with special built-in equipment for learning activities in such fields as mechanics, woodworking, electrical trades, radio, plumbing, air conditioning, etc.

The area in square feet of these rooms includes any storage and other service areas opening into and serving as adjuncts to particular shoprooms.

Number and Area of Technical Education Rooms

Technical education rooms are specialized classrooms designed or provided with special built-in equipment for learning activities in such fields as electronics, technical drawing and cosmetology.

The total area in square feet includes any storage and other service areas opening into, and serving as adjuncts to, particular technical education areas.

Number and Area of Homemaking Rooms

A homemaking room is a special classroom designed, or provided with special built-in equipment, for learning activities involving such things as the selection, preparation, serving, conservation, and storage of food; the selection, care, renovation, and making of clothing; the care and guidance of children; the selection, use, and conservation of home equipment; and the selection and care of the house and its furnishings.

The total area in square feet includes any storage and other service areas opening into, and serving as adjuncts to, particular homemaking classrooms.

Number and Area of Music Rooms

A music room is a special classroom designed, or provided with special built-in equipment, for learning activities involving choral and instrumental music.

The areas of practice rooms, robe rooms, music library rooms, and instrument storage rooms are included in the area of music rooms but are not counted as individual music rooms. The total area is given in square feet.

Number and Area of Special Education Rooms

A special education room is a classroom designed, or provided with special built-in equipment, specifically for accommodating classes organized for the particular purpose of providing instruction to exceptional children. Examples are sight-saving classrooms, classrooms for children with defective hearing, and orthopedic classrooms. Classrooms provided for mentally deficient children are included in this category.

The total area in square feet of special classrooms for exceptional children in a building includes any

182

storage and other service areas opening into, and serving as adjuncts to, particular special classrooms for exceptional children.

Number and Area of Business Education Classrooms

A business education classroom is a classroom designed, or provided with special built-in equipment, specifically for accommodating classes organized for learning activities in such subjects as Business Machines, Typing, Shorthand and Transcription, Bookkeeping, Clerical Practice, Business Law, Business Mathematics, Business English, Distributive Education, and General Business.

Number and Area of Administrative Rooms

An administration area is an area devoted to school business, pupil personnel management, or public relations activities of a school, or a combination of these activities, where such an area is not designated for other purposes. Storage and other service areas opening into, and serving as adjuncts to, a particular school administration area are considered as parts of that area. The kinds of areas included are the principal's office which includes areas for administrative, secretarial, and clerical assistance; guidance area; clinics; and miscellaneous areas such as conference areas, instructional storage, and textbook storage.

The number of administrative areas does not include closets, toilets, and similar spaces serving as adjuncts to a particular room. The total area in square feet includes any storage or other service areas opening into, and serving as adjuncts to, particular administrative area.

Area of Library or Instructional Media Center

The total area in square feet of school library areas in a building including any storage and other service areas opening into, and serving as adjuncts, to the library area.

Area of Auditorium

The total area in square feet of auditoriums of a building, including the stage, dressing room, balcony, storage, and other service areas opening into, and serving as adjuncts to, the auditorium.

Number and Area of Gymnasiums

The total area in square feet includes any training, storage, or other service areas opening into, and serving as adjuncts to, the gymnasium.

Cafeteria/Cafetorium Area

The total area in square feet includes any storage or other service areas opening into, and serving as adjuncts to, the cafeteria or cafetorium.

SCHOOL CODE	TYPE OF CONSTR.	RATED CAPACITY	NO. RMS.	GROSS FLOOR AREA	YR. ORIG. BLDG.	YR. OF ADMN. 1st	2nd	3rd	LST. ADD. NO.	LST. ADD. YR.	BSMT.	BUILDING SIZE 1st FLR.	OTHERS	TOTAL	CONTRACT	ARCH. ENG.	CONSULT. LEGAL	INSP.
*33	1																	
105	2	790	25	75062	94	52	55				6486	47657	12761	388225	380174	7156		895
110	1	610	19	41702	49	49	51	53	5	56		38415		504404	476889	25746		1770
120	1	350	11	33141	53	54	56					30145		364779	343683	19378		1718
125	1	460	16	17750	56	37	39	53				16590	11991	213331	201922	11105	150	303
130	2	60	6	28058	31	27					470	12655		283303	218507	14535		2446
135	1	760	24	11435	26	51	53	56				9700		59884	56495	3390		2171
140	1	550	17	43846	51	55	58					39753		518370	489296	26628		
150	2	230	7	31035	55	49						28516	15049	460357	434174	23880		
155	1	530	17	8559	43	30	40				7711	7845	8545	67738	63904	3614		
160	1	650	21	32829	28	23	34	37				14972		175206	165286	9917		2487
165	1	960	30	37672	10	56	57	63	4	30		16470		155574	151511	8063	580	234
170	1	490	15	46307	53	49	50	53			739	43215	11403	550539	518829	28643	1802	
175	1	790	24	32346	34	11	19	20				16017	14934	419670	395695	21939		
180	1	440	14	45795	09	49	49	58			11789	13077	9124	166977	156888	10089		543
185	1	440	14	29676	30	49	53					17466	10904	305343	289111	16232		
190	1	760	24	24902	29	23	30	33				11327	20187	261923	248390	13533		83
193	2	360	12	47395	22	64					7179	21769	11318	242567	221606	12785		
195	1	500	16	19218	55	28	30					17237		151287	195094	8563		
200	2	200	6	34042	11	50						11667		144601	142724	7118		
205	2	470	15	11021	49	57	58					9501	13428	249072	137483	13087	942	
210	1	440	14	25947	50	03	40	48			8291	23658		262118	228583	13988		
215	2	440	14	31689	94	10	19					14085	8064	81692	248131	3844	2428	
220	2	880	28	28298	10	51	52	53	5	58	1854	8258		534748	78648	26709		
225	3	320	10	45569	49	40						41939		81281	505611	4601		1732
230	2	520	16	23098	36	55						20233		365826	76681	17546		1249
235	1	320	10	27321	54	55	58					25141		264739	346548	13685		
240	1	320	10	19573	52	30					1143	17594	8320	106550	249805	6031		
244	1	290	9	21043	27	56	58	59	4	64	1166	8348		265816	100519	14201		
245	1	380	12	20078	54	30	49					14891		197435	248429	9981		
250	1	550	11	25079	27	56						12001	8857	275361	187455	14288		1299
255	1	580	18	20560	51	19	28	30			1538	19185	15199	155677	259775	8536		
260	4	550	17	36270	11	55	63					15205	8835	516692	142267	24089		2190
263	1	290	9	38084	52	30			5	50		26128		239099	437990	12255		1114
265	1	620	20	15862	63	63					5320	14506		214283	222815	10177		
268	2	760	24	46590	23	28	33				365	18455	18060	562173	204106	29653	663	2641
270	1	500	16	35102	60	52	53	54			1403	33345		216490	528228	11956		
275	1	640	20	33292	23	33	40					28487		390526	204534	19013		
280	1	640	20	35948	51	54	56					33204	11199	414329	369674	21177	567	1177
285	1	440	14	35607	51	37	48	49			512	32605	22207	215534	391196	11557	259	1956
295	1	980	32	28149	28	23	30	49			7935	13704		306786	202005	16686	368	
300	1	610	19	63610	10	19	30	33	4	49		27055	14739	252969	285424	13951		
305	1	500	16	36207	03	23	26	40			1594	16954	13170	127500	238650	7216		
308	2	200	6	31208	11							13608		82069	120283	17278		
315	1	410	13	8009	64	55	56		6	65		7621		332991	314142	18898	1571	1718
320	1	430	13	24868	55	50	52	53	4	58	1373	22996	9612	597488	576443	21975	605	913
325	2	560	18	23262	49	40	48	49				20991	4426	415091	391598	17839	601	
330	2	260	8	33557	37	51	53	56			361	18897		349899	330409	14834		1070
335	1	760	24	30937	50	59						23723		295428	278845	23936	1027	1109
340	4	640	20	19099	53	54	56	58	6	56	478	17399		456013	429749	29036	594	689
343	1	550	17	40025	37	40	48	51				36071		533369	503049	11006		1209
344	1	290	9	38001	63							33898		256346	241708	9424		1178
				16106	65							14659		248991	235600			

*The numbers represent individual schools.

185

Note 3. Painting Record

Name of School _____

Number of Classrooms _____

	OUTSIDE			INSIDE																	ANNEXES		
	Entire Outside	Cornice	Outside Doors	Entire Inside	Classrooms	Library	Cafetorium	Kitchen	Auditorium	Playroom	Clinic	Admin. Area	Toilets	Boys' Gym	Girls' Gym	Combination Gym	Corridors	Locker Rooms	Shops	Swimming Pool	Exterior	Interior	Toilets
19 – 19																							
19 – 19																							
1962 – 1963																							
1963 – 1964																							
19 – 19																							
19 – 19																							
19 – 19																							

LAST RECORDING

1. January	1962		
2. February	1963		
3. March	1964		
4. April	1965		
5. May	1966		
6. June	1967		
7. July	1968		
8. August	1969		
9. September	1970		
10. October	1971		
11. November	1972		
12. December	1973		

SPECIAL NOTES

3.
4.
5.
6.

1. List by coats – 1c, 2c, 3c.

2. If entire classrooms and toilets are not painted as a unit – list 1962-63 as Classrooms 108, 211, 311, on Back of Sheet or Toilet #101, 2, 3, etc.

TYPE AND SUB-TYPE OF EQUIPMENT

006 Amplifiers

   0 = None

   1 = Built-In

   2 = Portable

007 Audiometers

   0 = None

   1 =

   2 =

008 Earphones

   0 = None

   1 = Crystal Hi-Fi BA-200

   2 = Magnetic

   3 = Stereo HS-1

009 Filmstrip Projector

   0 = None

   1 = Manual Control

   2 = Remote Control

   3 = Controlled Reader

   4 = FS/Slide Combination

010 Intercom/Central Sound

   0 = None

   1 = Tube Type

   2 = Transistorized

011 Language Laboratory

   0 = None

   1 = Portable

   2 = Fixed

012 Lecturnette

   0 = None

   1 = AC or Battery

   2 = Battery only

013 Microphones

   0 = None

   1 = Crystal Hi Z

   2 = Dynamic Low Z

014 Opaque Projector

   0 = None

   1 = 300-500 W

   2 = 750-1000 W

015 Overhead Projector

   0 = None

   1 = Reflector/Condenser

   2 = Fresnell 400 W

   3 = Fresnell 600 W

016 Radio

   0 = None

   1 = AM Tube, AC

   2 = FM Tube, AC

   3 = AM-FM Combination Tube, AC

   4 = AM-FM Tuner - Tube, AC

   5 = AM Transistor, Battery

   6.= FM Transistor, Battery

   7 = AM-FM Combination Transistor, Battery

   8 =

017 <u>Record Player</u>

0 = None

1 = 3-speed Record Player-Tube Type

2 = 4-Speed Record Player-Tube Type

3 = Record Player, 3-Speed-Transistorized

4 = 4-Speed Record Player-Transistorized

5 = Combination Player - Radio Tube Type

018 <u>Screens</u>

0 = None

Tripod

1 = 50 x 50

2 = 60 x 60

3 = 60 x 70

4 = 70 x 70

Wall mounted

5 = 50 x 50

6 = 60 x 60

7 = 72 x 72

8 = 72 x 96

019 <u>16 mm Projector</u>

0 = None

Tube Type

1 = Separate Speaker

2 = Built-In Speaker

3 = Built-In & Separate Speaker

4 =

Transistorized

5 = Separate Speaker

6 = Built-In Speaker

7 = Built-In & Separate Speaker

8 =

020 <u>Slide Projector</u>

0 = None

1 = Manual Control

2 = Remote Control

3 =

021 <u>Speaker</u>

0 = None

1 =

2 =

022 <u>Tape Recorder</u>

0 = None

Tube Type

1 = Two Speed

2 = Three Speed

3 =

Transistorized

4 = Two Speed

5 = Three Speed

6 =

023 <u>Miscellaneous</u>

0 = None

1 =

2 =

MANUFACTURER

00	Not listed	43	Kalart	84	Techmaster
		44	Ken-A-Vision	85	Teck-Ni-Tilt
01	American Optical	45	Keystone	86	Thermofax
02	Amplicall	46	Kodak	87	Traveler
03	Ampro			88	Trimm
04	Apeco	47	Lecturnette	89	Turner
05	Arcturos				
06	Astatic	48	Magnascope	90	Vibratone
07	Audiomaster	49	Magnavox	91	Victor
		50	Maico	92	Viewlex
08	Baloptican	51	Masco	93	Viking
09	Bell & Howell	52	Minnesota Mining		
10	Beltone	53	Monitor	94	Webcor
11	Beseler	54	Motorola	95	Webster
12	Bioscope	55	Musicmaster		
13	Bogen				
		56	Newcomb		
14	Califone				
15	Capitol	57	Otometer		
16	Channelmaster				
17	Clevite/Brush	58	Paulmar		
18	Columbia	59	Pentron		
19	Concert	60	Philco		
20	Concord				
		61	Quam		
21	Dalite				
22	Decca	62	Radiant		
23	Delmonico	63	Rawlins		
24	Dukane	64	RCA		
25	Duosonic	65	Recordio		
26	Dynavox	66	Revere		
		67	Rheem		
27	Educ.Develop.Lab.	68	Robbins		
28	Eico	69	Roberts		
29	Electrovoice				
30	EZ Viewer	70	Sawyer		
		71	Sentinel		
31	Galaxy	72	Shure		
32	Gerrard	73	Signet		
33	General Electric	74	Silvertone		
34	Graflex	75	Sonocraft		
		76	Soundcraft		
35	Harmon-Kardon	77	Soundmaster		
36	Harwald	78	Standard		
37	Heathkit	79	Steelman		
38	Honeywell	80	Stereosonic		
		81	Stromberg-Carlson		
39	Ideal	82	SVE		
40	Instructomatic	83	Symphonic		
41	Jensen				
42	Jerrold				

OVERHAUL MONTH

01	Jan.	07	July
02	Feb.	08	August
03	Mar.	09	Sept.
04	April	10	Oct.
05	May	11	Nov.
06	June	12	Dec.

CONDITION

E – Excellent

G – Good

F – Fair

P – Poor

NOTE 5. PARTIAL SUMMARY ELECTRONIC EQUIPMENT AND MAINTENANCE RECORD

CODE	IDENTIFICATION	YR MAN	YR PUR	COST	COND	LOC	REPAIRS # LAST	OVERHAUL # LAST	TOTAL MAINT	YR DIS
	MAINT						1 4-67	*	5	
							1* 67		5*	
016 716 0601	RADIO AM/FM TRAN B CHNL 6518 61416	00	62	69.50	G	325				
016 716 0602	RADIO AM/FM TRAN B CHNL 6518 61717	00	62	69.50	G	412				
016 716 0779	RADIO AM/FM TRAN B CHNL 6506	00	00	.	G	250				
016 716 0780	RADIO AM/FM TRAN B CHNL 6518 31359	00	62	69.50	G	250				
016 716 0781	RADIO AM/FM TRAN B CHNL 6518 28114	00	62	69.50	G	375				
016 716 0848	RADIO AM/FM TRAN B CHNL 6518 60122	00	62	70.00	G	125				
016 716 0849	RADIO AM/FM TRAN B CHNL 6518 60930	00	62	70.00	G	275				
016 716 0850	RADIO AM/FM TRAN B CHNL 6518 60757	00	62	70.00	G	295				
016 716 0851	RADIO AM/FM TRAN B CHNL 6518 61371	00	62	70.00	G	340				
016 716 0852	RADIO AM/FM TRAN B CHNL 6518 59137	00	62	70.00	G	410				
016 716 0853	RADIO AM/FM TRAN B CHNL 6518 57386	00	62	70.00	G	415				
016 716 0854	RADIO AM/FM TRAN B CHNL 6518 61504		62	70.00	G	390				
	MAINT						1 3-67	*	13	
							1* 67		13*	
016 716 0889	RADIO AM TUBE AC CHNL 6518			.		268				
016 716 0890	RADIO AM TUBE AC CHNL 6518			.		330				

816

NOTE 6.   CODE FOR MOTORIZED EQUIPMENT

EXPLANATION OF INVENTORY

CODE - Property Classification

040 = Truck	Type	Brand	Size
X = Type	0 Dump or Dump Bed	0 Chevrolet	0 ½ Ton
	1 Electrical	1 Dodge	1 3/4 Ton
X = Brand	2 Pickup	2 Federal	2 1 Ton
	3 Panel or Package	3 Ford	3 1¼ Ton
X = Size	delivery		
	4 Stake or Platform	4 GMC	4 1½ Ton
XXXX = Equipment	5 Tractor	5 International	5 2 Ton
Number	6 Utility	6 Studebaker	6 2½ Ton
	7 Van	7 White	7 3½ Ton
	8 Winch	8 FWD	8 5 Ton

041 = Car	Type	Brand	Size
X = Type	0 Carryall	0 Chevrolet	0 2-door
	1 Sedan	1 Ford	1 4-door
X = Brand	2 Station Wagon		
X = Size			
XXXX = Equipment			
Number			

042 = School Bus	Type	Brand	Size
X = Type	0 Bluebird	0 Buick	0 24 passenger
	1 Superior	1 Chevrolet	1 36 passenger
X = Brand	2 Ward	2 Dodge	2 48 passenger
	3 Unknown	3 Federal	3 54 passenger
X = Size	4 Excell	4 Ford	4 60 passenger
	5 Carpenter	5 GMC	5 72 passenger
XXXX = Equipment		6 International	6 73 passenger
Number		7 White	7 75 passenger

043 = Tractor	Type	Brand	Size
	0 Gasoline	0 Allis-Chalmers	0 Light
X = Type	1 Diesel	1 Case	1 Heavy
X = Brand		2 Caterpillar	
		3 Ferguson	
X = Size		4 Ford	
		5 International	
XXXX = Equipment		6 Minneapolis-Moline	
Number		7. MRS	
		8 Oliver	

EXPLANATION OF INVENTORY (continued)

044 = Equipment, Heavy	Type	Manufacturer
X = Type	0 Back Hoe	0 Ateco
	1 Casie Dump	1 Austin-Western
X = Brand	2 Crane, Crawler	2 Caterpillar
	3 Crane, Portable	3 Gallion
X = Size	4 Grader	4 Hobbs-Schronrock
	5 Scraper	5 Huber
	6 Scraper, Hydraulic	6 Le Tourneau
XXXX = Equipment Number	7 Scraper, Towed	7 Texas
	8 Roller, Motorized	8 William Bros.
	9 Roller, Towed	9 Browning
		Bucyrus
		Hughes & Keenan
		Northwest
		Wayne Roy

045 = Equipment, Landscape	Type	Brand	Size
	0 Mower, Hammerville	0 John Bean	0 2 Bu. Hr.
X = Type	1 Mower, Rotary	1 Dobbins	1 42 inch
	2 Planter	2 Ford	2 80 inches
X = Brand	3 Rotavator	3 Hinderliter	3 50 gal.
	4 Machine, Spray	4 Howard	4 Unknown
X = Size		5 Whirlwind	
		6 Woodbros	
XXXX = Equipment Number			

046 = Equipment, Supply	Type	Brand	Size
	0 Plane Loader	0 Baker-Rowling	0 1,000 lb.
X = Type	1 Lift, Fork	1 Buda	1 2,000 lb.
	2 Lift, Yard	2 Clark	2 3,500 lb.
X = Brand		3 Ross	3 4,000 lb.
			4 6,000 lb.
X = Brand			5 Unknown
X = Size			
XXXX = Equipment Number			

047 = Equipment,
Miscellaneous

XX = Type

X = Brand

XXXX = Equipment
Number

Type

00 Cleaner, Steam
01 Compressor, Air
02 Compressor, Rotary
03 Ditcher, Trench
04 Engine, Gasoline
05 Jack or Pump, Mud
06 Kettle, Roofing
07 Machine, Paint
08 Marker, Line
09 Mixer, Concrete or
   Cement
10 Pot, Sandblast
11 Scratcher, Gravel
12 Sprayer, Termite
13 Spreader, Asphalt
14 Trailer
15 Trailer, Semi
16 Trailer, Utility
17 Tug
18 Welder

Manufacturer

(Aeroil
0 (Aircorps
(Blackwell

1 (Chicago
(Clark

2 (Davis
(Essick   Devilbiss

3 (Fordson
(Gilson Bros.

4 (Good Roads
(Hercules

5 (Hobart   Homelite
(Ingersol-Rand

6 (Jaeger
(Koehring

7 (Lincoln
(M&B Corp.

8 (Quick Steam
(Ruemlin   Westinghouse

9 (Shop Built   Target
(Wisconsin

EXPLANATION OF INVENTORY (Continued)

Identification

XXXXXXXXXXXX (12) = Name of Item

XXXXXXXXXXXX (12) = Manufacturer

XXXXXXXXXXX (11) = Serial Number

XX (2) = Size

Other Information

XX   = Year Manufactured

XXXXX   = Cost

Maintenance

X   = Condition A = Excellent   B = Good
                         C = Needs Repair
                         D = Salvage Parts
                         E = Junk

XX   = Total Number of times repaired

XX   = Last year repaired

X   = Total number of times overhauled

XX   = Last year overhauled

XXXX   = Total maintenance cost in dollars

Disposition

XX   = Year

X   = Reason

Note 7. PARTIAL SUMMARY - MOTORIZED EQUIPMENT

CODE			DESCRIPTION	YR MANU	YR PUR	COST	COND	LOC	# RPR	YR LAST	# OVH	YR LAST OVH	YR LST MAINT COST	ACC	BY
040	015	0003	TRUCK DUMP DODGE 82629409 2T	54	54	300.	G		6	67			42		
040	015	0004	TRUCK DUMP DODGE 82629458 2T	54	62	250.	G		5	67	1	65	276		
040	028	0010	TRUCK DUMP BED FEDERAL 45GAI153903 5T	51	62	500.	G		5	67	1	66	511		
040	028	0011	TRUCK DUMP FEDERAL 21866 5T	51	62	450.	G		5	67			46		
040	034	0002	TRUCK DUMP FORD F5RICH16816 1 1/2T	51	61	200.	F		3	66			31		
040	036	0005	TRUCK DUMP FORD F75N9U43281 2 1/2T	59	59	500.	G		9	67			145		
040	037	0009	TRUCK DUMP FORD T75F9U43282 3 1/2T	59	59	1000.	G		14	67	1	65	935		
040	046	C006	TRUCK DUMP GMC 12212 2 1/2T	51		350.	F		1	65			12		
040	046	0007	TRUCK DUMP GMC 12214 2 1/2T	51		350.	G		3	67	1	65	64		
040	046	0008	TRUCK DUMP GMC HC451622 2 1/2T	51	59	350.	F		1	66			4		
040	054	0001	TRUCK DUMP INTERNATNL A802 1 1/2T	51	62	300.	G		2	67			13		
040	058	0012	TRUCK DUMP INTERNATNL A3376 5T	53	58	400.	G		3	67	1	66	628		
040	078	0013	TRUCK DUMP WHITE 404770 5T	51	63	500.	G		11	67			351		
040	078	0014	TRUCK DUMP WHITE 402083 5T	51	63	500.	G		6	67	3	67	524		
040	078	0015	TRUCK DUMP WHITE 404792 5T	51		500.	G		7	67	1	65	528		
040	186	0101	TRUCK ELECT FWD 5112252 2 1/2T	51	62	200.	G		1	66			19		
040	200	0201	TRUCK PICKUP CHEVROLET 5HPK34452 1/2T	50	58	150.	G		6	66			229		
040	200	0202	TRUCK PICKUP CHEVROLET 3JPL-4573 1/2T	51	57	150.	G		2	66			49		
040	200	0203	TRUCK PICKUP CHEVROLT H54K023883 1/2T	51	61	200.	G		2	66			16		
040	200	0204	TRUCK PICKUP CHEV 3A56S030120 1/2T	56	60	500.	F		8	67			114		
040	200	0205	TRUCK PICKUP CHEVROLT 5KPI-17948 1/2T	52	57	175.	G		2	66			17		
040	200	0206	TRUCK PICKUP CHEVROLT 9KPI-8376 1/2T	52	57	175.	G		2	66			44		
040	200	0207	TRUCK PICKUP CHEVROLT 5KPI-17883 1/2T	52	58	175.	G		7	67			93		
040	200	0208	TRUCK PICKUP CHEVROLT 5JPB10503 1/2T	51	61	150.	G		2	67			225		
040	200	0209	TRUCK PICKUP CHEVROLT 5JPC12039 1/2T	51	60	150.	G		4	67	1	67	30		
040	200	0210	TRUCK PICKUP CHEV 3A57K118342 1/2T	57	63	450.	G		3	67			61		
040	200	0211	TRUCK PICKUP CHEV 3A57K118288 1/2T	57	63	450.	G		3	66			87		
040	200	0212	TRUCK PICKUP CHEVROLET 5HPJ31535 1/2T	51	63	150.	G		3	66			41		
040	200	0213	TRUCK PICKUP CHEV 3A57S112773 1/2T	57		500.	G		2	67			206		
040	200	0214	TRUCK PICKUP CHEVROLT 21JP114227 1/2T	51	63	150.	G		8	67			210		
040	200	0215	TRUCK PICKUP CHEV HS55K025312 1/2T	56		500.	F		1	66	1	66	32		
040	200	0216	TRUCK PICKUP CHEV 3A57K118583 1/2T	57		500.	G		9	67			61		
040	200	0217	TRUCK PICKUP CHEVROLET 59B1184 1/2T	57		650.	G		4	67	1	65	147		
040	200	0218	TRUCK PICKUP CHEV H29537V8711 1/2T	60	61	150.	G		2	67			41		
040	200	0219	TRUCK PICKUP CHEV M255S047188 1/2T	55		450.	G		10	67			218		
040	200	0220	TRUCK PICKUP CHEVROLET 5HP128818 1/2T	50	60	150.	G		3	67			263		
040	200	0221	TRUCK PICKUP CHEVROLET 9KPI-8853 1/2T	52	57	175.	G		8	67	1	66	305		
040	200	0222	TRUCK PICKUP CHEVROLT 55P130035 1/2T	51	60	150.	G		4	67	1	67	308		
040	200	0223	TRUCK PICKUP CHEVROLT 5JP-130025 1/2T	51		150.	G		1	67	1	67	15		
040	200	0244	TRUCK PICKUP CHEV 3A59K105275 1/2T	59		575.	G		3	67			18		
040	200	0245	TRUCK PICKUP CHEV 3A57K137769 1/2T	57		475.	G		6	66			132		
040	200	0246	TRUCK PICKUP CHEV 3A57K122892 1/2T	57		475.	G		3	66			44		
040	200	0252	TRUCK PICKUP CHEV 1/2 TON 3A56K029794	56	65	500.	G	72	3	66			227		
040	201	0224	TRUCK PICKUP CHEV 3E57K129800 3/4T	57	61	500.	G		3	66	1	66	39		
040	202	0225	TRUCK PICKUP CHEV 5FSG2500 1T	48	46	100.	G		3	67			51		
040	202	0226	TRUCK PICKUP CHEV 5FG2485 1T	48	54	100.	G		3	66			8		
040	202	0249	TRUCK PICKUP CHEV 5FSG-2497 1T	48	48	100.	F		2	66	1	65	3		
040	210	0227	TRUCK PICKUP DODGE 82196443X 1/2T	50	57	100.	F		1	66			9		
040	210	0228	TRUCK PICKUP DODGE 82299367 1/2T	52	63	175.	G		3	67			37		
040	210	0229	TRUCK PICKUP DODGE 82300686 1/2T	52		200.	F		1	66			11		
040	210	0250	TRUCK PICKUP DODGE 1/2 TON 1161567311	65	65	2250.	A	193							
040	210	0251	TRUCK PICKUP DODGE 1/2 TON 82298437	52	65		G	72	4	67			37		
040	210	0255	TRUCK PICKUP DODGE #82299737 1/2 TON	52	67	60.	G	33	1	67			11		

WORK ORDER

Maintenance Dept.   **Oklahoma City Public Schools**

DATE:_____PROJECT NO._____

BUILDING: _____

INSTRUCTIONS

Front

ROUTING

_____   _____   _____   _____

_____   _____   _____   _____

_____   _____   _____   _____

_____

Date Started_____Date Completed_____

Completed Satisfactorily: Work Order Approved:

_____   _____

Supervising Foreman   Supervision of Maintenance

NOTE 8. WORK ORDER

INITIATING DEPARTMENT: (1) Federal Projects (2) Food Service (3) Vocational (4) Laundry (5) Manpower (6) Safety (7) School (8) Engineering (9) Administration (10) Supply

WORK CLASSIFICATION: (1) Scheduled P&SM No._____
(2) Emergency (3) Vandalism (4) Normal Maintenance
(5) Add. Facilities (6) Preventive Maintenance

DO NOT WRITE IN THIS SPACE

School_____Proj. No._____Init. Dept._____Man Hours_____

Date Started_____Date Completed_____Work Class_____

Job and Craft Code_____

Back

TIME CARD

Maintenance--

Name _____

Craft _____

Rate _____ Date _____

WorkOrder No.	Project No.	Hours	Amount	
TOTAL				

I certify that the above time has been spent in gainful
employment for the Oklahoma City Board of Education

Approved By _____

NOTE 9. TIME CARD

STOCK REQUISITION

Deliver to _____ — 19 ____

No. 37513

K

Code No. 1—8	Quantity 9—11	Sch. No. 56—58	Work Order No.	√ if already issued 11/79	11/80

Principal _____

NOTE 10.   STOCK REQUISITION

```
┌─────────────────────────────────────────────────────────────────────┐
│                                                                       │
│                              Employee No._____        │
│                                                                       │
│  Name_____Address_____  │
│                                                                       │
│  Date of Birth_____Home Tel. No._____   │
│                                                                       │
│  Married_____Wife's Name_____No. Dependents_____   │
│                                                                       │
│  No. Children at Home_____  _____    │
│                                      In Emergency Notify              │
│                                                                       │
│  _____  _____  _____        │
│  Position     Rate of Pay    Date employed by Board of Education      │
│                                                                       │
│  Remarks_____      │
│                                                                       │
│  _____     │
│                                                                       │
└─────────────────────────────────────────────────────────────────────┘
```

NOTE 11.

MAINTENANCE DEPARTMENT PERSONNEL INFORMATION

ABSENTEE RECORD

NAME _____ NO. _____

ADDRESS _____

CRAFT _____ TEL. NO. _____

Date	Sick Leave			Date	Vacation		
	Earned	Used	Bal.		Earned	Used	Bal.

NOTE 12.   ABSENTEE RECORD

Appendix C

NOTES FOR CHAPTER 7.

This list of tools should help those persons responsible for equipping the skilled workmen with the minimum tools for maintenance. The number and kind will differ in the separate school districts depending upon the number of maintenance employees and the kinds of maintenance services. Various hand tools are omitted, such as screw drivers, pliers, wire cutters, hammers, rules, regular shovels, and short tapes.

During summer operations, water cans should be provided on trucks or projects.

Note	List of hand tools by crafts	Page
1.	Carpentry	205
	Clocks and signals	205
	Concrete	205
	Drayage	205
	Drivotrainer	205
	Electrical	205
	Filters	206
	Garage	206
	Heating and air conditioning	206
	Heavy equipment	206
	Instructional equipment	206
	Landscape	206
	Machine shop	207

Notes for Chapter 7. (Cont'd.)

Note	List of hand tools by crafts	Page
	Masonry	207
	Motor Winding	207
	Paint	207
	Plaster	207
	Playground and Fences	207
	Plumbing	207-208
	Roofing	208
	Sheet Metal	208
	Welding	208

NOTE 1. Hand Tools - Various Crafts

Carpentry

Brace and bits	Hand plane	Routers
Drill motors	Mitre box and saw	Sabre saw
Electric screwdrivers	Power plane	Sander
Hand saw	Power saw	Vibrator sander
		Window groover

Clocks and Signals

Drill motor	Socket set	Voltmeter
Millivolt meter	Soldering gun	

Concrete

Aluminum levels	Concrete shovels	Margin trowel
Asphalt rakes	Crescent wrenches	Pipe vise
Asphalt shovels	Dirt picks	Pipe wrench
Bolt cutter	Drill motor	Post hole digger
Box wrenches	Extension cord	Sharp shooter
Caulking gun	Framing square	Steel finishing trowels
Cold chisels	Hacksaw	Tape
Concrete hones		Tin snips

Drayage

Flat four wheel dollies	Stair step dollies	Roller dollies
Mule dollies	Two wheel dollies	

Driver Training

Drill motor	Soldering gun	Voltmeter
Hacksaw	Soldering iron	

Electrical

Allen wrenches	Hand lantern	Reamer
Amp meters	Masonry bits	Soldering gun
Chisels	Nut driver set	Star bits
Cotton rope	Oil can	Star drills
Crescent wrenches	Pipe benders	Test light
Drill motor	Pipe dies	Tin snips
Extension cords	Pipe wrenches	Vise
Fish tape	Punches	Wire puller
Knockouts	Rattail file	Wood bits
Hacksaw		

NOTE 1. Hand Tools - Various Crafts

Filters

Allen wrenches	Hand lantern	Socket wrenches
Crescent wrenches	Pipe wrenches	Tin snips
Dust mask		

Garage

Air wrench	Ring squeezer	Torgue wrench
Drill motor	Tire tool	Tow chain
Honing tool	Valve clamp tool	

Heating and Air Conditioning

Absolute pressure gauge	Gauge glass cutter	Refrigerant pump
Amp meter	Grease gun	Refrigeration Thermometer
Amprobe	Hacksaw	Scale
Cap check kit	Hand lantern	Sheave puller
Chain tong	Heating thermometer	Socket wrenches
Crescent wrenches	Micro amp meter	Soldering gun
Drill motor	Oil can	Torch
Extension cord	Orifice drills	Tubing bender
Fish tape	Pinch off tool	Tubing cleaning kit
Flaring tool	Pin vise	Tubing cutter
Freon leak detector	Pipe threading tools	Tubing tool kit
Fuse holder	Pipe wrenches	Welding gun
Fuse puller	Punch	

Heavy Equipment

Chains	Greese guns

Instructional Equipment
Roof Antennas and Central Sound

Combination tool kits	Soldering guns	Tap and die set
Crescent wrenches	Stud nut drivers	Wire stripper
Long shank nut drivers		

Landscape

Axes	Grubbing hoe	Rake
Balling spade	Hedge shears	Scoop shovel
Chain saw	Lapping shears	Spray gun
Crosscut saw	Pruning saw	Spray hose
Dirt pick		

NOTE 1. Hand Tools - Various Crafts

Machine Shop

Bushing tools	Impact tool	Tap and die set SAE
Deep socket wrenches	Reamers	Tap and die set NC
Drill motor	Shallow socket wrenches	Valve seating kit
Gear pullers		

Masonry

Air gun	Caulking gun	Mortar hoe
Brick hammer	Extension cord	Plumb rule
Brick tongs	Levels	Spacing rule
Brick trowel		

Motor Winding

Amprobe	Gear puller	Side cutter
Armature tester	Insulator tester	Tachometer
Gear knocker		

Paint

Brushes, various sizes and kinds	Putty knives	Spray guns
Hand scrapers	Rollers	

Plaster

Cold chisels	Levels	Plaster hawks
Extension cord	Margin trowels	Trowels
Electric grinder	Mortar hoe	Water brushes

Playground and Fencing

Bolt cutters	Dirt pick	Pipe wrenches
Cold chisels	Drill motors	Wire cutters
Concrete mixing hoe	Pipe cutters	Wire stretchers
Crescent wrenches		

Plumbing

Allen wrenches	Force cup	Running rope
Basin wrench	Hacksaw	Sewer cleaning cables

NOTE 1.   Hand Tools - Various Crafts

Plumbing (Cont'd)

Caulking irons	Ladle	Socket wrench set
Chain tongs	Lead tools	Soldering iron
Closet auger	Level	Swedging tool
Cold chisel	Mattox	Tap and Die set
Crescent wrenches	Oil can	Three way stock & dies
Dirt pick	Packing iron	Tin snips
Drill bits	Pipe cutters	Top snakes
Drill motors	Pipe reamers	Tubing cutters
Extension cords	Pipe threaders	Wire grips
Files	Pipe wrenches	Yarning irons
Flaring tool	Ratchet die set	

Roofing

Caulking gun	Hand scraper	Tin snips
Cold chisels	Margin trowel	Water hose
Hacksaw	Pole ax	

Sheet Metal

Drill bits	Rivet set	Soldering iron
Drill motor	Scratch awl	Tin snips
Metal punch		

Welding

Clamps	Electric grinder	Level
Chipping hammer	Framing square	Torch igniter
Crescent wrenches	Goggles	Welding gloves
Drill motor		

208

GLOSSARY

Ancillary—The additional areas in a school plant other than the regular prescribed areas. These areas do not exist in all school plants of the small grade level.

Automation—A process in which equipment performs functions normally generated by human hands.

Cafetorium—The space adjacent to a food service kitchen which may be used for eating and/or assembly purposes. In addition this space may be used for other instructional purposes as the local school program is defined.

Combustible—A material or structure which may burn (combustible is a relative term).

Custodial Services—Those services performed by school plant employees such as cleaning, care and operating equipment, general care of the physical plant, and policing.

Data Processing—The process of collecting, selecting, arranging, categorizing, and analyzing data.

Economic Obsolescence—The external conditions which accrue to a school plant, such as neighborhood infiltration, legislation, zoning, and changes in transportation facilities.

Educational Environment—All the objects, forces, and surroundings which affect the individual through stimuli (such as by shape, by color, by light, and by cleanliness) he is able to perceive.

Efflorescence—The white deposit which appears on the surface of brick walls. This condition is caused by soluble salts contained in the brick and/or mortar being dissolved by water penetrating the brick or mortar. The film is deposited on the surface of the brick as the water evaporates.

Electrolysis—The overall process of chemical decomposition on account of the passage of electrical currents from water pipes, gas pipes, and electric cable sheaths to the earth or another body. The electrolysis occurs when the current leaves the metal underground structures to flow in the earth, i.e., when the structures are positive to the earth.

Frequency of Service—The local determination of the cycles of time between maintenance services, such as the outside painting of a building every four years.

Fire Prevention—The predetermined measures planned and/or operated which avoid the inception of fire.

Fire-Resistive—The quality of materials in a design which resist the effects of any fire to which the material or structure may be expected to be subjected.

Functional Obsolescence—Accrued inadequate conditions for the educational program caused by poor planning, outmoded style, size, and improper location.

Job Description—An outline of the duties of an employee consisting of one or more tasks as his capabilities fit into a particular organization.

Maintenance—This service is synonymous with "repairs" and "upkeep" and is a continuous process of restoration of any piece of property, whether school plant site or buildings or equipment, as nearly as possible to the original condition or efficiency. The restoration is made through repair or by replacement with property of equal value and efficiency.

Modernization—The adapting of existing facilities and spaces to meet the needs of changing educational programs.

Nonscheduled Projects—The emergency jobs which were not foreseen at the time of the inspection of the physical properties for defects.

Physical Deterioration—An accumulation of defects which occur to a school plant because of wear and tear, decay, cracks, dry rot, and structural failures.

Potable Water—Water which is free from impurities and suitable for drinking.

Rehabilitation—The general overhauling of a complete school plant or major section thereof to adapt the school plan for continued use for the school program.

Remodeling—A change in structure or a major structural improvement to a building.

Security of Plant—The provisions made by responsible personnel to protect all parts of the school plant from vandalism and from illegal entry.

Scheduled Maintenance—The approved repair items collected from the inspection of the school plant, the annual request of the principal, and the local frequency of service. These selected items are formulated into a planned program and often called preventive maintenance.

Standards—Those accepted statements indicating what is desirable or ideal in a school plant according to a defined pattern.

Waste Space—Unfinished or unusable rooms or space not serving either instructional or auxiliary purposes.

Work Orders—Written orders made by the supervisor of maintenance prescribing the work to be performed on a certain project and directing the crafts to proceed with the execution of the order.

Work Request—A written suggestion made by authorized personnel to perform maintenance work on a particular element of the school plant.

BIBLIOGRAPHY

BOOKS

Part I: Administrative Practices.

American Association of School Administrators. *Curriculum Handbook for School Administrators.* Washington, D.C.: The Association, a Department of the National Education Association, 1967. Deals with the phases of modern curriculum development. Chapter II treats Safety Education.

American Association of School Administrators. *Safety Education.* Eighteenth Yearbook. Washington, D.C.: The Association, a Department of the National Education Association, 1940. The different phases of safety education related to all hazards of life are discussed. Special stresses of school safety in all departments are treated. The accident prevention in industry and transportation is applicable to school maintenance.

American Association of School Administrators. *Schools For America.* A report of the AASA Commission on Buildings, 1967. Washington, D.C.: The Association. Discusses all phases of the school plant. Chapter 14, Plant Management, outlines the responsibilities in keeping the school plant efficient in order to provide better learning environments.

Baker, Joseph J. and Peters, Jon S. *School Maintenance and Operation.* Danville, Illinois: The Interstate Printers and Publishers, 1963. One part of the book deals with the administration of the maintenance program. Maintenance services and frequencies are treated in detail.

Engman, John David. *School Plant Management for School Administrators.* Houston, Texas: Gulf School Research Development Association, 1962. A practical handbook for school administrators. Includes suggestions in fifteen areas of plant management which should assist administrators in studying the maintenance program of a school district.

Florio, A. E. and Stafford, G. T. *Safety Education.* New York: McGraw-Hill Book Company, Inc., 1962. This book deals with the scope and methods of safety education. Stresses the areas of driver, fire, and vocational safety.

Gabrielsen, M. Alexander and Miles, Caswell M. *Sports and Recreation Facilities: In School and Community.* Englewood Cliffs, N.J.: Prentice-Hall, Inc., 1958. This book details the different material elements contained in each sport facility for the different areas of the nation.

211

Linn, H. H. (ed.) *School Business Administration.* New York: The Ronald Press Company, 1950. Treats the basic areas of school business administration. Discusses special phases as personnel administration and school plant operation and maintenance, and the interrelationships of these areas.

MacCrehan, W. A., Jr. *Small Plant Management.* A Guide to Practical, Know-How Management. New York: McGraw-Hill Book Company, Inc., 1960. Copyright by the American Society of Mechanical Engineers. Discusses concepts of management in the organizing, operating, supervising, and controlling of small plants.

March, C. A. *Building Operation and Maintenance.* New York: McGraw-Hill Book Company, Inc., 1950. Deals primarily with operation and maintenance services to all buildings. It is of value in assisting to determine the scope of maintenance services in school plants.

National Council on Schoolhouse Construction. *Guide for Planning School Plants.* East Lansing, Michigan: The Council, 1964. A most excellent guide in the planning, construction, and remodeling of school plants. (Now Council of Educational Facility Planners, Columbus, Ohio.)

Sack, Thomas F. *A Complete Guide to Building and Plant Maintenance.* Englewood Cliffs, N. J.: Prentice-Hall, Inc., 1963. This book treats the many phases of school plant maintenance from a custodial standpoint. The stress on efficiency of each separate phase is noteworthy.

Stack, H. J., Seibrecht, E. B., and Elkow, J. D. *Education for Safe Living.* New York: Prentice-Hall, Inc., 1949. Gives the general principles and specific precautions regarding effective machine guarding and correct work practices.

Stahl, Glen O. et al. *Public Personnel Administration.* Third edition. New York: Harper & Brothers, 1950. Treats employee problems on national, state, and local levels. The scope of understanding these problems by the administrator should be enlarged.

Part II: Daily Maintenance Problems.

American Association of School Administrators. *EDP and the School Administrator.* Committee on Electronics Data Processing. Washington, D.C.: The Association, 1967.

Bruno, Louis. *Modernization of School Buildings: A Feasibility Study.* State Department of Public Instruction. Olympia: The State Board of Education of Washington, 1963.

Finchum, R. N. *Administering the Custodial Program.* Office of Education Bulletin OE-21005. Washington, D.C.: U. S. Government Printing Office, 1961.

————. *Organizing the Maintenance Program.* Office of Education Bulletin, 1960, No. 15. Washington, D.C.: U. S. Government Printing Office, 1960.

————. *School Building Maintenance Procedures.* Office of Education Bulletin, OE-21207. Washington, D.C.: U. S. Government Printing Office, 1964.

Schaefer, John W. *What is Operations?* A Handbook for School Business Officials. A special report prepared by the ASBO Research Committee in Maintenance and Operations. Research Bulletin No. 6. Chicago: Research Corporation of the Association of School Business Officials, 1967.

Sessions, E. B. *Rehabilitation of Existing School Buildings or Construction of New Buildings.* Research Bulletin No. 2. Chicago: Research Corporation of the Association of School Business Officials, 1964.

MAGAZINE ARTICLES

Boles, Harold W. "25 Significant Economies in New School Buildings," *American School Board Journal,* 148:19–20, January 1964.

Cohen, Louis and Bogg, Ridley M. *The Administration of Non-Instructional Personnel in Public Schools.* Research Bulletin No. 1. Chicago: Research Corporation of Association of School Business Officials, 1963.

Connecticut State Department of Education. *Structural Considerations in School Building Economy.* (School Building Economy Series No. 5). Hartford, Connecticut: State Department of Education.

Educational Facilities Laboratories. *The Cost of a Schoolhouse.* New York, N.Y.: The Laboratories, 1960.

Emory, Vance. "Vandalism and Protective Devices," *1966 Proceedings.* Association of School Business Officials, p. 233–237.

Finchum, R. N. *Fire Insurance Economies Through Plant Management.* U.S. Department of Health, Education, and Welfare, Office of Education. Washington: U. S. Government Printing Office, 1965.

———. "Check List Tells How To Schedule Maintenance Work," *The Nation's Schools,* 72:76–80, October 1963.

Gardener, John C. "Security Readiness Via Two-Way Radio Control," *American School and University,* 39:55–56, July 1967.

George, N. L. "Maintenance Combines Men, Materials and Methods Effectively," *American School Board Journal,* 148:30, No. 4, April 1964.

———. "Heating, Lighting and Ventilation," *The Nation's Schools,* November 1958. pp. 71–72.

Interstate School Building Service. *Economies in School Construction.* Nashville, Tennessee: George Peabody College for Teachers, 1962.

Records, Samuel H. "Benefits of Planned Maintenance in the Public Schools," *Modern Sanitation and Building Maintenance,* 10:24–26, 46, January 1958.

Seagers, Paul W. "A Different Approach to Ventilation," *The Nation's Schools,* 42:60, October 1948.

Tonigan, Richard F. "Budgeting for Sound Maintenance," *American School and University,* 37:39–40, No. 4, December 1964.

———. "Lighting Maintenance," *The Nation's Schools,* 66:97–98, September 1960.

Wolffer, Wilfred C. "Recruiting and Selecting Non-Instructional Personnel," *American School Board Journal,* 146:37, June 1963.

ORGANIZATIONAL ARTICLES

Selected Articles from the Annual Proceedings of The Association of School Business Officials of the United States and Canada. Chicago: The Association.

Bagwell, Walter M. "Pros and Cons of Carpeting." Proceedings of the Fifty-First Convention, 1965. pp. 346–351.

Bruning, Walter F. "Minimum Maintenance Planning for School Grounds." Proceedings of the Forty-Ninth Convention, 1963. pp. 293–302.

Bush, George H. "Care and Operation of Stadia." Proceedings of Forty-First Convention, 1955. pp. 292–299.

Corwin, Ralph G. "Building Materials Standards Which Reflect Long-Term Maintenance and Operations Savings." Proceedings of the Forty-Eighth Convention, 1962. pp. 414–421.

Finchum, Ralph. "Doors and Hardware." Proceedings of the Forty-Fifth Convention, 1959. pp. 116–119.

George, N. L. "Facility or Building Item Rating Form." Proceedings of the Forty-Seventh Convention, 1961. pp. 114–120.

Higgins, E. Eugene. "Long Range Survey of Maintenance Needs." Proceedings of Forty-First Convention, 1955. pp. 299–304.

Ladd, G. H. "Organization of Maintenance and Operations Department in Medium Sized Districts." Proceedings of Fortieth Convention, 1954. pp. 94–98.

McEwen, F. W. "Contracts Versus School Maintenance." Proceedings of Forty-Third Annual Convention, 1957. pp. 107–113.

Richardson, James F. "Roofs." Proceedings of the Fifty-Second Convention, 1966. pp. 313–315.

Sansbury, S. S. "Present and Future Status of Electricity For Heating School Buildings." Proceedings of the Forty-Sixth Convention, 1960. pp. 156–172.

Wenger, Charles C. "Specifications for Turfed Athletic Fields." Proceedings of Fortieth Convention, 1954. pp. 240–255.

MISCELLANEOUS INFORMATION

Property Protection Manual. New York: Detex Watchclock Corporation, (n.d.).

National Safety Council. *Accident Prevention Manual.* Chicago: The Council (n.d.). (Chapter 15 titled Building Construction and Maintenance by Clement J. Lucpke.)

National Safety Council. *Alphabetical Index Industrial Safety Data Sheets* (including Special Categories). Chicago: The Council, 1966.

Selected National Council Safety Education Data Sheets. Chicago: The Council.

No. 2 Matches, 1945
No. 5 Falls, 1959
No. 6 Cutting Implements, 1946
No. 7 Lifting, Carrying, and Lowering, 1946
No. 8 Poisonous Plants, 1958
No. 9 Electric Equipment, 1946
No. 14 Chemicals, 1946
No. 15 Hand Tools, 1947
No. 24 Places of Public Assembly, Grandstands, Bleachers, and Auditoriums, 1948
No. 29 Play Areas, 1957
No. 33 Traffic Control Devices, 1949
No. 39 Bad Weather, Hazards, Precautions, Results, 1949
No. 46 Safety in the Woodshop, 1950
No. 47 School Fires, 1958

No. 50 Safety in the General Metals Shop, 1951
No. 52 Highway Driving: Rules, Precautions, 1957
No. 53 Safety in the Machine Shop, 1958
No. 55 Motor Vehicle Speed, 1951
No. 56 Welding and Cutting Safety, 1951
No. 57 Safety in the Auto Shop, 1958
No. 69 Playground Apparatus, 1956
No. 73 School Bus Safety, Operating Practices, 1956
No. 74 Playground Surfacing, 1956
No. 76 Safety in Bad Weather Conditions, 1956
No. 78 Safety for Amateur Electricians, 1957
No. 82 Office Safety, 1957
No. 83 Safety in the Sheet Metal Shop, 1957
No. 87 Safety in the Electrical Shop, 1958
No. 88 Vision and the Driver, 1959
No. 90 Flammability of Wearing Apparel, 1959

American Mutual Insurance Alliance. *Tips on Fire Safety.* Chicago: The Alliance (n.d.).

Kemper Insurance. *Pocket Guide to Construction Safety.* Chicago: the Company (n.d.).

Moore, Robert L. *How to Inspect for Accident Prevention Physical Condition of Buildings.* Chicago: Kemper Insurance Companies (n.d.).

Kemper Insurance Publications:

Consultation Sheet #13   titled "Public Liability Inspection Check List."
Consultation Sheet #29   titled "Inspection to Determine Condition of Buildings"
Consultation Sheet #30   titled "Plant Inspection Check List"
Consultation Sheet #640   titled "Building Collapse"
Consultation Sheet #641   titled "Floor Loading"
Form ZA 6341   titled "Physical Plant Survey"

Chicago: Lumbermans Mutual Casualty Company (Robert L. Moore, Superintendent of Engineers).

A Cost Analysis of School Heating Systems, *American School Board Journal,* 146:39, April 1963.

Heating Boilers, Maintenance and Operation. Chicago: Lumberman's Mutual Casualty Company and American Motorists Insurance Company (n.d.).

Notes on the Care and Operation of Heating Boilers. Hartford, Connecticut: The Hartford Steam Boiler Inspection and Insurance Co. (n.d.).

U. S. National Bureau of Standards, *Fuel Oils.* Commercial Standard, CS 12. Washington: U. S. Government Printing Office, 1940.

U. S. National Bureau of Standards, *Standards for Gas Service.* Circular C405. Washington: U. S. Government Printing Office, 1934.

Periodicals Featuring the Maintenance of School Plants:

The American School and University   *Institutions*
The School Product News   *The School Bus Fleet*
Buildings   *American School Board Journal*
School Management   *Nation's Schools*
Turf-Grass Times   *School Executive*

Index

A

Absentee record, 65, 202
Accidents:
  causes, 52
  handling, 52
Actual time, 23
Address, change of, 43
Administration:
  benefits, 45
  better tools and equipment, 87
  clerical or administrative paper work, 89
  general and committe meetings, 89-90
  handling and transportation of materials, 88
    from shop to locations within district, 88
    within shop, 88
  idle time, 89
  manpower, 85-86
  material savings, 86
    availability of stock items, 86
    pooling of requests for purchase, 86
    right materials, 86
    salvage materials, 86
    standardization of parts, 86
  methods of operation, 87-88
  safety program, 88-89
  summary, 90
  upgrading personnel, 91-95
  (see also Personnel, upgrading)
  work time, 89
Administrative and health areas, master check list, 164
Age, a qualification, 35
Age of school plant, 132-133
Air conditioning and heating hand tools, 206
Allied services:
  concrete, 111

Allied services *(Cont.)*
  drayage, 112-113
    aims, 113
    common problems, 113
    scope, 112-113
  fire protection, 117-118
  garbage, 113-115
    aims of services, 114
    common problems, 114-115
    scope, 114
  key shop, 116-117
  machine shop, 115
  sheet metal, 111-112
  snow removal, 115
  summary, 118
  vandalism restoration, 117
  welding, 112
Amount and cost of maintenance, 4-5
Ancillary, definition of, 209
Ancillary areas, services:
  central administration plant, 129-130
  data processing room, 126-127
  federal projects, 130-131
  food facility, 130
  greenhouse, 128-129
  mobile laboratory, 127
  other ancillary services, 131
  school stadia, 127-128
  summary, 131
  swimming pool, 128
  television studio, 129
Annual request, building principal's, 15
Appearance, personal, 35
Application form, 65
Applying for job, 33-34
Apprentices, 27, 38, 91
Area mechanics, 37-38
(see also Personnel policies)

Attitude, a qualification, 35
Attractiveness of plant, 3
Authorities, public, 31
Automation, definition of, 209

B

Benefits, wage and employee, 41-42
Birds, 124
Boiler rooms, master check list, 157
Boilers, 63, 103
Budget:
    allowance, 15-16
    finalizing, 16
    planning, 140
Building:
    criteria for judging, 135-136, 138-139
    maintenance pointers, 142-143
    manuals, 29
    updating codes, 5

C

Cafetorium, definition of, 209
Carpenter services, 105-106
    (*see also* Services in school plant areas)
Carpentry craft hand tools, 205
Carpet services, 125
Ceiling finishes maintenance pointers, 144
Central administration plant, 129-130
Central service plant:
    central maintenance shops, 67
    desirable requirements, 67
    determination of supply control, 67-68
        maintenance control, 68
        warehouse control, 68
    determining size of shop area, 69-71
        large school district, 69
        minimum shop areas, 69
        other site areas, 71
        specific accommodations areas, 69, 71
        specific requirements, 71
    general building requirements, 68-69
    housekeeping, 83
    service centers, 71
    shop equipment and tools, 78-83
        equipment, 78
        tools, 78-83
        (*see also* Tools)
    summary, 83-84
Characteristics of personnel, 34
Checklist, master, 149-166
Cillie, 11
Circulation areas, master check list, 154-155
Civil service commissions, sources of personnel, 38
Classes of services:
    nonscheduled, 14
    scheduled, 13
Classrooms, master check list, 158-161
Cleaning time, 23-24
Climate, 4

Clocks and signals, tools, 205
Codes, updating building, 5
Coding systems and definitions, 170-184, 187-190, 192-195
Color finishes maintenance pointers, 145
Combustible, definition of, 209
Communications, developing:
    control, 30
    elements, 29-30
    flow, 30
    media, 30-31
        radio, 31
        telephone, 31
    methods, 30
Communications time, 23
Component parts, standardized, 7
Concrete craft hand tools, 205
Concrete services, 111
Conferences, 15
Construction, criteria for judging, 136-138
Construction maintenance pointers, 145
Controls of maintnance functions, 20-32
    (*see also* Functions, controls of maintenance)
Coordination of work, 8, 11
Cost and amount of maintnance, 4-5
Courses, local short, 92
Crafts, hand tools listed by, 203-208
Custodial quarters, master check list, 163
Custodial services, definition of, 209

D

Daily report, 25
Data processing, definition of, 209
Data processing room services, 126-127
Day, length of, 40
Death of employee, 42
Delays, 24-25
    (*see also* Time study)
Demonstrations, 92
Dependability, 35
Descriptions, job, 27-28
    (*see also* Job descriptions)
Design for preplanned maintenance, 4
Disasters, 52
Discharge, employee, 42-43
Discussion groups, 92
District map, 63
Door finishes maintenance pointers, 144
Drayage hand tools, 205
Drayage services, 112-113
    (*see also* Allied services)
Drinking, 35
Driver training hand tools, 205
Drivotrainers service, 119

E

Economic obsolescence, definition of, 209
Economy methods, 3, 7
    (*see also* Maintenance)

Educational environment, definition of, 209
Educational level, a qualification, 35
Efficiency, 12
Efflorescence, definition of, 209
Electrical craft hand tools, 205
Electrical maintenance pointers, 145-146
Electrical services, 101-102
(*see also* Services in school plant areas)
Electrical services, master check list, 165
Electrolysis, definition of, 209
Electronic equipment, 63
Electronics coding system, 187-190
Electronics equipment and maintenance record, 191
Electronics service, 120
Elevator repair services, 123
Employee benefits, 41, 45
Employee organization, 47
Employment form, 65
Equipment:
  amount and cost, 5
  critria for judging, 139-140
  maintenance pointers, 147-148
Evaluation, applying constant, 18-19
Evaluation of performance, 45-47
Experience, a qualification, 35
Exterior finish maintenance pointers, 143
Exterior of building, master check list, 151-153

F

Federal projects services, 130-131
Fencing hand tools, 207
Filters, hand tools for, 206
Filters, heating, 103
Finishes, maintenance pointers, 143-144
(*see also* Pointers, preplanned maintenance)
Fire drills, 51-52
Fire prevention, definition of, 209
Fire protection, 117-118
(*see also* Allied services)
Fire-resistive, definition of, 209
First-aid, 51
Flying insect control, 124
Food facility services, 130
Foreman, general, 27, 37-38
Frequency of service, definition of, 209
Fuels, 103
Functional charts, 17
Functional obsolescence, definition of, 209
Functionalism, 11
Functions, controls of maintenance:
  building manuals, 29
  developing adequate communications, 29-31
  (*see also* Communications, developing)
  establishing standards, 25-26
    frequencies of service, 26
    parts, 25
    policies of replacement, 26
  human relations, 31-32
  (*see also* Human relations)

Functions, controls of maintenance (*Cont.*)
  job descriptions, 27-28
  (*see also* Job descriptions)
Functions, controls of maintenance:
  methods of detection of repairs, 20-21
    authorized personnel, 20-21
    disposition, 21
    needed information, 21
    work requests, 21
  ordering right materials, 27
  responsibility for records, 29
  (*see also* Records)
  summary, 32
  time study, 23-25
  (*see also* Time study)
  use of records, 28-29
  (*see also* Records)
Functions, method of performing, 5-6
Furniture:
  criteria for judging, 139-140
  maintenance pointers, 147-148
  repair, 106-107
  (*see also* Services in school plant areas)
  school, 63

G

Garage hand tools, 206
Garbage services, 113-115
(*see also* Allied services)
General foreman, 27
Goodwill, 12
Greenhouse services, 128-129
Grounds and landscaping, 109-110
(*see also* Services in school plant areas)

H

Hand tools listed by crafts, 203-208
Handling time, 23
Health and administrative areas, master check list, 164
Healthful conditions, 3
Heating, 102-103
(*see also* Services in school plant areas)
Heating and air conditioning hand tools, 206
Heating facilities maintenance pointers, 147
Heavy equipment, hand tools for, 206
Hindrances to effective maintenance, 6-7
(*see also* Maintenance)
Human relations:
  general public, 31-33
  public authorities, 31
  salesmen, 31
  school personnel, 31-32

I

Imagination, use of, 133-134
In-service training, 91-92
(*see also* Personnel, upgrading)
Industrial arts equipment, 64

Industry, source of recruitment, 38
Insect control, 124
Inspection check list, 166
Instructional equipment services:
  drivotrainers, 119
  electronics, 120
  instructional media equipment, 120-121
  sound systems, 121
Instructional equipment, tools for, 206
Intelligence, a qualification, 35
Interior finishes maintenance pointers, 143-144
Inventory and stock, 65

J

Job description, definition of, 210
Job descriptions:
  apprentices, 27
  general foreman, 27
  journeyman, 27
  laborers, 28
  plasterer's helper, 27-28
Journeyman, 27, 38

K

Key shop services, 116-117

L

Labor, organized, 47-49
Laboratory services, mobile, 127
Laborers, 28
Landscaping and grounds, 109-110
  (*see also* Services in school plant areas)
Landscaping hand tools, 206
Laundry repair services, 123
Learning laboratory, value as, 3
Length of day, 40
Life cycle of school plant, 132
Linn, 13

M

Machine shop hand tools, 207
Machine shop sevices, 115
Mail, personal, 43
Maintenance:
  amount and cost, 4-5
    climate, 4
    design, 4
    local school plant situation, 4-5
    "machine" politics, 5
    managerial efficiency, 5
    standards of service, 5
    supplies, materials, equipment, 5
    technological advances, 5
    updating building codes, 5
    use, 4
    wage levels, 5
  classes of services, 13-14
  (*see also* Classes of services)

Maintenance (*Cont.*)
  definition of, 210
  economy methods, 7
    purchase locally if practical, 7
    quality checking, 7
    school plant detail, 7
    standardized component parts, 7
    time, 7
  hindrances, 6-7
  list of hand tools by crafts, 203-208
  local determination of activities, 13
  master check lists, 149-166
  methods of performing functions, 5-6
  objectives, 3-4
    attractiveness, 3
    continued use, 3
    economies, 3
    healthful conditions, 3
    protection of property, 3
    safety, 3
    value as learning laboratory, 3
  organizing, 8-19
  (*see also* Organizing for maintenance)
  principal's annual request, 167-168
  programming, 14-19
  (*see also* Programming for maintenance)
  promising preplanned pointers, 141-148
  (*see also* Pointers, preplanned maintenance)
  summary, 7
Maintenance services, allied, 111-118
(*see also* Allied services)
Man-hours by craft, 17
Managerial efficiency, 5
Manpower, 85-86
Manuals, building, 29
Map of district, 63
Masonry, 107-108
(*see also* Services in school plant areas)
Masonry hand tools, 207
Master check lists, 149-166
Master plan, 140
Material procurement time, 23
Materials:
  amount and cost, 5
  arranging for, 17-18
  savings, 86
(*see also* Administration)
Mechanical safeguard, 54
Mechanical services, 104-105
(*see also* Services in school plant areas)
Mechanical services maintenance pointers, 146-147
Mechanics, area, 37-38
(*see also* Personnel policies)
Meeting areas, master check lists, 162
Meetings, general and committee, 89-90
Microfilming records, 65
Modernization, 3, 210
Motor winding, 207
Motorized equipment, 64, 192-195
Motors, 63
Mowing services, 121-122

N

Noise, 25
Non-productive time, 24-25
(*see also* Time study)
Nonscheduled projects, definition of, 210

O

Objectives of maintenance, 34
(*see also* Maintenance)
Organization charts, 17
Organization, employee, 47
Organizing for maintenance:
   classes of services, 13-14
   (*see also* Classes of services)
   local determination of activities, 13
   master checklists, 149-166
   principal's annual request, 167-168
   principles, 8-12
      coordination, 8, 11
      efficiency, 12
      funtionalism, 11
      promising practices, 11-12
      service, 12
   programming, 14-19
   (*see also* Programming for maintenance)
   summary, 19
Overtime, 41

P

Painting, hand tools for, 207
Painting records, 186
Painting services, 98-99
(*see also* Services in school plant areas)
Paper work, 89
Parts:
   standardization, 86
   standards for maintenance, 25
Payrolls, 64
Performance evaluation ratings:
   forced choice, 47
   ranking method, 45, 47
   self rating, 47
Personal appearance, 35
Personnel policies:
   duty of area mechanics, 37-38
      foremen, 37-38
      journeymen, 38
      other labor, 38
   employee organization, 47
   establishing qualifications, 35
   freedoms, 34
      employment, 34
      pressures, 34
   garnishments, 44
   miscellaneous working relationships, 43-44
      change of address, 43
      emergency telephone numbers, 44
      keeping informed, 44

Personnel policies (*Cont.*)
   miscellaneous working relationships (*Cont.*)
      personal mail, 43
      personal visitors, 44
      solicitations, 44
      subscriptions, 44
      talkfests, 44
      telephone calls, 43
      use of shops, 44
   performance evaluation, 45-47
      administration benefits, 45
      employee benefits, 45
      forms, 45
   methods of rating, 45, 47
      positive steps in rating, 47
      scope of qualities, 45
   personnel characteristics, 34
   place to apply, 33-34
      dependent organization, 34
      independent unit organization, 33
   recognition, 49
   records, 201
   recruitment, 38
   relations with organized labor, 47-49
      able maintenance administrator, 48
      collective bargaining, 48
      conducting negotiations, 48
      improvement in security, 48
      labor-management framework, 48
      leadership in organized labor, 48
      many union organizations, 48
      record of communications, 48
   selection, promotion, retention, 38-41
      induction, 40
      interview, 40
      promotions and transfers, 40
      retention, 40
      review of applications, 40
      selection, 40
      terms of employment, 40-41
      tests, 40
   severance, 42-43
      death, 42
      discharge, 42-43
      employee resignation, 42
      suspension, 43
   specific skill qualifications, 35-37
      area men, 37
      head of maintenance, 36-37
      supervision, 36
   summary, 49
   transportation, 44
   wage and employee benefits, 41-42
      employee benefits, 41
      other personal benefits, 41-42
Personnel records, 64-65
Personnel, upgrading:
   formal training, 92
      institutional, 92
      local short courses, 92
      state departments, 92

Personnel, upgrading (*Cont.*)
  in-service training, 91-92
    apprentice training, 91
    demonstrations, 92
    discussion groups, 92
    local workshops, 92
    safety committee, 92
  instructional methods and services, 94-95
    devices, 95
    methods, 94
  recommended practices, 93
    testing, 93
    visitations to other school districts, 93
  short term schools of instruction, 94
    organization, 94
    short term schools, 94
    trade shows, 94
  sources of helpful information, 95
  summary, 95
  using available school plant information, 93
Pest control:
  birds, 124
  domestic rodents, 124
  flying insects, 124
  insects, 124
  miscellaneous pests, 124-125
  termites, 124
Physical ability, a qualification, 35
Physical deterioration, definition of, 210
Plant, central service, 66-84
  (*see also* Central service plant)
Plant life, 109
Plant records, partial summary of individual, 185
Plasterer's helper, 27-28
Plastering, 108-109
  (*see also* Services in school plant areas)
Plastering hand tools, 207
Play equipment, 110
Playground hand tools, 207
Plumbing, 63
Plumbing hand tools, 207-208
Pointers, preplanned maintnance:
  building spaces, 143
  construction, 145
  electrical services, 145-146
  equipment and furniture, 147-148
  exterior finish, 143
  interior finishes, 143-144
    color, 145
    ceilings, 144
    doors, 144
    safety, 144-145
  mechanical services, 146-147
    heating facilities, 147
    sanitary facilities, 147
    ventilating facilities, 147
    water systems, 146-147
  summary, 148
  total building, 142-143
  total site layout, 142

Portable classroom service, relocating, 122
Portable water, definition of, 210
Precautions, safety, 56-60
Principal's annual request for maintenance, 167-168
Priorities, establishing, 16
Productive time, 23-24
  (*see also* Time study)
Programming for maintenance:
  applying constant evaluation, 18-19
  arranging for materials, 17-18
  budget allowance, 15-16
  building principal's annual request, 15
  conferences, 15
  establishing priorities, 16
  finalizing budget, 16
  inspection by capable personnel, 14
  inspection by responsible craftsmen, 14-15
  organizing staff, 16-17
    (*see also* Staff, organizing)
    functional charts, 17
    man-hours by craft, 17
    organization charts, 17
    supervision, 17
  recommendations of instructional staff, 15
  tooling up, 18
Promotion, 38-41
Property Accounting for Local and State School Systems, 63
Protection of property, 3
Public, general, 31-33
Purchase requests, pooling, 86

Q

Qualifications, job, 35-37
  (*see also* Personnel policies)
Quality checking, 7

R

Radio, 31
Rating, methods of personnel:
  forced choice, 47
  ranking, 45, 47
  self rating, 47
Records:
  absentee records, 202
  code for motorized equipment, 192-195
  coding system—electronics, 187-190
  coding systems and definitions, 170-184
  maintenance personnel information, 201
  managing, 62-65
    (*see also* Records, managing)
  painting, 186
    partial summary—electronics equipment and maintenance record, 191
  partial summary—motorized equipment, 196
  partial summary of individual plant records, 185
  responsibility, 29
    adjacency of offices, 29
    kinds of records, 29

Records (*Cont.*)
  responsibility (*Cont.*)
    number of copies, 29
    people responsible, 29
  stock requisition, 200
  time card, 199
  use, 28-29
    contractual, 29
    control, 28
    cost, 28
    inventory, 28
    school plant, 28
  work order, 197-198
Records, managing:
  basic, 62-63
    as built plans, 62
    individual property records, 62-63
    map of district, 63
    one line, scaled drawings, 63
    original plans and specifications, 62
    photographs, 63
  inventory and stock, 65
  maintenance operations, 64
    budget, 64
    payrolls, 64
    record of materials, 64
    time card, 64
    work orders, 64
    work requests, 64
  microfilming, 65
  parts of school plants, 63-64
    boilers, 63
    electronic equipment, 63
    industrial arts and vocational equipment, 64
    motorized equipment, 64
    motors, 63
    painting, 63
    plumbing, 63
    school furniture, 63
  personnel records, 64-65
    absentee record, 65
    application form, 65
    employment form, 65
  summary, 65
Recruitment, 38
Referrals, union, 38
Rehabilitation, 3, 210
Relatives, a qualification, 35
Relocating portable classroom service, 122
Remodeling, 2, 210
Repair, 3
Replacement policies, 26
Replacements, 3
Requests, work, 21
Requisition, stock, 200
Residence, a qualification, 35
Resignation, employee, 42
Retention of personnel, 38-41
Rodent control, 124

Roofing, 99-101
(*see also* Services in school plant areas)
Roofing hand tools, 208

S

Safety, an objective of maintenance, 3
Safety committee, 92
Safety program, 55, 88-89
Safety, responsibility of administrator:
  precautions, 56-60
    certain parts of school, 57-60
    specific operations, 56-57
  responsibilities, 51-56
    disasters, 52
    fire drills—schools, 52
    fire drills—shop, 51-52
    first aid—dispatched personnel, 51
    first aid station, 51
    handling of accidents, 52
    inspection, 54
    mechanical safeguard, 54
    safety program, 55
    study causes of accidents, 52
    teaching methods and techniques, 55-56
    training in operation procedures, 54-55
  scope of responsbility, 51
  strict enforcement of rules, 60
  summary, 61
Salesmen, 31
Salvage materials, 86
Sanitary facilities:
  maintenance pointers, 147
  master check list, 156
Savings (*see* Administration)
Scheduled maintenance, definition of, 210
School personnel, 31-32
School Plant Management, 17, 69
School plant life cycle, 132
School plants, upgrading existing, 132-140
(*see also* Upgrading existing school plants)
School site, master check list, 150
Security of plant, definition of, 210
Selection of personnel, 38-41
Service:
  classes of, 13-14
  frequencies of, 26, 209
  instructional equipment, 119-121
  (*see also* Instructional equipment services)
  principle of organization, 12
  standards, 5
Service plant, central, 66-84
(*see also* Central service plant)
Services for ancillary areas, 126-131
(*see also* Ancillary areas, services)
Services in school plant areas:
  carpenter, 105-106
    goals, 106
    inside parts of school building, 105-106
    outside school building, 105
    outside surfaces of school building, 105

Services in school plant areas (*Cont.*)
  electrical, 101-102
    common problems, 101-102
    scope, 101
  furniture repair, 106-107
    common problems, 106-107
    materials, 107
    scope, 106
  grounds and landscaping, 109-110
    outside instructional areas, 109
    plant life, 109
    play equipment, 110
    site improvements, 109
  heating, 102-103
    boiler controls, 103
    boilers, 103
    filters, 103
    fuels, 103
    systems, 102
    water treatment, 103
  managing allied, 111-118
    (*see also* Allied services)
  masonry, 107-108
    responsibilities, 107-108
    methods of repair, 108
  mechanical, 104-105
    aims, 104
    common problems, 104-105
    sanitary facilities, 104
  painting, 98-99
    contract, 99
    glazing, 99
    interior, 99
    outside, 99
  plastering, 108-109
  roofing, 99-101
    causes for failure, 100
    methods of repair, 101
  summary, 110
  ventilation, 103-104
Severance:
  death, 42
  discharge, 42-43
  employee resignation, 42
  suspension, 43
Sheet metal hand tools, 208
Sheet metal services, 111-112
Shops, use of, 44
Signals and clocks, tools, 205
Site, criteria for judging, 134-135
Site layout maintenance pointers, 142
Skill qualifications, 35-37
Smoking, 35
Snow removal, 115
Solicitations, 44
Sound systems, 121
Sources of personnel, 38
Specialists, use of, 133
Stadia services, 127-128

Staff, organizing:
  functional charts, 17
  man-hours by craft, 17
  organization charts, 17
  supervision, 17
Standards, definition of, 210
Standards of maintenance, 25-26
  (*see also* Functions, controls of maintenance)
State departments, 92
Stock and inventory, 65
Stock items, availability, 86
Stock requisition, 200
Subscriptions, 44
Summer hours, 41
Summertime repairs, 25
Supervision, 17
Supplies, amount and cost, 5
Supension, 43
Swimming pool services, 128

T

Talkfests, 44
Technological advances, 5
Telephone, 31
Telephone calls, 43
Telephone numbers, emergency, 44
Television studio services, 129
Termites, 124
Testing of tools and equipment, 93
Time, 7
Time card, 64, 199
Time study:
  daily report, 25
  noise, 25
  non-productive time, 24-25
    delay due to others, 24
    other delays, 24-25
    unavoidable delays, 24
  productive time, 23-24
    actual, 23
    cleaning, 23-24
    communications, 23
    material procurement, 23
    transportation and handling, 23
  summertime repairs, 25
Tooling up, 18
Tools:
  better tools and equipment, 87
  care, 78
  control, 78
  list for a particular district, 79-83
  listed by crafts, 203-208
  necessary tools and equipment, 79
  records and inventories, 79
  storage, 78
Trade shows, 94
Training of personnel
  (*see* Personnel, upgrading)

Transportation, 44
Transportation time, 23

U

Union referrals of personnel, 38
Upgrading existing school plants:
  criteria for judging, 134-140
    building, 135-136
     existing construction, 136-138
     furniture and equipment, 139-140
     interior building elements, 138-139
     site, 134-135
     supplemental educational requirement, 136
  educational responsibility, 133
  life cycle of school plant, 132
  master plan, 140
  planning budget, 140
  school plant's age, 132-133
  setting upgrading program, 140
  summary, 140
  use of imagination, 133-134
  use of specialists, 133
Upkeep, 3

V

Vandalism, 4
Vandalism restoration, 117
Ventilating facilities maintenance pointers, 147
Ventilation, 103-104
  (*see also* Services in school plant areas)
Visitations, 93
Visitors, personal, 44
Vocational equipment, 64

W

Wage and employee benefits, 41-42
Wage level, 5
Waste space, definition of, 210
Water systems maintenance pointers, 146-147
Water treatment, 103
Welding, 112
Welding hand tools, 208
Work orders, 64, 197-198, 210
Work requests, 21, 64, 210
Work time, 89
Working with others, a qualification, 35
Workshops, local, 92